Disasters and Dilemmas

728

UNIVERSITY OF BRISTOL
Department of Philosophy

9 Woodland Road
Bristol
BS8 1TB

Disasters and Dilemmas

Strategies for real-life decision making

Adam Morton

Basil Blackwell

Copyright © Adam Morton 1991

First published 1991

Basil Blackwell Ltd
108 Cowley Road, Oxford, OX4 1JF, UK

Basil Blackwell, Inc.
3 Cambridge Center
Cambridge, Massachusetts 02142, USA

British Library Cataloguing in Publication Data

A CIP catalogue record for this book is available from the British Library.

Library of Congress Cataloging in Publication Data

Morton, Adam.
Disasters and dilemmas: strategies for real-life decision making / Adam
Morton.
p.   cm.
Includes bibliographical references and index.
ISBN 0-631-16216-x
1. Decision-making.   2. Conflict (Psychology)   I. Title.
BF448.M67   1991
153.8′3—dc20   90-37129
CIP

Typeset in 11 on 13 pt Ehrhardt
by Graphicraft Typesetters Ltd., Hong Kong
Printed in Great Britain by
Billing & Sons Ltd, Worcester

Contents

Introduction

Here is how the eco-mystics of South Devon make decisions. They make a pendulum with a crystal – different people argue strongly for different crystals – and they swing it from a string held between the thumb and first finger of the left hand (to engage the right hemisphere). Then as the pendulum swings they think hard about the actions they are choosing between and associate each with a simple cyclic pattern – circle, ellipse, figure of eight, and so on. Then the crystal begins to follow one of these patterns. That tells which action to perform. Often the crystal chooses an action that the person had not thought very promising or reasonable, but often when the action is performed it turns out to have hidden virtues and unexpected advantages.

Here is how the really tough-minded economists of the world make decisions. They list all the courses of action they are choosing between: for example putting their money in the bank, in a government bond, in a secure investment trust, in a speculative unlisted stock. And they list all the natural and human events that might affect the outcome of the action taken: the possible rates of inflation, the possible behaviour of the stock market, the possible bank rates. Then for each outcome and each possible action they list the probability of that outcome's occurring if the action is performed, and the relative desirability of the resulting situation. For example there may be a 0.2 chance that after I have made a speculative investment there will be a stock market crash, and the desirability of the resulting situation might be measured as minus −100 on a scale in which making a fortune counts as 100 and coming out even counts as 0. Then each action is given a ranking according to the sum of all these probabilities each multiplied by the corresponding desirability. The top-ranked action is chosen.

Each of these methods may seem mad, in very different ways. Decision-by-pendulum seems to allow no room for careful consideration of the consequences of possible actions, and it seems to allow arbitrary whims of hand and brain to govern the direction of one's life. On the

other hand it gives a way in which unconscious preferences and unconscious knowledge can affect a decision, and it allows a certain feedback
between the course of the decision and the preferences on which it is
based. (I mean: if the pendulum begins to trace a figure eight, and your
heart sinks because that means you must stay with your spouse, the sink-
ing of your heart will no doubt cause a crystal of any intuitive power at all
to jump quickly into another pattern.) Decision-by-calculation, in contrast, seems thoroughly methodical and to take the consequences of
actions thoroughly into account, but it presupposes a superhuman knowledge of probabilities, of one's own desires, and of what the consequences of
one's actions would really be like.

This is a book about decision making. I describe some decision-making
strategies and I argue that they are both usable and give good answers.
They may well seem more in the spirit of decision-by-calculation than
decision-by-pendulum. Probably they are. But they are meant to connect
with intuition as well as calculation, and they are meant to take into
account the fact that we usually have no very clear ideas about how likely
the world is to go one way rather than another and how we would like it
if it did.

The most important claim I make for these decision-making strategies
is that they apply in situations where one has to make a decision on the
basis of 'incomparable desires'. That is a term I shall use to cover a variety
of cases in which desires are not ranked in a simple linear way: one cannot
say 'I want A more than I want B'. There are both trivial and heartbreaking examples. You may have to choose between a film and a concert, or between your self-respect and your career, and you don't seem to
have a simple preference between them. There are very different cases
here, and I try to distinguish them, but in all cases I try to develop 'non-
balancing' strategies: strategies which do not force one to find a balance
or a tradeoff between very different things.

Non-balancing strategies are useful also in situations in which one
does have clear, or at any rate clearer, preferences and some grasp of
probabilities. I discuss some issues about risk-taking and about coordination problems in order to show this. Moreover, non-balancing strategies
apply to moral dilemmas as well as to non-moral dilemmas. And as a
result, or so I claim, when one begins to think in terms of them the distinction between moral and non-moral ('practical') decision making begins
to break down. Chapter 5 discusses a very basic and very puzzling question, essentially 'Are there decisions one should avoid making?', just
because it arises in both moral and non-moral contexts. And chapter 11 is

in fact an attempt to argue that the moral/non-moral distinction is a very unclear one.

(I use the word dilemma to mean what it usually means: a situation where it is very hard to decide what to do. So a moral dilemma is a situation in which it is very hard to decide what one ought morally to do. In recent moral philosophy the word has come to be used rather differently, to mean a situation where one will regret whatever one does. I will not use the word this way, though I discuss a number of moral, and non-moral, problems exhibiting the double regret trap.)

Though this is a book about making decisions it does not bear a simple relation to what is usually called 'decision theory'. Decision theory tries to give precise procedures by which, given a fixed list of options and relatively clear beliefs and desires (or probabilities and utilities), one can choose a 'best' action to perform. The heart of decision theory lies in its analysis of the relation between degrees of desirability of simple and of complex situations. (So it should tell you, for example, how much it is reasonable to want a gamble offering a 0.6 chance of soup or bread and a 0.4 chance of a ride on the roller coaster, compared to how much you want soup, bread, and a ride on the roller coaster.) The emphasis in this book is rather different. I am concerned with strategies for getting complex, vague, incomparable, or otherwise recalcitrant beliefs and desires into a form in which one could apply the procedures of decision theory. I am interested in an earlier stage of the process.

In fact, one of the aims of the book is to defend the possibility of a helpful theory of the 'middle level' of decision making. The bottom level, on this metaphor, consists of fairly precise reasoning about how, given a list of options, one is to choose one to perform. That is the domain of traditional decision theory. And the top level is the search for promising options. Thinking of options is like any other kind of creative thought: it is unpredictable, mysterious, and not governed by any very obvious rules. And while no doubt the central clue to actually making good decisions is to think of the right options, it seems no more likely that there are simple how-to-do-it rules for thinking of the right options than that there are simple rules for making scientific discoveries or finding gripping plots for novels.

But there is a level between these two, between the mechanical and the mysterious. At this middle level of decision making we do such things as: judge which ideas about what to do are live options and which are non-starters, think through what criteria are to be used in a decision, and assess the reliability of the beliefs that will have to be brought to bear on the question. It is this middle level that concerns me, and my claim is that there is a lot to be said about it.

(It is not like doing arithmetic, or verifying a formal proof. Nor is it like finding a proof in the first place. More like solving equations. Like solving differential equations, in fact, in the presence of complicated boundary conditions.)

Some of the topics I discuss, for example coordination problems and decisions involving risk, are traditional concerns of decision theory proper. But, I think, we miss some important points if we do not see that some of the difficulties of decision making in these areas arise at the middle level: from the difficulty of getting our beliefs and preferences into a usable form. And sometimes what decision theory tells us is that there is no ideal solution to such a problem. That still leaves us with the problem of cobbling together a way of getting on with life given that rationality cannot give all that we want. (It is a bit like the problem of putting together a workable political system given that every voting procedure has serious flaws.)

The book is written in short chapters, which are meant to be relatively independent of one another. Moreover, it is divided into three sections, which are also relatively independent of one another. The middle section, 'Theory', is a little heavier going than the other two. Some readers may want to skip it at first reading. Since I wanted the book to be accessible to a wide range of readers I have tried to keep the main text as free as possible from technical terms and free from very local issues from moral philosophy, economics, decision theory, and statistics. For the same reason I have avoided discussing particular people's work in the main text. But this may give the impression that I am claiming more originality for some of the ideas than I should. The notes at the end of the book make connections with more technical questions and with the work of others.[1]

I wrote the first draft of this book in the autumn of 1988. I then inflicted the very rough result on a number of people. I am grateful to Tim Akrill, Paula Boddington, John Broome, Keith Graham, Rex Hollowell, Mac McCarthy, Walter Sinnot-Armstrong, and Mike Talibard for their comments. And I am grateful to Stephan Chambers at Basil Blackwell for treating that rough draft as if it were a respectable book manuscript, and for frequent encouragement. Nick Scott-Samuel helped me with proof-reading and index-making. Roger McGough's poem 'Worry' at the head of chapter 7 is reprinted by permission of the Peters Fraser and Dunlop Group Ltd.

Part I
Problems

1

Patterns of Desire

Some decisions are painful but not hard. If a mugger gives you a choice of being killed or parting with the gold watch your mother gave you when to everyone's surprise you got a university place, you will give up the watch with regret but without much hesitation. Or you have promised to take your daughter to see a film but a friend phones and is evidently near to suicide. Then with a different kind of regret but no more hesitation you break your promise and attend to your friend.

I am not concerned with these decisions, but with decisions which are inherently difficult. In the situations I shall discuss the deciding itself is difficult. You don't know what you should do. There are no end of such cases: I discuss some below. In all of them you understand the situation fairly well but do not know what the best thing to do is. (And so in other cases which are similar but with the added complication that you do not understand the situation at all well, or are uncertain what you want, making the decision is even harder.) If you do manage to make the decision you may then feel unhappy at what you have had to renounce in order to get something else, but your problem is first getting to the point where it hurts. It is situations like this that I call dilemmas.

The difficulty of a dilemma is often due to the pattern of one's desires: the way in which your wants for different things are related to one another. I think that when one sees how many patterns desires can take one begins to appreciate the real difficulty of decision making. But one also begins to see that dilemmas are not all unfortunate and insoluble traps. There are good and not so good strategies for dealing with them.

1.1   Qualified Trumps: The Fragile Driver

A comes to live with B and C and their children after a catastrophic end to a calamitous marriage. She finds their household a refuge and a revelation: that people could live at close quarters with so little aggression. Her self-esteem is very low, and B and C do all they can to protect her from her sense that everything she does is likely to end badly. One function she can play in the household is to drive the children to school and to their music lessons, and of course she would like to be useful and friendly in this way. There is a problem, though. B and C have ridden with her and been terrified: her lack of confidence makes her an impulsive and unpredictable rather than a reliably cautious driver. They are very unwilling to have their children driven by her. They seem to have to choose between damaging her fragile confidence and endangering their children's lives.

Now in this case one can think of various tactful ways out which might allow B and C to prevent the issue arising. But whether or not any of these will work, given the details of the case, the root of the dilemma remains. It is that the two possible harms that B and C are steering between are very different, and intrinsically difficult to balance. For the danger to the children is of a really quite small probability of something definitely awful, while the threat to A's self-esteem is of a larger probability of something which, while clearly undesirable, is much less irreversible and much less awful. No wonder that it is hard to stay on that particular tightrope.

The way in which these weights resist balancing is also found with much graver dilemmas. In chapter 8 I discuss it in connection with such things as the distribution of health care resources: how to balance between measures which preserve life, such as sophisticated apparatus and advanced surgical techniques, and measures which alleviate suffering, such as decent nursing care. The general problem here is of dealing with trumps. Saving life trumps alleviating suffering, both when distributing health care and when choosing who is to chauffeur the kids. But does this mean that we must have a health system in which almost no one dies but millions live in squalid institutions? Or that B and C must be so cautious with their children's lives that they damage A's fragile equilibrium?

In the case of the fragile driver issues about comparing life with lesser goods interact with issues about risk. The issues about risk are fundamentally quite similar; they too turn on the question of how much a greater value can trump a lesser one. (See chapters 5, 6 and 7.) In fact I am wrestling with various forms of the trumping problem throughout this book. In the form of it we have here we have to compare two kinds of desire, or more properly desires for two kinds of things (e.g. one's children's safety and one's friends' sanity.) Desires of each kind are often fairly easy to compare among themselves. But they are for the most part hard to compare with desires of the other kind, with one exception: very large amounts of one kind of thing (e.g. high probabilities of death) uncontroversially outrank ordinary amounts of the other kind of thing. As a result we have trouble reconciling the decisions we make at different times: we normally balance small amounts of either thing against one another in a rough and ready way, but when the stakes get high we stop balancing and take one desire to trump the other.

Call this pattern of desires *qualified trumps*. (Trumps for obvious reasons, qualified because the trumps don't always trump.) We have many desires which fit this pattern. One reason why the dilemmas they lead to are so often rather acute is the shifts of perspective they can expose one to. This will happen in the marginal area where it is not clear whether the 'trump' values are to be taken as trumping all others. Suppose, for example, that you are B and you think it just possible but not very likely that your children will be harmed if you let A drive them. So you let her, for the sake of her self-respect. But there is an accident and a child is killed. Then very likely in retrospect you would see the decision you took as not merely ill-fated but negligent: in retrospect threats to life will trump opportunities to help your friends even when they will not in prospect. So the difficulty of balancing desires in these cases is compounded by the possibility of remorse.[1]

1.2 Simple Incomparables

Qualified trumps are a form of incomparable desire. The way I will use the term, a pair of desires are incomparable whenever neither one is preferred to the other, but they are not equal in desirability either. There are much simpler examples of this.

Suppose for example that you want to go to a concert and to a meal. Among the concerts available you prefer the Stravinski concert to the opera, and among the meals available you prefer the Indian meal to the Chinese meal. But if asked to choose between any concert and any meal you cannot say more than that no clear comparison is possible. The situation can be pictured as follows:

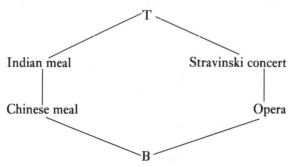

This structure allows the preferences between meals and between the concerts to be perfectly definite, while making no comparisons between the meals and the concerts. In fact, it not only does not equate the desirability of any meal with that of any concert, it actually forbids us to equate incomparability with equality of desire. For if the Indian meal is equal in desirability with the Stravinski concert since neither is desired more than the other, so is the Stravinski concert and the Chinese meal. But then the Chinese meal would be equal in desirability to the Indian meal, which is not the case.[2]

The diagram also shows a desire marked T for 'top', preferred to all restaurants and concerts, and one marked B for 'bottom', to which all restaurants and concerts are preferred. There nearly always are such desires: almost anyone whose desires fell into the situation described would prefer a present of a million pounds to going to either the most favoured restaurant or the most favoured concert, and would prefer either of them to spending the night in a police cell. (Though neither the million pounds nor the night in the cell need be things one could get at will.) For all that, everyone surely has large numbers of mutually incomparable desires among their wants. For many objects of desire are for many people incomparable: freedom and security, career success and a happy family life, chalk and cheese.

Incomparable as these desires are, they may not be *deeply* incomparable: the incomparability may disappear when the issues are better understood or when one rethinks the situation in different terms. This might be the case. It might also be the case that when one reflects carefully on one's desires other less easily thought-away incomparabilities appear. So careful thought may produce more incomparability. That is a difficult question which should not be prejudged: a good dilemma-managing strategy should accept that simple incomparabilities occur in the desires people find themselves with. In dealing with the resulting dilemmas the strategy may find ways of reducing them to more comparable desires, or it may not. (There is much more about incomparability in chapter 3.)

1.3 Second Order Desires

George has always been indifferent to music. In fact he has developed rather an aversion to all things musical, since he feels excluded by the mystical importance others sometimes attach to music. George has a daughter, Helen, who suffers from a fairly severe mental handicap. George loves Helen and worries what her life way be like. A teacher at the special school Helen goes to discovers that Helen has a great musical gift. After very little instruction she can play the violin by ear and can recall and repeat quite complex music on first hearing. She struggles to learn to read music; the struggle seems to give her a chance of learning to read prose, and the interaction with her music teacher improves her command of language. George Knows that Helen's music must be encouraged, and he knows that the best way to do this is to become interested himself, to learn to listen intelligently, perhaps to learn an instrument himself, and above all somehow to come to like the stuff.

Consider George's resolve to become interested in music. There are many obvious ways in which he can carry it out. (None of them guarantee success, but he will just have to try and see what works.) If any of them succeed he will have desires that he does not now have. He will want to hear particular pieces; he will want to buy records or go to concerts; he will even want to hear (and not just see) his daughter practise. But he cannot tell in advance *which* desires he will acquire. So in now wanting to acquire them he is not now wanting to go to concerts, buy records, and argue with Helen about tempi. The object of his desire is more general: he wants to have wants of a certain kind, and many different wants will do.

These are second order desires: wants to have other wants.[3] They can conflict with ordinary or first order wants. George will have to give up some television watching and his Saturday rugby match if he is to acquire and live up to his second order desire. It is not at all obvious how to compare first and second order desires when they conflict. Their objects are so different. In this case it seems intuitively clear that the second order desire should win; George ought to de-emphasize sports and television and put the effort into music instead. But the comparison here is in part based on a comparison of first order desires: George's desire that Helen realize her potentiality is surely stronger than his desire for sports and diversions. In other cases it is much less obvious how a conflict between first and second order desires should be resolved. Here is one such case.

Carol comes from a family of proud, conservative, and respectable people. Some would say snobs. She shares her family's contempt for social or cultural slovenliness: it is an important part of her self-respect that there is a distance between herself and most of the world. When Carol is eighteen she goes to University and lodges with a large, happy, unedu-cated family. At first she is appalled at the amount of time they spend watching TV serials, the carelessness with which they speak, and their general unawareness of anything cultural. But then she comes to appre-ciate the warmth of the family atmosphere and the support they give each other in their troubles. She finds herself liking them. When she returns home at Christmas she finds herself appreciating her family less, and is less convinced that they are part of a small minority of people who really matter. This shakes her image of herself; she finds herself less confident that she likes the way she is. She realizes that liking her host family is upsetting her. She resolves to like them less and to suppress her desires for the easy friendly social life they represent. The first step is to fing somewhere else to live.

This is a case of someone whose second order desires – not to want the qualities represented by the host family – conflict with particular first order desires, for example to be with members of that family. But in this case it is not at all clear how the conflict ought to be resolved. Would Carol be better off ignoring her 'values', her conception of the kind of person she wants to be, and just following her particular desires as they occur? One couldn't begin to say without knowing a lot more.

1.4   Unspecified Desires

Rupert is a man of enthusiasms. More than most people he is seized by the interests and experiences of the moment, finding it impossible to feel the tug of desires that he had previously or knows he will have later. At the moment he is collecting 1950s sports cars and in love with a yachtswoman. (It helps to be rich, if you have enthusiasms.) Last year he was writing a book in mathematical statistics and in love with a violinist. He knows that within a few years he will have quite different interests again. And then of course there is the (to him) unimaginably distant future when he is old and has needs that he cannot now even imagine. He is offered the chance to become part-owner and director of a unique venture: a museum and track in which classic racers and sports cars will be restored, exhibited, and raced. (The grounds will contain miles of the kind of deserted country road that, before motorways and mass ownership of cars, made open and agile cars so attractive.) The investment must be accompanied by a commitment: he will have to direct the venture for a decade or more, and it is very unlikely that anyone will buy him out.

There is a bad argument Rupert can use to justify the investment. 'I love cars of that period,' he could say, 'and the life they represent, and I want anything that connects me to them. This is a once-in-a-lifetime opportunity to do what I most want, and I should not let it pass.' It is a bad argument because it supposes that since he wants something, getting it will improve his life. ('A once-in-a-lifetime opportunity.') In this case that is not true: within a few years his interests will have shifted, and he will find himself trapped in a life that is no longer his.

It is not so easy to say what Rupert should do. He could be very cautious and invest all his money in an annuity which will provide a decent income for the rest of his life, while preventing him from ever tying the capital to any one project. (Protecting his future selves from one another.) But that would be a very dull life, not one that Rupert could bear. In fact, present interests and future interests are usually hard to compare, and, as usual when balancing the unbalanceable, a simple compromise between the extremes may not be the best answer.

The interest of cases like this is that in them an agent has to satisfy desires which he not only does not have but whose objects he does not know. One wants to make a good life for oneself and that includes – among many things – ensuring the satisfaction of some of one's present desires, not because what one wants for now conflicts with what one wants for the future, but because what one now wants – for now or the future – conflicts with what one will in the future want. Another dimension of complication arises, and arises in very ordinary cases, when the nature of those future desires depends in part on one's present decisions. In deciding whether to marry someone, or whether to have a child, one is deciding among other things what kinds of thing one will want in the future. So one cannot think out the decision in terms of 'if I do this then I'll get this that I want, but if I do that then I'll get these other things.' For one will have different desires, depending on what decision is made.

1.5 A Diagnosis

In none of the situations I have been describing is it obvious what the person should do. And in none of them does it seem as if finding out what should be done involves simply finding the best way of satisfying a determinate set of clear desires. The problems are deeper than that.

The diagnosis I am developing of the difficulty of decision making traces many difficulties to various patterns of incomparability among our desires and values. One reason why we find many decisions hard to think through – and when we do manage to think them through find it hard to say how we did it – is that we are caught between two apparent platitudes. One is that we very often cannot compare the relative strengths of competing desires, values, and obligations. And the other is that rational decision making consists in going for what you want most, or, pushing it a bit further, going for as much as you can of what you want. The 'best' decision is the one that allows you to expect the greatest satisfaction of your present desires. (And similarly for values, obligations, and the like.) If both platitudes are right then many, perhaps most, decisions are impossible.

My suggestion is that we drop the second platitude. The 'best' decision is not always the one that gives you the most of what you now want. Sometimes a good decision will maximize future rather than present wants; sometimes it will maximize the chances of a good life; sometimes nothing as simple as either of these. In fact, once one begins to doubt that rationality consists in maximizing the satisfaction of present desires a great variety of decision-making methods, of 'dilemma-managing strategies', opens up. The problem then is not to find ways of thinking through the problems of incomparable desires, but to classify and evaluate all the ways that human ingenuity produce.

(This makes it sound as if the solution is to jettison the whole tradition of desire maximization. Or expected utility or cost-benefit analysis: optimization for short. That is not so. For one thing this tradition gives us the best, almost the only, hold we have on situations which have to be thought out in terms of probabilities. Dilemma-management and optimization have to fit together. The answer, crudely, is that dilemma-management largely consists in setting things up so that maximization can be sensibly applied. But the details of that, too, will have to emerge.)

I discuss some dilemma-managing techniques as applied to some pretty trivial cases in the next chapter, and later chapters discuss harder, more 'vital' dilemmas. It is important to me to present the trivial cases and the crucial or heartbreaking cases as made of the same basic materials, difficult for the same reasons and yielding to the same techniques. However, the non-trivial cases are more complex, and the stakes are higher.

Complexity is itself a non-trivial matter. I end this chapter with one more example, both to show the kinds of problems complexity generates and to introduce yet another reason for doubting that rational action consists in trying to satisfy definite pre-existing desires.

You are deciding whether to buy a new car. At first the pros and cons seem to be simple: if you buy a new car you will have a reliable and comfortable vehicle instead of your rough and rusty old banger, but the expense will make it necessary to live more frugally in other ways. You are beginning to think out how this advantage weighs against this disadvantage, and have tentatively decided that the increased driving comfort is worth the decreased domestic luxury, when you find that things are more complicated. If you keep your old car then in a year or two it may be possible to buy one whose fumes cause less environmental damage than those available now, but if you buy a car this year you will not be able to afford not to keep it for five or six years. The possibility of being able to minimize damage to the environment seems to outweigh the greater comfort of getting a new car now, and so your next tentative decision is not to buy it. But then yet another factor occurs to you. A new car would be safer than your present one – the brakes would be better and it would give more protection in a crash. It is true that the new car might lure your spouse into driving more dangerously, but you do not think this very likely, and in fact it seems to you that the safety factor outweighs the environmental one, and so you conclude, still tentatively, that you should buy the new car. But then another thought strikes you, and then another.

You could go on forever like this, getting deeper and deeper into the ramifications of your decision. It is bad enough that there are so many possibly relevant factors, and that weighing them against one another is such a very uncertain business. But that is not the most worrying thing. The most worrying thing is that there seems to be no natural point at which to stop considering more factors. For a simple possibility like having or not having a new car is not really something one can see in isolation. Whether the simple possibility is desirable or not depends on the surrounding circumstances: having a new car but being injured in a crash is presumably undesirable, and not having a new car but living in a less polluted environment desirable.

So in choosing 'new car or not new car' one is really choosing between various bundles of possibilities: probability p of having a new car and probability q of being severely injured; and probability p of having a new car and probability q of being severely injured and probability r of an improved environment. And so on ... The more one thinks about one's options, the more completely one describes these bundles. And if one could think things out completely the bundles would be descriptions of whole possible worlds: one would see one's options in terms such as 'probability $p1$ one of a world like this, and probability $p2$ of a world like that, and ...' But a whole possible world isn't really something one can have a desire for either: it is too complex; no real person could keep all the information together in their head.

There is no problem here if you know that you want something regardless of the accompanying circumstances. Money and happiness are the usual choices. But it is pretty rare that the circumstances can be ignored. (Wanting money for its own sake is pretty crazy; happiness is really no single thing that you can want.) So in most real cases you must either frame your desires in terms too crude for real deliberation (car or not car) or make a stab at possibilities so complex you cannot really hope to understand them.

The practical dilemma here is simply that you do not know when to stop deliberating.[4] With every further stage of deliberation the conclusion seems to change, so that you just oscillate between one choice and the other. There is a theoretical puzzle underlying it, which I tried to describe. A quick way of bringing out the edge of the theoretical puzzle is to ask yourself: what is it you want in making a decision such as whether to buy a new car. Is a new car all by itself an object of desire? Surely not. Is a complex of possible worlds, each of them more detailed than you could possibly imagine, what you are trying to bring about? Surely not. Is it something in between, and if so what? These are very hard questions.

2

Dilemma-Management: Easy Cases

We are often forced to choose between very different things, things we wouldn't even try to choose between if the situation did not force us to. Life is stuffed with such situations. My aim in this chapter is to begin to describe a way of thinking, really a family of ways of thinking, which allows incomparables to be left incomparable. The patterns of decision making I will describe are very ordinary and unsurprising; in fact my discussion of them will inevitably seem to be labouring the obvious. But the point is to show that we do have ways of thinking that do not require us to balance the unbalanceable, and to begin to develop a vocabulary that helps reveal how we do this. In later chapters (see especially chapters 4 to 8) these ideas are developed further and applied to more complex and more troubling problems.

2.1   A Broken Promise

Consider first how we think through some moral non-dilemmas. That will help us to see what is going on in some non-moral dilemmas. The example concerns broken promises.

I promise to meet you at my office at 10 o'clock. You tell me that the meeting is about something fairly important, and I say I'll be there. As I am walking to my office that morning at 9.30, after a leisurely breakfast and a thorough reading of the morning papers, I see a car hit a child and drive off. No one else is in sight. The child is alive but injured, probably with a broken limb but I don't trust my judgement on such matters. I go to a nearby house and persuade the occupant, herself busy with small children, to telephone for an ambulance and then I wait with the child until it arrives. As I wait I realize that I will be very late for our appointment, and that you may well not have been able to wait for me. When I get to my office you are not there, but I tell myself that I had no choice: although I had promised to be at the office it would have been crazy to keep that promise at the expense of an injured child.

Surely I was right. I had no choice but to break my promise. (And that is an interesting point in itself, another example of the fact that any commitment can be outweighed by strong enough other ones.) But the story cannot end there; I cannot leave things there. The first thing I must do is to find out what the consequences of the missed appointment are for you. Suppose I discover that you have failed to get a job application in by its deadline. Then I must try to get the deadline waived for you, and if that is not possible try to find out about other jobs I can help you apply for. None of these would have been my concern if I had not missed the appointment.

Now imagine me sitting with the child waiting for the ambulance and worrying about the missed appointment. You had said it was important and so I know I may be making difficulties for you. So I may worry, both about my neglected obligation and about your reaction. Both worries can be lessened when I realize that the situation does not end with my failure to turn up on time. Since by not being on time I am taking on a responsibility to minimize the resulting harm to you, and since I know and accept this, I have something to offer my conscience and your annoyance. And what I am offering is not just a compensating present, a good turn to offset the bad turn. It is a way of honouring my obligation. Put it this way: I had two conflicting obligations, to the child and to you, and I chose, as I had to, to live up to one with direct and immediate attention and to the other with indirect and long-term attention. And indirect attention is not neglect at all; in the long run it may cost me more.

This situation is straightforward, in that it is clear roughly what I must do. (The details of my obligation are not so clear, though. To what lengths must one go to clear up unexpected results of a broken promise?) But it makes explicit something that can be applied to real dilemmas: that is the contrast between direct and indirect attention. The contrast can be applied in a variety of ways. Consider the options I have if the situation is slightly different so that, on the one hand, the child is not badly hurt and I phone its parent rather than the ambulance, and on the other hand I know that it is quite crucial, a life-and-death matter, that I get to the appointment on time. The child asks me to stay till its parent arrives. Then instead of giving direct attention to the child and indirect attention to the appointment, I might give direct attention to the appointment and indirect attention to the child. I might rush off to the appointment, asking a neighbour to keep a distant eye on the kid, and later check back to see what I must do to compensate for any distress that I have allowed. There is a risk, of course, when I check back I may find that the child has died. But then if I stay with the child and miss my appointment I may find the consequences of that just as severe.

The point is that in deciding which obligation to attend to immediately I do not think in terms of the relative strengths of the two. (How would I compare a sincere promise about a relatively minor matter to an accidental involvement in something more serious?) I think instead in terms of the relative availability of indirect attention. Call this *the rain-check strategy.* It consires in turning the choice between two conflicting obligations or desires into a question of which one to satisfy immediately and which one to defer. Deferring one will usually mean that it cannot be satisfied directly. Some sort of indirect attention directed at an indirect satisfaction will be called for. (There is obviously a lot more to say about indirect satisfaction.) If I think one of the indirect follow-ups is easier or less risky than the other, then I should perform the action which commits me to that follow-up rather than the other. And if I cannot see any important difference between the two follow-ups then I may toss a mental coin, or take whatever option happens to be my whim knowing that I am prepared to follow up my responsibility to the other neglected option.

The rain-check strategy does not guarantee that things will go smoothly. Indirect attention to neither horn of the dilemma may be very appealing. The responsibility treated indirectly may develop disastrously. But very often it will solve the problem, without requiring a comparative weighing of the two issues. And this is the point to remember in seeing how the same kind of thinking applies to other case. Begin with a particularly trivial case, even by the standards of this chapter.

2.2   Sleep or Film: Indirect Satisfaction

At the end of a long day you arrive home from work hoping to be able to get to bed early so that the next day may not be so exhausting. Leafing through the newspaper you see that tonight is the last showing a few miles away of a film that you have long wanted to see. You are torn: desperate for a long sleep and very reluctant to miss the film. No clever device will allow you to do both. Now it may be that you are just stuck, and there is no more to it than a choice of which strong desire to leave unsatisfied. But that need not be so. To see why, consider seven reasons for taking one or another of the options.

   1   Sleep – because you'll regret missing the film. If you don't see the film then you will have frustrated some strong desires. You must find out which: they may for example be desires to see films by that director, or of that genre, or they may be desires for experiences of a certain kind, such as those given by romantic or exciting films. If you can discover what the *roots* of the frustrated desire to see that film are then you can attend to those roots, find books or other films or other experiences satisfying them. So you can neglect your desire for the film, and treat your neglect like a broken promise, to be dealt with by indirect attention. Put it this way. The desire to see that particular film could hardly be an isolated quirk of your psychology, unconnected with anything else you want, People do have quirky random desires, but these are usually pretty weak – easily overruled by other more important desires – or at any rate they usually fade quite quickly once they can no longer be satisfied. The desires that clamour for satisfaction, and grumble persistently when they are neglected, are desires with roots, with deep connections to one's most fundamental and permanent wants. And these connections and the deep desires they connect to are usually pretty hard to understand clearly. So if your desire to see the film is strong and insistent – if you know you'll regret not seeing it – then it has roots. What will be unsatisfied and cause regret is not just the desire for that film but needs or persistent strands of motivation which will remain after the possibility of seeing the film has passed. So if you have a hope of finding some other way of satisfying or expressing these needs you can promise them they will eventually dealt with, and go to bed.

2   *Film – because you can sleep the next night.* The roots of the desire to see the film may not be so easily satisfied. Other films by that director, or of that genre, or other experiences with that quality may not be coming your way, And you may have no idea what the roots of these roots are. On the other hand the desire to sleep can be satisfied the next night, at the price of a weary day before you can get it. So if you think you can struggle through the next day without a major disaster you can give immediate satisfaction to the desire which cannot wait, and go to the film.

3   *Either – because you can compensate either.* It may not be clear whether it is easier to find indirect satisfactions for the desire for the film or the desire for sleep. Then you might as well do either. Flip a coin. One will then be neglected. You will then want to look for indirect attention for the neglected one.

4   *Sleep – because the film desire will go away.* Perhaps you know that your enthusiasms are pretty fickle, and that the next day you will not regret having missed the film. Then indirect attention to the roots of the film desire will be easy, as there aren't any.

5   *Film – because the desire to sleep will pass.* Perhaps you know that early evening exhaustion followed by a brief sleep is usually followed by a reasonably bearable following day.

6   *Film – because the film desire will go away.* If you miss the film to sleep then you will not want to see a film again for a while, and will there-

fore have missed a rare opportunity to leave the work–supper–bed rut your life has slipped into.

7 *Either – because both desires will go away.* So indirect satisfaction will be trivial in either case.[1]

These are trivial considerations. It would not be an intellectual feat to act in accordance with any one of them. Moreover, they recommend different courses of action. But for the most part their different recommendations are based on different assessments of various facts, mostly about one's capacities for future satisfaction and future change of desire. And it might not be at all trivial finding out which of these assessments is really right. In a trivial everyday case like this one would just guess, but in deeper dilemmas, where more is at stake, the decision can turn on very hard questions about what patterns of future desire–satisfaction will be satisfactory.

First dilemma-managing principle: the rain–check principle. *Look for indirect satisfactions of desires and responsibilities. Choose the action which is least susceptible to indirect satisfaction.*

There can be something paradoxical about the rain–check strategy. For it can tell you to go for the thing you want less. In the first of the seven cases above, for example, it may be that you want to see the film more than you want a good night's sleep, but because you think the film desire will be satisfied with seeing two of that director's other works at a film festival in six months' time you decide to go to bed early tonight. I make no excuse for the paradoxicality of this. I think it reveals something which we accept in our decisions every day, surprising though that may seem. Sometimes the sensible thing to do is to choose the thing you want less.

2.3 Do You Like Chess? Wants Versus Values

You read in the newspaper that someone you knew at school will give an exhibition chess match tomorrow. 'That's nice,' you think, 'I haven't seen her for years, and I haven't so much as thought about chess for almost as long.' Then you find that you are committed to talking to your child's teacher that evening about the child's awful behaviour, so you cannot go.

You are annoyed. But not really upset, for this is just the kind of frustrated want that yields to indirect satisfaction. But then you have to think: what was it that you wanted? Was it to see your friend, or to touch again your former liking for chess? Or perhaps just not to have to face your child's outraged teacher. Whichever motive it was – or, more realistically, whatever the comparative strengths of these motives – you will be able to find an indirect satisfaction. But they demand quite different satisfactions. You could start reading the chess columns of newspapers, or teach your child to play. Or you could write to your friend, suggesting a meeting at some other time. Or you could take up some other intellectually demanding pursuit, perhaps learn to program a computer. There are many things you could do. There are always may things to do.

You may find some of these attractive. You may find all of them attractive. But none of them are the same as what they substitute for: seeing that person give that exhibition that evening. There is a distinction that it is important to make here, between what I shall call *wants* and *values*. Wants are for particular things and events, for example to go to that particular exhibition match. And values, not necessarily moral values, are underlying patterns of preference – for example a fondness for old friends or a liking for chess – which reveal themselves in one's wants for particular things. It is easier to know one's wants than one's values, but it is values rather than wants that are important in thinking through long-term patterns of action.

(The objects of one's values are usually particular kinds of things, situations, and activities. But one may not have simple names for them. So making one's underlying values explicit may involve some linguistic or conceptual ingenuity.)

So in thinking through the dilemma you have to find out which values are involved in your wanting to go to the match. This is not really a matter of self – analysis. What you need to know is which kinds of future actions you can promise yourself, so that looking back later you will not regret your choices. Or, putting yourself now into that retrospective position, what you need to know is the actions you can promise yourself which will allow you to go ahead without thinking you are neglecting something important. Perhaps all, or a large variety, of the likely indirect satisfactions – taking up chess, re-establishing the friendship, learning to compute, and so on – will work. Any of them will allow you to miss the match without a sense of regret or of something left unfulfilled. Then it may be that your wanting to see the match was based on many different values, any one of which could be indirectly satisfied. But more likely it would mean that no values are involved and it was just a whim, a want of the moment not tied to any pattern of motives. Then you could have shrugged your shoulders and let the match pass, without any of these complicated thoughts.

There is a lot more to say about the distinction between wants and values, and what it is for a want to be based on a value. It is a central theme of the next chapter. For the moment let me leave it vague and express it as a bit of advice to accompany the rain-check principle: distinguish between wants and values; remember that there is usually a choice of values which can be used to satisfy a want indirectly.

2.4   Bundle-balancing

Things get more complicated when the choice is not between two simple possibilities but a series, among some of which one has preferences. Let me explain with another trivial example.

You have a free evening in London and find that there are a number of concerts that interest you. You are also hungry and there are a number of restaurants you can afford. You know which concerts you prefer and which meals you prefer, but choosing between combinations of concerts and meals is more difficult. Your first choice among concerts is for a concert by the Birmingham Symphony; the second choice is a performance of the *St Matthew Passion*; third is a recorder recital. Your first choice among meals is a particular Armenian restaurant; second is a particular Italian restaurant; third is a particular Chinese restaurant. Unfortunately the Birmingham symphony begins early and the Armenian restaurant opens late, so you cannot have both of your first choices. In fact, the only choices allowed by the opening times and the problems of getting from place to place are (1) Chinese meal plus Birmingham Symphony, (2) Italian meal + *Matthew Passion*, and (3) Armenian meal + recorder recital. And you find that although you have clear preferences about music and clear preferences about food, you cannot compare music and food. Your preferences about music and food do not lead easily to preferences between bundles of food + music.

Options (1) and (3) each have an appeal, since each gives one side of your nature full expression. But then (2) has a very different sort of appeal, the appeal of compromise, since it allows neither kind of desire to be completely frustrated. What should you do?

I am going to argue against compromise in bundle-balancing. You should choose between (1) and (3). If need be make an arbitrary choice between them. Nothing I can say can be conclusive here, and no doubt the details of some situations make compromises like (2) attractive. So the general message is just: beware of compromises. Here are some reasons for caution.

First just imagine that you were faced with a series of food-versus-music choices. Once a month for the next year you will have an evening in London with essentially the same choices. Suppose you choose a compromise solution, and each time you have an acceptable but not first-choice meal followed by a pleasant but not really exciting concert. How boring! Anyone faced with such a series of choices, who really liked both food and music but had no preferences between them, would surely arrange or resolve a series of best meals and best concerts. One would probably care less whether there were more meal-dominated or music-dominated evenings than that there be very few evenings in which both values were frustrated.

What goes for a series goes for a single choice. For even if you were setting up a series of such evenings for a series of different people you would probably arrange that they divided between the extremes, avoiding the doubly frustrating middle. But if the compromise were as good as one of the extreme options for a single unrepeatable choice then the fact that (for example) the food is not bottom choice would compensate for the fact that the music is not top choice. This would amount to giving points for quality of meal and quality of concert: 1 point for bottom choice, 2 for middle, and 3 for top, say. Then each of the three options would get 4 points. So they all should be equally good. But then a series of compromise choices (for distinct people, so the position in the series is irrelevant) would be as good as a series of extreme choices. But it is not. So we cannot assign such points. So compensation doesn't apply, and there is nothing to recommend the compromise solution.

But suppose that you dislike Chinese food so much that the pleasure of getting the concert you want would be spoiled if it were preceded by a Chinese meal. Then you might prefer the compromise solution. But in that case you *do* have preferences between bundles of music and food. Or, to put it differently, compensation is possible. You would give up some musical pleasure to avoid gustatory displeasure.

So, supposing that compensation is not possible, the extreme solutions are better than the compromise. Here is another argument for this. Suppose that you discover that you have more options than you thought. Suppose you discover a new place to eat, a Japanese restaurant, and a new concert, a performance of *La Traviata*. Your orders of preference are now 'Armenian, Italian, Japanese, Chinese', and 'Birmingham Symphony, *La Traviata, Matthew Passion*, recorder recital'. Now consider the earlier compromise option, Italian meal + *Matthew Passion*. It no longer looks like much of a compromise, since it combines the second best meal with the second worst concert. It seems biased toward food. The fact is that the very idea of a compromise does not make sense unless you can compare decreases in one value with compensating increases in another.[2]

So there is a lot to be said for taking one of the two extreme options. And there is not much to be said in favour of the compromise option, unless in fact bundles of food and music can be compared to one another. Of course if the choice is taken in isolation taking one of the extremes means neglecting one value, food or music. The other then is a candidate for indirect satisfaction. (There may be a natural candidate for indirect satisfaction. Perhaps there are good *Indian* restaurants at home.) The full power of this strategy, of choosing the extreme of one value for direct satisfaction leaving the other for indirect satisfaction, will have to wait until the discussion of 'revaluing' in the next chapter. For the moment let me sum it up in a principle.

---

*Second dilemma-managing principle (*anti-compromise*): be suspicious of compromises. Often an option that allows both values a mediocre satisfaction leads to neither value being well satisfied, either directly or indirectly.*

2.5   Compensation: Freddie and Marilyn

The anti-compromise principle has a big proviso attached to it: be suspicious of compromises when combinations of the two values cannot be compared. But with a little ingenuity they often can be compared. One way of stimulating some ingenuity is to think in terms of compensation.

Instead of thinking of one person choosing between food and music consider two people facing the same dilemma. Imagine Siamese twins or an emotionally inseparable couple of whom one, Marilyn, is interested in music and not food and the other, Freddie, in food and not music. They cannot separate, Marilyn going to the Birmingham Symphony and Freddie going to the Armenian restaurant. They must go to the same restaurant followed by the same concert. Suppose that they choose (3), the bottom musical choice and the top food choice. Then Marilyn has reason to complain. Freddie can still her complaints in several ways. One way is to offer her compensation. Consider only compensations that do not involve food or music. Freddie can offer Marilyn anything – a holiday, shoes, a book, or simple callous money – with a question 'if this were added to option (3) would you be as happy as you would be with option (1)?'

Suppose Marilyn can say that she would freely exchange option (1), her top musical choice, for (3), her bottom musical choice, plus a given present. Then, of course, Freddie can give her the present, sweeten the bundle, and get the meal he wants, without making her unhappy. But, more to our purposes, Freddie can use such compensations to find out just how much Marilyn prefers (1) to (2) to (3). What is the smallest present (easiest to think just in terms of money now) which Marilyn will freely accept in exchange for (3) rather than (1)? Or for (2) rather than (1)?

Marilyn can explore the force of Freddie's preferences in the same way. And they can vary the technique in many ways, for example by asking each other how they would compare a given sweetener to a 50/50 gamble between (1) and (3). In these ways they can scale the musical and the food options: they can discover, for example, whether the *Matthew Passion* is for Marilyn just a little or a lot less desirable than the Birmingham Symphony. And if they can find things – presents, situations, amounts of money – which they both have much the same attitude to (longing, abhorrence, or indifference) then they can begin to compare Freddie's food preferences to Marilyn's music preferences. They might, for example, conclude that Marilyn has varying shades of indifference to all three musical options while for Freddie there is a world of difference between the most and the least attractive meal.

The importance of these comparisons is not particularly that they should compensate one another for not getting their first choice. (Though some of the sweetened bundles may appear among their more considered options.) The real importance is that they can measure the values of the bundles of food music on something like a common scale. For example, if Marilyn doesn't really care about music while food matters immensely to Freddie they should choose (3). Suppose, on the other hand, that each one likes their top choice about as much as the other does, and dislikes their bottom choice about as much too, but for Marilyn the *Matthew Passion* is almost as good as the Birmingham Symphony and for Freddie the Italian restaurant is almost as good as the Armenian restaurant. Then they should take the compromise (2) – *Matthew Passion* and Italian restaurant – since it satisfies both of their desires pretty well and frustrates neither of them very much.

Now return to the one-person case. Freddie and Marilyn were just symbolic images of two strands of one person's values. Exactly the same procedure that they went through to compare their preferences can be carried out by 'you' in choosing between options (1), (2) and (3). You can imagine situations in which the various options are sweetened in various ways. You might, for example, find that you are indifferent between bare (1) – Chinese meal + Birmingham Symphony – and a sweetened (3) – say Armenian meal + Recorder recital + tomorrow morning off work. Suppose you are also indifferent between bare (3) and a similarly sweetened (1). And suppose, lastly, that you decide, by simple introspection or by other imaginary compensations, that the *Matthew Passion* is almost as good as the Birmingham Symphony and the Italian restaurant is almost as good as the Armenian restaurant. Then, just as with Freddie and Marilyn, the compromise solution – Italian restaurant + *Matthew Passion* – is a reasonable choice. For it is almost as good as the extreme choices on both counts.

It makes an important difference, then, whether the components of a bundle can be compared, using real or imaginary compensations. But it isn't always a matter just of ingenuity or self-knowledge whether the comparison is possible. Values which can be compared and values which cannot are just very different, so quite often nothing like the Freddy and Marilyn game is possible. And even when it is possible a nagging doubt remains that the comparison has been forced harder than it should be. One reason for this is that the wants involved in many dilemmas are neither simply incomparable nor simply comparable.

Third dilemma-managing principle: compensation. *Try to calculate compensations by comparing options with other possible or imaginary compensating additions. In particular, do this with additions that can be compared among one another, like amounts of money or days of holiday. Then choose the option that would require least addition to make it as desirable as any other option.*

2.6   Catching a Whim

It is hard to satisfy a desire that won't stay still. Consider a problem for indirect satisfaction. You know that you often have a whim to buy small unnecessary items in shops. Ties, earrings, decorative notebooks, magazines whose cover pictures seize your eye. Sometimes you can give the purchase to someone, retrospectively justifying it, but usually they just accumulate at home. You also know that if you can resist the whim, you never later wish you had not. Suppose now that you are walking down the street and in a shop window you see a little china frog, attractive but not beautiful. You stop to buy it, and then realize that there is nothing in your pockets but a little cash. If you buy the frog you cannot buy the book you came into town for, and if you don't buy it you will never miss it.

There are several problems here for the rain-check strategy. First of all the advice has been to give indirect satisfaction to the desire which can most easily have it, letting its rival be satisfied directly. It is easy to satisfy the desire for the book indirectly – come back tomorrow with cash or credit card. But indirect satisfaction of the desire for the frog is impossible: you won't want it once you have passed by. So the rain-check strategy seems to advise buying the frog and coming back tomorrow for the book.

That seems crazy. Buying the frog is throwing money away. Much better to buy the book and forget about the frog. There seem to me to be in fact two non-crazy choices. Buy the book and forget about the frog, or buy the book and indirectly satisfy the frog desire. Let me explain the second of these, the less obvious one, and after that say why the example does not refute the rain-check principle.

What might be the point of indirectly satisfying a whim for a china frog? One point might be to avoid becoming a mechanical, calculating, inflexibly end-directed person. Another might be to satisfy some deep craving for small pretty possessions. (Who knows, perhaps your big brother used to hide your toys.) Different such reasons would suggest different indirect satisfactions, for they point to different values underlying the whim. (The value of having whims, or the value of having small pretty things.) Supposing there is an underlying value, then the indirect satisfaction is clear: you give in to other whims occasionally, or you start a collection of really interesting small pretty things. (netsuke, perhaps, or cigar boxes.)

In this way the roots of the whim, whatever you took or discovered them to be, would be attended to. (There might be no roots; the whim might be a pure whim. But that is not likely if there is a pattern in the objects of your whimsy.) So more of what you want would have been satisfied than if you had just suppressed the whim in order to buy the book. That is the justification for indirectly satisfying the whim. But why not directly satisfy the whim and indirectly satisfy its unwhimsical rival?

The answer is obvious. You would not at the end of the day have got much of what you wanted. Looking back later, the frog would mean nothing to you and the purposes for which you wanted the book would have been less easily satisfied. The rain-check strategy is meant to satisfy as many as possible of the values underlying one's moment-to-moment desires. It is, that is, meant to allow one to look back and see one's actions as things one does not regret having done. There is a lot more to say about this but it is enough to explain why the rain-check strategy does not suggest that you should prefer to satisfy a whim rather than a desire with roots. Briefly: indirect satisfaction is directed at values rather than wants.

The idea that choice should be based on the way one might later retro-spectively evaluate one's actions is important. I call it the looking back principle.

Fourth dilemma-managing principle: the looking back principle. *Make choices which can later be seen as a coherent expression of a set of under-lying values. Look ahead to how you might look back.*

This is the most basic of the principles I discuss in this chapter. It is very hard to state it correctly. I shall have more to say about it, as late as the last chapter of the book. The looking back principle should not be taken as an injunction not to satisfy whims, or as a requirement that everyone have their life planned in advance. Its main meaning, at this stage, is that you shouldn't make choices which you know will mean nothing to you later.

2.7 Manipulating the Agenda: Unequal Opportunities

Given a list of options it is often hard to choose which one to take, or what further plans for further action to join to one's decisions. But, for all that, the general shape of the decision is often determined before that stage, by the selection of options from which the choice is made. So in thinking through a dilemma it is often worth considering whether one is using the best way of presenting choices to oneself. In chapter 5 I consider a series of techniques for relating the choice of options for serious consideration to the problem at hand. Now consider just one example.

You are on a committee which is making an appointment to a job. It is important to you to get the best person for the job. The job is open to both men and women but there are disproportionately many men in that department and, if only for the sake of the company's public image, you would like to appoint a woman. But you cannot say how much weight the need to appoint a woman has compared to the need to appoint the other-wise best candidate. if the best candidate is a woman you will have no problem, and if there is a tie between a man and a woman you will appoint the woman, but you know that things rarely work out so nicely.

Here is one way in which the committee can deal with its problem. Suppose that appointments are made in the standard way: the job is ad-vertised and then the committee goes through the applications of people who have responded to the advertisement and selects a shortlist of people to be given intense scrutiny. Then the people on the shortlist are interviewed and the most impressive of them is offered the job. Often it is decided in advance how large the shortlist is to be. In many cases the basis for the decision is something pretty superficial, like the amount of time it would be convenient to spend interviewing. Now suppose that you determine in advance the maximum and minimum size of the shortlist, for example that it will contain at most six and at least three people, and that at least three of them will be women. Then you follow the standard procedure, except that when you draw up the shortlist you are constrained to have three women on it, even at the expense of having a longer list than usual.

If you can persuade your colleagues to adopt this procedure, you will have increased the likelihood that the job will go to a woman, without compromising the principle that the committee should choose the best person or forcing you to balance qualifications against gender. (Note that the apparent suitability of candidates usually changes a lot from the rough scrutiny that gets them on to a shortlist to the more intense consideration before and during the interview. So one thing that manipulating the shortlist does is to increase the chances that one of the people whose rough acceptability turned on closer examination into real suitability will be a woman.)

The general trick here is to avoid having to balance gender and qualifications by instead balancing gender and administrative effort. (If you had an even stronger commitment to equal opportunities you could have resolved that two-thirds of the shortlisted people would be women and that the shortlist would, if need be, contain twelve names. But then you would have to be prepared to put a lot more time into investigating and interviewing the candidates.) That gives a fifth dilemma-managing principle.

Fifth dilemma-managing principle: unequal opportunities. *sometimes a value that cannot easily be balanced against another can more easily be balanced against some aspect of the decision-making process. In that case a suitable procedure for finding options to decide between may remove the need to compare the two hard-to-compare values.*

These five dilemma-managing principles show the rationale of a whole family of strategies. There are important differences between them. But they all manage incomparable desires by avoiding simple maximization. And they all do this by shifting the task of balancing competing desires elsewhere: either from the immediate choice to a pattern of future choices or from one part of the decision-making process to another. They raise a number of questions, though. Can something more systematic be said about indirect satisfaction? How are wants related to values? When, more exactly, is compromise a reasonable solution? What is it for a history of choices to be a coherent expression of a set of values? And, most importantly, what makes one dilemma-managing strategy rather than another reasonable for a particular person in a particular situation? These are not questions to which I shall give complete and definitive answers. But, as we shall see, there is more to say about them.

Part II
Theory

3

Incomparabilities

3.1 *Dimensions of Incomparability*

You want a successful career and also to be a conscientious parent. You had not realized that life would force you to choose between them, and when you find that your occupation, your spouse, and your own limitations make it necessary to choose or compromise, you find you are just not prepared with any coherent preferences.

Possibly if you think hard enough about your situation you will come up with some coherent preferences, and these may just possibly involve a tidy tradeoff between family and career. Or it may be that the harder you think the more complicated and obscure your preferences become. So you may conclude that you can give neither value a clear priority in your life. But you are not simply indifferent between them either. You could not give up either one in favour of the other and regard yourself as having come out just as well as if you had found a comfortable balance between them. Family life and your career are incomparable values for you.

The point of this book is to present strategies for making decisions based on desires which cannot be straightforwardly compared to one another. Incomparable desires certainly cannot be straightforwardly compared. The whole topic of incomparability of desires is veiled in confusion and controversy. Some people deny that there are any incomparable desires.[1] The aim of this chapter is to say what I mean by incomparability, why I take it to be just a fact of life that many of our desires are incomparable, and why it makes an enormous difference to decision-making what patterns of incomparability our desires exhibit. There are many ways in which desires can be incomparable, and the zoo of types of incomparability I describe here is only scratching the surface of their variety. That is the main thing I have to show.

You prefer one thing to another when you want it more than you want the other. In fact, preference is a clearer idea than wanting: as I sit at my desk trying to concentrate I would prefer to be interrupted by a friend than by a salesman, but I just don't know whether I want to be interrupted by either. (But perhaps I do want an interruption; the work is getting me down. The point is that it can depend on a fine shade of meaning for 'want' although the facts about 'prefers' are perfectly straightforward.) You are indifferent between two things when you want them equally, when you would happily exchange either for the other. But sometimes you neither prefer one thing to another nor are you indifferent between them. Then they are incomparable for you.

If two things are incomparable for you then you will not be able to choose between them just on the basis of your preference between them. Since everyone has trouble choosing between some options there is a very weak and obvious sense in which desires can be incomparable: often one does not know which of two things one wants more, while being not at all certain that one wants them equally. The restaurant-versus-concert examples of the last chapter describe situations like this.

Sometimes you cannot decide on the relative weight to give to two things you want, but if you think about the question it becomes quite clear what your preference ought to be. This usually happens because you come to understand the connections between the two options and other matters about which your preferences are quite clear. Thus you may find it very hard to decide whether to go to a film or to get some much-needed sleep – the desires for the film and for sleep do not by themselves fall easily into an order – but when you remember that you have an interview the next morning for a job you desperately want, it becomes clear that you ought to go to bed.

On the other hand, sometimes when you think about your choices your preferences become less rather than more definite. Sometimes this is a sign of wisdom. Suppose for example that you have a sum of money which you wish to give away so as to do the most good. You are choosing between an emergency fund set up to benefit thousands of starving refugees from war and famine in Africa, and a development fund for a region of Central America. At first it seems to you obvious that the disaster fund is the one you should benefit, since the people it helps cannot wait and their immediate plight is awful. But then troubling thoughts occur to you. One is: famines and other large-scale calamities receive more publicity than the continuing endemic misery of much of the world's population, and thus receive disproportionately much private and public aid. You should therefore contribute to the neglected rather than the well-publicized cause. As you consider this you become more and more uncertain. (One of the deep questions you are having to worry about is the relative weight of saving life and alleviating misery. See chapter 8.)

I take it that many choices are like this. The more we think about them the more connections with things we want, fear, and value appear, and the harder it becomes to take account of uncertainties in the information available and inherent risks in the situation. There may be an ultimately correct preference, which one could arrive at if one was intelligent enough and thought long enough. But on the spot, with limited time and brainpower, one has to choose an option and has no idea which thing one wants more.

The first dimension of incomparability is thus what we might call *depth*: how much thought and how many comparisons with other wants the inability to choose will survive. Another dimension is what we might call *generality*, whether the incomparability concerns just individual wants or also the values that usually underlie them. The incomparability in the restaurant-versus-concert examples was between particular wants – for example to eat in this restaurant tonight or go to that concert tonight – but in discussing them I tacitly assumed that there must be an incomparability between the values the person attaches to food and to music. In the family-versus-career example the incomparability is clearly between the underlying values, and pretty clearly these values are themselves related to others, rather harder to articulate precisely, concerning love, success, the opinion of others, work, accomplishment, duty and the like.

People sometimes claim that there are incomparabilities between their political and social values. For example it might be claimed that although equality and freedom are both valuable – you ought to want there to be more equality rather than less equality and more freedom rather than less freedom – there is no objective way of comparing the two.[2] This will matter when one has to compromise between them, for example when one can gain equality at the price of freedom or vice versa. Then there would be no telling which compromises are acceptable. A similar claim might be made about values occurring in the lives of individuals, such as love and accomplishment. (Notice that these claims are for an incomparability not only of a great generality but also of a great depth: the fundamental values involved will remain or become incomparable even after one has completely thought through their relations to one another.)

It is controversial whether deep and general incomparabilities exist. I take it to be pretty clear that shallow incomparability of both general and particular wants is common: that is, that a moderate amount of reflection often does not tell you which of two particular options to prefer or which of two values to give priority to in your life. (Although a little reflection does tell you that you should not think of them as interchangeable.) I take it, too, that the depth of many incomparabilities is fairly great: it would take a very non-trivial application of human intelligence to establish a simple preference. That is enough to establish a serious decision-making problem: we need ways of making decisions that we can use when our preferences leave many things incomparable.

(I have ignored one possibility: are there deep non-general incomparabilities? Pretty clearly there are. One could have two pure whims – to buy a china frog or to do a cartwheel in the street – and not only not know which whim was stronger, but also find that no amount of thinking told one which whim it made more sense to indulge. I don't think this is a very interesting or important fact, though.)

3.2   Preference Orderings

Comparable preferences are easy to understand: they just form a linear series from the most (or more) wanted to the least (or less) wanted. Incomparable preferences are harder to think about; they are arranged in more complicated patterns. Some of these patterns are quite easy to imagine spatially. Doing so is the easiest way to understand some of their basic properties.

Very rarely are two desires incomparable in the most simple possible way, which would happen if one's desire for something were simply incomparable with any of one's other desires. it couldn't be compared to anything. (So it would not be more desirable than the destruction of the world or less desirable than the achievement of all one's hopes and ambitions.) Usually, in fact I would think always, a desire will be comparable to some others and incomparable to others. The simplest form this can take is the *diamond pattern*.

Consider, for example, a pattern of five desires. You are considering various holidays, and on reflection your order of preference is as follows:

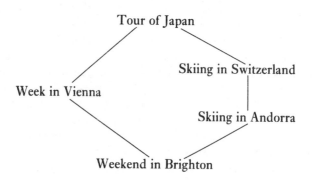

That is, you prefer Japan to any of the other options shown, and Brighton least. Skiing is better in Switzerland land than in Andorra, but you cannot compare skiing options with ordinary touring options. (Japan is an extraordinary touring option.)

It is clear in this case that although Switzerland (for example) is incomparable with Vienna, the two do not have the same desirability. For Andorra is also incomparable with Vienna, and if these two also have the same desirability then so do Switzerland and Andorra, which is just not true. (If Switzerland = Vienna and Vienna = Andorra, then Switzerland = Andorra.) So the difference between incomparability and indifference comes out very clearly.[3] It is also clear that we can say something about the relation between Vienna and the skiing holidays even though they are incomparable. We can say, for example, that Vienna and both skiing holidays lie between Japan and Brighton in preference: so if you would pay £500 for a tour of Japan and you would pay £50 for a weekend in Brighton then all three of the other holidays are worth between £500 and £50. (This might actually be a useful consideration: you wonder how much you would pay for a Swiss skiing holiday and you draw the upper limit at the least for which you could get a tour of Japan.)

The diamond pattern is very common. The restaurants–versus–concerts example was of diamond-shaped preferences. (An even simpler diamond has just four members: For example if we removed one of the skiing holidays from the diagram above. But this would illustrate the difference between incomparability and indifference less well.) The overall structure of most people's preferences must contain diamonds within diamonds. In a diamond-shaped set of preferences many preferences are incomparable but they are linked by their relations to other possibilities. In this way the choices one can make are restricted. For instance, if you are forced to choose between Vienna and Andorra you may choose either one consistently with the preferences as pictured. You can choose one way today and the other way tomorrow, supposing you were forced to choose again. But you cannot choose Andorra rather than Vienna if Switzerland is available. (It is quite alright to choose Andorra over Vienna if Switzerland is not available.)

(This ignores two important questions. How should you compare Vienna and, say, a 50/50 gamble between Japan and Brighton? And how should your choices show the fact that you would rather not be forced to choose between Vienna and Switzerland?)

A yet more complex pattern of choice is produced by the next pattern of incomparability, *zig-zag*. Imagine you are choosing between holidays in Bali and Colorado. You cannot choose between, say, seven days in one place and seven days in the other. But you would prefer, say, eight days

in Bali to five days in Colorado. And you would prefer eight days in
Colorado to five days in Bali. And in general, a stay in either place is
incomparable with a stay in the other as long as one is not more than two
days longer than the other, but beyond that point a preference for longer
holidays takes over. So you find you have a pattern of preferences like this:

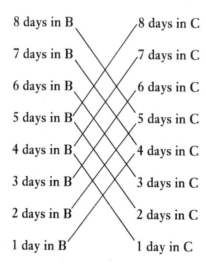

When you realize that this is the pattern of your preferences you might
well decide to simplify things by preferring n days in either place to m
days in the other as long as n is greater than m. In this case the difference
in your choices would not be great. But there are other cases where it
would make an important difference. For example it would eliminate an
important aspect of the preferences involved in 'qualified trumps' where
large amounts of one thing are comparable with small amounts of another
(for example large amounts of pain are worse than small probabilities of
death) but large or small amounts of either one are incomparable with
similarly large or small amounts of the other.

The last pattern of preference I shall describe is also linked with
qualified trumps. Call it the *shifting horizon*. Start with a zig-zag pattern,
for example the Bali/Colorado pattern. Suppose that someone who had
those preferences began to doubt whether five days in Colorado really
were preferable to two days in Bali. They might then revise their preferences so that stays in either place were incomparable unless there was a
difference of more than four days in their duration. Then the diagram of
the preferences would look exactly the same except that the lines representing preferences between stays in the two places would slope down
more steeply.

Suppose that the person on some occasions chose as if their preferences had the first pattern ('five in Colorado better than two in Bali;
four in Colorado incomparable to two in Bali') and on other occasions
chose as if they had the second pattern ('six in Colorado better than two in
Bali; five in Colorado incomparable to two in Bali'). (Imagine the person
to be a travel agent making assumptions about other people's holidays.)
Then this person's preferences would have the general shape of the zig-
zag pattern, except that the slope of the connecting lines would wobble:
sometimes they would be more steep than at others.

So this represents another possible pattern, in which incomparability
occurs at a higher level: the person's choices hover between one zig-zag
pattern and another. This is not easy to describe in unconvoluted
language, but the picture is easy to grasp.[4] One has a number of fixed
outcomes in two or more categories, and instead of a fixed set of preferences between members of different categories there is a variety of
'horizons' of definite preference between them. And it is clear how this
can also model some 'qualified trumps' preferences. For example sometimes one's preferences between losses of money and risks to one's life will
fall into one zig-zag pattern and sometimes into another. The horizon of
incomparability shifts, within limits.

By now it should be clear what an enormous variety of patterns there is
for preferences to take. My examples of preference patterns have all
involved a small number of preferences, and so an interesting question is
whether the variety becomes greater or smaller when we consider something nearer to a person's whole system of preferences. I tend to think that
there is a normal pattern to the rough global structure of a typical person's
preferences, and that it looks like a family of rough diamonds determined
by a system of shifting horizons.[5] (Within that overall structure, though,
there would be an enormous variety of local substructures.) That may or
not be right: even to pose the question is to move well beyond what we
understand. What is clear is that more limited sets of preferences can have
a great variety of patterns, and that the appropriateness of a decision-making strategy depends sensitively on the pattern of the relevant preferences.

3.3 Beliefs Shaping Desires

The significance of some patterns of incomparability becomes clearer if we
add another ingredient to the brew: the influence of beliefs on desires.
Consider an example to illustrate this influence. I will have to develop the
point before the connection with incomparability appears.

You would love to go hang-gliding. The idea of floating quietly in the air and climbing on thermals like a bird, with the feel of the air on your face and the sense that the wings holding you up are controlled directly by your body, is overwhelmingly enticing. But you don't do anything to achieve this dream, and in fact you take measures to keep yourself away from hand-gliding sites, for you think it is just too dangerous.

Would it be accurate to say that you want to go hang-gliding? On the one hand you have a very strong impulse to do it, and you know you would enjoy it, and on the other hand you carefully and deliberately avoid it. In everyday English we might say that you wish you could go hang-gliding but, all things considered, do not think you should. In fact in English we have a rich variety of terms and constructions to express distinctions like this. We speak of wants and whims and desires and wishes and hopes, and of what one would like or what one really wants.

There is a basic fact here that has to be acknowledged on any theory of decision making. One way of expressing it is that a person can want something very much and yet give it a very low weight when making choices, because of the consequences they think choosing it would have. Another way of putting it is that a person can change the preferences that are revealed in their decisions without changing anything very fundamental about what they want, just because their information about the world is changing. (You learn that hang-gliding is after all not very dangerous; in fact the tranquil state it induces can prolong your life. You immediately sign up for lessons. But not because your urge to fly has increased, or your concern for safety decreased.) There is therefore a problem: how can we characterize that aspect of a person's preferences which is not just a reflection of their beliefs?

3.4   Ultimate Descriptions

There are two attractive types of solution to the problem. Let me begin with what is perhaps the less natural or obvious of them, as it is, for all that, the most common one among decision theorists. I'll call it the *ultimate descriptions model*. I call it a model because it gives a simplified picture of the relation between a person's beliefs and their desires, a relation which can be the core of a whole theory of decision making. The central idea here is that if we describe our desires more carefully we find that the preferences that change in response to changes in belief are not the same as the preferences which do not change. For example what 'you' want to a great degree is something like 'flying in immediate contact with the air without bad consequences' and what you want very little is death or injury. Neither of these is changed if you gain new information about the dangers of hang-gliding. But new information will change your attitude to a more indefinite option like simply 'hang-gliding'.

So, on this picture, when revising one's desires because of new information or changes in one's beliefs what one does is to begin with one's preferences with respect to the most detailed descriptions one can get of all the relevant possible situations. ('I go hang-gliding and enjoy it very much and for several years go up once a month with great enjoyment and without injury, but on my sixtieth flight I am caught in a downdraught and crash breaking both legs' would be on the way, but only on the way, to such a detailed description.) Then for each less detailed description of a state of affairs (e.g. 'I take hang-gliding lessons', 'I live to be 100') you calculate its 'new' desirability in terms of how likely it is on each basic situation and what the 'old' desirability of that situation is. You reason along lines like: if I take up hang-gliding then I am very likely to be in situation A and a little less likely to be in situation B and very unlikely to be in situation C; A is an awful situation, B is slightly uncomfortable, and C is very nice; so I should see the attractiveness of hang-gliding as somewhere between that of A and C but nearer to A. (There are standard formulas for making quantitative judgements along these lines.[6]) The less detailed descriptions that matter most are those like 'I take hang-gliding lessons', which describe possible actions, since you should perform the action which is preferred to all others on the new desirability scale.

So if you could describe all the situations you and the world around you might be in, and if you had definite preferences between all of these situations, the problem would be solved.[7] You could take your constant 'underlying' desires to be given by your preferences between these totally specific situations. These would generate different 'working' desires for less specific objects depending on your changing beliefs. (This is not to deny that your most fundamental desires can also change. But your more superficial desires – what car you want to buy or what political party you want to win the next election – can obviously change without any change in your more basic preferences.) But can anyone have such a complete and detailed set of preferences?

Imagine someone who could. Imagine a person who is so intelligent that she can imagine everything that might possibly happen. Call her Superia. For each possible world – each completely detailed specification of a way things could be – Superia knows exactly how much she wants it and how likely she thinks it is that the real world is or will be that way. You can describe to her the most unlikely state of affairs and she can tell you just where it ranks in her preferences, and what she takes its probability to be. For any particular proposition, for example the proposition that she quit her job to become an author, she knows exactly which detailed states of affairs – which possible worlds – would make it true. (It would be true if she spends the rest of her life working on a novel which she never finishes; or if she finds she cannot write fiction and spends forty years as a hack journalist; or if she finds her niche as a writer of popular philosophy; or if . . . Of course all of these are infinitely less detailed than the possible worlds Superia would actually have to imagine.) And for each of these possibilities she knows exactly how likely she thinks it is. So, in order to decide how much she wants such a particular proposition Superia can go through all the possible worlds in which it is true and form a mental sum of them, weighted by the likelihood that such a world represents the actual future. So she knows how much she wants to become a writer by seeing all possible future lives she could live and knowing how much she wants each one of them.[8]

3.5 Complexity and Incomparability

Real people are not like Superia. We are inferia mainly in that we cannot imagine, let alone form preferences between, possibilities beyond a certain degree of complexity. So we just do not have attitudes to whole possible worlds. Instead we have preferences between and beliefs about propositions we can express in our limited vocabularies and grasp with our limited imaginations. Anything with far-reaching consequences (for example anything such as a career or investment decision which will have consequences at every moment of future time) will thus be too much for us if we try to think it through in these terms.

How do we do it, then? One way is obvious. We know, to some extent, what we are trying to get in life (for example comfort, love, excitement, self-respect) and we evaluate both actions and possible detailed situations in terms of these. (So we start in the middle, as it were: we have prior attitudes to general characteristics of our lives and we have to think our way 'down' to possible situations, inasmuch as we can grasp them, and 'up' to possible actions.) This is just the distinction I drew in chapter 2 between desires and values. By a value I shall mean a desire for something fairly general, like having a million dollars or being the object of someone's love, which plays a constant role in a person's motivation over a period of time. Some values outrank others: for most people having a million dollars is more desirable than having a thousand dollars. This ranking of values may not be the same as that of wants for particular things, like having a cup of coffee or pressing the red button half-way down the coffee machine. Desires are different from values both in their objects and in the fact that preference between them depends in part on one's beliefs.

Consider a simple two-level model, then, the *basic values model*.[9] Assume that every person has two sets of preferences: value-preferences and desire-preferences. Value-preferences hold between general aspects of situations and actions, and together with the person's beliefs they generate the desire-preferences between particular actions and more detailed situations. (The first represents what a person 'really wants', if you like, and the second what they 'would choose all things considered'. But if you speak this way you must remember that the two attitudes have characteristically different objects.)

What you desire-prefer is what will achieve more of what you value, if the world is the way your beliefs represent it. I shall assume, to sharpen the contrast with the ultimate descriptions model, that desire-preferences are derived from value-preferences by deduction from one's beliefs: one action or possibility, A, will be at least as good in desire-preference as another, B, for a person if it follows from the person's beliefs that if A were to happen then all values that would thereby be achieved would be at least as good in value-preference as those that would be achieved were B to happen. Obviously very often options or possibilities will be incomparable to each other in desire-preferability on this model. A trivial way in which this can happen is that each of them can bring with it the achieving of some value incomparable to all those that the other would bring.

More interestingly, on this model options or possibilities can be incomparable even when the underlying values have no incomparability. The basic fact here is the incompleteness of our beliefs. Suppose that a person has completely comparable value-preferences. The person might be a hedonist for whom degrees of pleasure are the only things that matter, the more the better. Then suppose the person confronted with a complex choice, for example one of the restaurant-versus-concert mini-dilemmas. They would, on the basic values model, produce some desire-preferences according to the rule: A is preferable to B if my beliefs entail that if A happens I will get more pleasure than if B happens. But, nearly always, the person's beliefs will leave many questions unanswered. (How well will the orchestra play? Would the asparagus be fresh?) And as a result many options will not be ranked with respect to one another. They will be left incomparable.

Thus even if there are no incomparabilities among one's values, there will almost inevitably be some among one's desires. (According to the basic values model, that is, but, I would say, also in reality.) These derived incomparabilities can be seen as part of a complexity-handling

strategy behind the basic values mode. For the full description of the
nature and consequences of the options before one may be beyond one's
understanding. All one can do is get more and more information about
them, approaching as near to one's limit as the occasion warrants. But, on
the basic values model, as long as the new information is consistent with
the previous information one will never have to reverse the desire-preference of two options. If one option is preferred to another relative to a set
of beliefs it will be preferred relative to any consistent enlargement of that
set. Thus we can see the incomparability of desire-preferences as a way of
holding the question of priority between options open, until enough information comes in to settle the question once and for all.

This does not happen on the ultimate descriptions model. On that
model if there are no incomparabilities in the preference-ranking of the
most complex and detailed possible situations there will be none in the
ranking of less complex ones. If our hedonist were described by this
model each restaurant and each concert would be comparable to each
other: one of them would always be preferred to the other. And as the
hedonist acquired more information about the cooking or the performance
this ordering would change: the order of some pairs would be reversed.

In describing the ultimate descriptions model and the basic values model
I have made them as different as possible. They differ in two fundamental
respects. One is that on the ultimate descriptions model one has fundamental preferences over the most complex possibilities, while on the basic
values model one has fundamental preferences over aspects or qualities (or
large sets of possibilities, if you want). The other contrast concerns the
relation between beliefs and preferences. On the ultimate descriptions
model the system of beliefs is assumed to be a complete assignment
of a probability to everything that can happen, and preferences between
actions and non-ultimate possibilities are obtained by taking a proba-
bility-weighted average. On the other hand, on the basic values model
there may be gaps in the system of beliefs, and preferences between
actions and possibilities are obtained by deducing a comparison, in the
way I have described. (So the ultimate descriptions model tries to encode
all ignorance and uncertainty in terms of probability, while the basic
values model leaves ignorance as ignorance, that is, as gaps in one's
beliefs.)

There are many positions between these two extremes, and one can
make models that cut across the two contrasts. For example one can introduce probabilities into the basic values model, retaining the distinction
between value-preferences and desire-preferences and still leaving gaps in
the system of beliefs. (Then the model could use a formulation something

like: what you desire-prefer is what will give a greater chance of achieving more of what you value.) But the components of each of the two extreme cases dovetail very naturally together, and each certainly represents an ideal form of one kind of practical reasoning. And contrasting them brings out an important link between complexity and incomparability: a model that accommodates our limited capacity to handle information is likely to generate incomparable preferences for complex situations even given comparable preferences for simple ones.[10]

3.6 Elasticity and the Effects of Reflection

The basic values model is only a model, a helpful simplification. Two levels would not really be enough to capture the ways in which people's desires respond to their beliefs; or for that matter for describing people's decision-making resources. But it is enough to get to grips with one very important characteristic of human wanting, its elasticity.

Elasticity is the capacity to snap back to a previous shape. You first believe that hang-gliding is dangerous and thus do not want-prefer it to bird-watching, but then come to think it safe and so reverse these preferences. Your value-preferences remain unchanged, though. And thus when your beliefs change yet again, to their original values – the person who persuaded you that hang-gliding is perfectly safe turns out to have taken out an insurance policy on you – your want-preferences snap back so that you again prefer bird-watching.[11]

That is not to say that when your beliefs change back to their original values your preferences will always revert to exactly their original values. One reason they may not is that your value-preferences may have changed. You may find that the very act of signing up for hang-gliding lessons shakes the grip that the value of safety had on you, so that exciting risky options now have much greater appeal.

The relation between complexity and incomparability gives a reason for something I asserted in the last chapter: that sometimes when one thinks over one's preferences the number of incomparabilities can increase rather than decrease. Reflection sometimes makes one's wants less clear. The reason is that when one reflects one makes finer discriminations between the ways the world might be or become. One thing that can then happen is that previously ignored aspects of situations come to mind, which are not comparable with the aspects previously considered. Consider an example that makes a connection both with the theme of avoiding compromises and with the theme of regret. You at first have a simple preference for option A – an evening spent at your first-choice concert, plus a poor meal, over option B – a rather worse concert plus a rather better meal. But then you reflect that the next day you may regret having had to eat so badly if you take option A, and you may regret having missed the best concert if you take option B. The regret would be less with B, though, since you will at least have had a decent concert, if not your top choice. So in terms of the pleasure of the evening you prefer A to B but in terms of likely regret you prefer B to A. And you find you have no easy tradeoff between pleasure and regret. So the decision has become harder. (Better decide quickly, before it becomes harder yet.)

The least compromising options are often the ones with the greatest possibility for regret. So non-compromisers often have to be fairly well regret-proofed. But that is not the main point now. The main point is just that the more you consider the fine structure of the possibilities before you the more you may find apparently simple preferences becoming clouded with incomparabilities.

3.7   Haste Makes Waste

You are becoming disgruntled with your job of analysing statistics on beverage consumption for a big food company. Over the past year the work has seemed much less interesting; routine work with the computer seems now to be the main focus of the job, while once it was just a means to the exploration of the maze of different tastes and habits of many different nationalities and social groups. Your uncle is part-owner of a chain of small hotels and holiday villages in the Mediterranean; he has been suggesting to you that you should quit your job and become manager of the chain, taking over his share when he retires. It is an attractive prospect, but you value the security of your present job and you remember that not long ago it was much more engaging.

In deciding whether to stay or to move jobs you have to consider the possible futures that could follow from either. But there are so many of them, and it is hard to know how likely any of them are.

If you are thinking in terms of ultimate descriptions you try to make up your mind exactly how much you prefer these possible futures: as many of them as you can think of and in as much detail as possible. Suppose you do this, and eventually decide that two possible lives are crucial. If you take the job in the hotel business then you will very likely find the mathematical side of your present job replaced by a human-interaction side. On the other hand if you stick with the food company job for another year or so you will probably be able to get a promotion to head a group of analysts and programmers, so that your work will mainly be concerned with statistical and programming problems that they cannot handle. How would the interest of that compare to the novelty and freedom of the hotel job? The appeals of these two very different future lives are very hard to compare, but eventually you decide that a change and human contact mean more to you than security and intellectual stimulation. So you take your uncle's offer. Within six months you find that while human contact may be a great good, it is not worth much when the humans you are contacting are peevish, petty, and unprincipled. You hate it. Disaster. To make things worse, it is not just a bad-luck disaster. If you had thought a little further you could have predicted it. One cause of the disaster was preferring the one option to the other before you had thought the question through.

(This is a common characteristic of disasters, that in retrospect one sees how they could have been anticipated. But, usually, it does not follow from this that they *ought* to have been anticipated. There are so many possibilities to think through, and so many of them contain potential catastrophe, that it is only in the light of an actual disaster that one particular set of dangers comes to stand out.)

Suppose that you had instead thought out your problem in terms of values. Much of your deliberation would have been the same, but there would have been a difference at the point at which you had to compare the two most likely possible lives, differing in intellectual stimulation and human contact. If you were thinking in terms of values rather than detailed lives you would most likely conclude that you could not compare these two possibilities. This would be not just because of the difficulty of comparing intellectual stimulation and human contact, but also because you would not have enough information to describe in real detail what the two lives would be like.

At this point it would make a big difference whether you were thinking just in terms of preferences which have to be hammered into a definite order, as ultimate descriptions suggests, or more subtly, in terms of preferences which when examined may crystallize into a definite order or may remain incomparable. On the latter mentality preferences which resist ordering signal a dilemma and suggest that you should do something subtler than just going for what seems to offer most of what you want. You will then be reluctant to take either course; you will look around for a dilemma-managng strategy. One element of a suitable strategy in this case might be taken from one of the 'spreading strategies' of chapter 5, which give different preferences different roles in the decision. Another would surely be to gather information which will help you to sort out what you want. For example in the next few months you could shift your emphasis in the firm more in the direction of customer-handling, to find out what kinds of human contact really appeal to you.

Moral: it is a mistake to act on the result of a short deliberation as if it were the result of a long one. We need ways of marking some preferences as tentative, to be treated with caution. Incomparability is one way of doing this.

3.8   Revaluing

I have taken values to underlie desires and to remain constant while desires change. The opposite can also occur, as it does in the dilemma-managing strategy I shall call *revaluing*, which is closely related to both the ultimate descriptions model and the basic values model. In fact it shows that there is something right about both of them. It amounts to finding new values for one's existing desire-preferences, and it does so by extending one's preferences to more nearly complete descriptions and then using them to underpin one's preferences much as a set of values would. To illustrate this let me consider the dilemma I started this chapter with, in which someone finds their desires for a happy family life incomparable with their desires for a successful career.

Your desires for family life are not a single thing but a bundle. The bundle contains desires for affection, for a part in the lives of children, for certain kinds of experiences and memories, and many more things. Central among them are desires for long-term connections with the lives of particular other people (not, typically, any other people, but the ones that you happen to love). The same goes for your desires about your career. You want the respect of others, an occupation you like, the sense of accomplishment, and, usually, a progression in a career hierarchy. Moreover, most of these are wanted not just for their own sake but also for their capacity to structure and coordinate the other things you do and want. In particular, the long-term involvement in the lives of a few particular people that is essential to family life gives a perspective in terms of which much else of what you do from adulthood to death can be placed, and the progression from one responsibility or task to another provided by many careers gives you a motivation to summon your energies to pass from one year of your life to the next. (that is why we speak of a satisfying career, but of a dead-end job.)

Everyone discovers eventually that they can't have all of both of these bundles (and would be damned lucky to have all of either of them.) One natural reaction is to tone down your ambition, to compromise. Another is to abandon one side of life and try to get all one can out of either your family or your career. It may seem just a matter of taste which of these solutions one adopts. But there are other, subtler, ways out.

To begin, think of the difficulty of compromise here. To compromise you have to find limited ambitions in each area of life, at which you have a reasonable chance of simultaneous success. But any set of limited ambitions is going to be unstable: little deviations from it will improve it in one direction at a small cost in another. Suppose, for example, that you work for an organization in which ambitious people get promotions about every five years, but being this ambitious requires working evenings and weekends and taking no holidays. You want more time with your spouse and children and so you decide to work a 'regular' 9 to 5 five-day week with three weeks off in the summer and a week at Christmas. The company will allow this but of course you will not get promotions nearly as readily and will at the end of your career not have advanced very far. But you will have had something more like a family life. Then one year a special project is under way in the company that calls for special skills, which you possess. If you work longer hours during the week and just the occasional weekend just for this one year you can be head of the project, and can expect a promotion and a salary increase at the end of it. This will further your career at a small cost to your family life. So you take it, but then you find you have in effect abandoned the compromise on which your life was based. You have no defence against other encroachments of ambition into the domain of attachment. (The encroachments could have gone the other way. A child could be beginning in a new and rather demanding school and you might decide that for one year you will pick the child up each day after school, so that you can talk over the day's challenges on the way home, even at the price of having to leave work early some days. Then too you could find that you had abandoned your compromise and had no easy way back to it.)

The problem of compromise between incomparables is that there is no stable point among the many possible compromises. This problem does not arise with extreme choices, which abandon one whole value completely. That is fine if you can make yourself do it, and if you can suppress or re-form your desires enough to get yourself on to the radical course and stay there. The danger is backsliding or nostalgia. If the desires involved are strong then something of the kind seems inevitable, for you are deciding not to get something that you want very much.

To avoid both instability and disappointment you would have to find a way of straightforwardly maximizing some values without abandoning anything that matters deeply to you. Now the main point is that sometimes this can be done. Suppose, for example, that advancement in your career, in the sense of occupying better-paid and more respected positions, does not matter crucially to you. What you do want from your work is that it provide a succession of interesting and rather different jobs, so that you can look forward to a change every few years, never get stuck in a rut. You may be able to arrange this without putting in the long hours and superior-stroking that conventional advancement requires. You might become your company's expert on rewriting defective software, or on handling morale crises in sub-departments, so that you would be transferred from one trouble-spot to another when your special skills were required. Or, on the other side of the balance, suppose that what matters to you about family life is not day-to-day contact but a sense of long-term involvment with the lives of your spouse and children. So you may be able to spend long hours at work, often not coming home in the evening, but devoting one day a week to a family excursion, chosen so as to allow real conversations and exchanges of feeling, and every year having a brief but intense and memorable family holiday.

More subtle solutions are likely to involve matching re-thinkings of both career and family ambitions. And they may well not be anything like as easy to state as the two simple-minded examples I gave. The vital point about all of them is that they find a pair of more precise values than just 'career success' and 'family life' such that you can hope to maximize both simultaneously. So the solution is stable – given an opportunity in either direction you take it – and minimizes regret, in that you find that the values you are not devoting effort to satisfying are ones that you do not care deeply about.

This is revaluing. It consists in finding new values on which to base your desires. The usual route to revaluing is to see a pattern in your choices which suggests that you could make most of your choices on the basis not of your existing values but of a different set. In effect you find that the new values make as much sense of what you found yourself choosing, and present you with fewer dilemmas.

Put abstractly like this revaluing may seem a very demanding process. But the 'career-versus-family' examples show how it can be a part of routine dilemma-management. And in fact some degree of revaluing is a routine part of life: as you revise your taste in music or friends or holidays you are in part guided by a reflection in which the choices you actually make lead you to refine your conception of what it is that you value. Even in these routine cases you often find that articulating the exact nature of the more refined values that fit your choices between particular things is not at all easy: conventional terms like 'food', 'friendship', 'comfort', 'excitement' will probably be much too clumsy to catch what you are really after.

Revaluing allows one to be uncompromising.[12] To that extent it is a development of the anti-compromising strategy I advocated in the previous chapter. For it allows one to maximize each of the revalued values without inhibitions derived from the other. In another way revaluing is the result of compromise, because it comes from a refining or cutting back of each of two competing values. But this lacks some of the characteristics of true compromise, for in a successful revaluing the values retained are the ones which most matter to one so that only the values which on reflection are less important are cut back. And, most importantly, there is no need to try to see how much of one value, new or old, is equivalent to a given amount of the other.

3.9   Changes and Discoveries

Revaluing is an opposite to the formation of desires from values that I described earlier. It forms preferences between general characteristics of one's life from preferences between particular things and actions. (I say 'an opposite' rather than 'the opposite' because it cannot be the only way of doing this.) When I described the process going the other way, from values to wants, it was as part of the 'basic values model', a rival and alternative to the 'ultimate descriptions model', which made all preferences lie between particular objects. (Counting a whole possible life as a particular object.) Revaluing partially vindicates the ultimate descriptions model, in that it confirms that, sometimes, one can get more satisfactory choices between actions by probing beneath the values that seem to govern one's life to the actual situations one might face.

Suppose, for example, that one is considering cutting back the general value one attaches to success at one's career to a more specific value attached to having interesting and varied work. In thinking through this possible revaluing one will have to imagine lives which differ only in that in some of them one's career succeeds on all standard criteria (salary, rank, responsibility, etc.) and in others it succeeds only on the criterion of providing interesting and varied work. If one finds that the latter possible careers are as attractive as the former ones, one is in a good position for this revaluation. But to find this out one will have to think in terms not of the values that seemed to shape one's choices but of one's preferences between the consequences that would follow from various possible patterns of choice.

The ultimate descriptions model is only partially vindicated, though. The possibility of revaluing does not remove the fact that limited human beings cannot conceive in more than very superficial detail all the possibilities relevant to their decisions. So when revaluing one moves towards somewhat more ultimate descriptions in order to have a new set of values which one will then use instead of detailed descriptions in future decisions.

We usually announce the results of a revaluing as if it were a self-discovery. 'I found I don't really want to spend such a lot of time with my children; it is special attention at special times that I can best give them.' But it does not have to be given this interpretation. All that really matters is that a coherent set of values now underlies one's desires for particular things, and allows one to make more satisfactory choices. It may be a fact about us that whenever we find values that we can actually live with and use it feels as if we have discovered what it is we always wanted.

4

Good Strategies, Good Decisions

4.1 What Makes a Good Decision?

One answer is very simple: a good decision is one that leads to your getting what you want. Or, just a little more carefully, to your getting more of what you want than you would have got if you had taken one of the other options open to you. The value of a decision, judged this way, depends a lot on luck: a carefully and lucidly thought out decision can lead to disaster, and an impulsive, misinformed, mad act can have great success, if the wind changes suddenly.

Luck plays a smaller role if we ask what makes a good decision-making method or policy. (We can then judge decisions by the policies that prompted them, acknowledging that good policies sometimes produce disastrous results.) We can take a particular conception of rational decision, for example one of the patterns of probabilistic reasoning described by a standard decision theory, and we can ask for its advantages and disadvantages. We can ask – to give a crude approximation to a range of different questions – how often people will get more of what they want if their decisions are formed in this way, than they would have had they reasoned differently. These are typically very hard questions. And we can ask similar questions about the advantages or disadvantages of the dilemma-managing strategies I have been describing in this book.

In the rest of this chapter I present a systematic view of the strategies discussed in this book, with an emphasis on how to evaluate them. My main aim is simply to show that one can talk sensibly of better and worse ways of thinking out the kinds of reorganizations of one's desires and priorities in questions. In doing this I make some general suggestions about how to take apart the decision-making process in order to evaluate different parts of it in different ways. I should say that I am more confident that some of the strategies I describe are reasonable ways of approaching complex decisions than that I have given the right account of *why* they are reasonable. The strategies could be fine even if my justification of them fails.

The first step has to be to state more systematically what the range of dilemma-managing strategies is. What are we talking about? The strategies discussed in this book are of three kinds. First there are what I call *partition-shifting strategies*, such as the rain-check strategy of chapter 2. In these a decision is made by shifting from one way of evaluating the results of actions to another; for example, the shift can be from thinking in terms of what you want most now to thinking in terms of what patterns of action will give most satisfaction in the long run. I state the general form of partition-shifting strategies more carefully below in the following secion. The second kind of strategies consists in *spreading strategies*, in which two or more different ways of evaluating the options are used simultaneously. Chapter 5 ('The Price of Choice') is the home of these strategies in this book. (The spreading strategies I consider are all agenda-manipulating strategies, like the 'unequal opportunities' example of chapter 2. There can be agenda manipulation strategies which are not spreading strategies, so agenda-manipulation is really another, overlapping, class of strategies.) And the third kind consists in *revaluing strategies*, in which to make a decision one changes one's preferences. (Usually it will be a permanent change, affecting future choices too.) This is the hardest kind, both to carry out and to talk clearly about. I put off discussing it until the end of this chapter.

(There is no reason to think that all worthwhile dilemma-managing strategies fall into one of these classes. In fact, it seems to me no more likely that there could be a simple and helpful classification of absolutely all the ways in which people can intelligently think through decisions than there could be a classification of all the ways in which people can invent new options or possible solutions to their problems.)

4.2 Partitions

Suppose that you are deciding whether to go to the beach or to a film. You might think along the following lines: 'if I go to the beach then either it will rain or it will not. If it rains then I will have a really miserable time, but if it does not then I will enjoy myself. If I go to a film then it will not matter whether it rains or not, but it will be crucial which film I am able to see. If I can get into "The Godfather, part 16", then I will be distracted a bit from my depression, but if the queue is too long and I have to go to "the categorical imperative" directed by Lars-Eric Jaspersson I will come out with a headache.' You might then go on to think out how likely it is that it will rain or that the queues will be too long for you to get into the film you most want.

This pattern of decision making is the standard one. It centres on a *partition*, a list of the situations that could result from the actions being considered.[1] In this case the partition has four elements: rain + long queue, rain + short queue, no rain + long queue, no rain + short queue. A more careful decision would use a larger partition, perhaps bringing in the possibility of a light shower or of a queue long enough to be irritating but short enough to allow you to escape the other film. Most decisions involve a partition, for pretty fundamental reasons. When you make a decision you have to think through the possible consequences of each option and evaluate them. And the consequences of different options must be compared in as near to the same terms as possible. A suitable choice of a partition allows this comparison. You classify everything that can happen in terms of a fixed set of possibilities: you know that one and only one of these possibilities is sure to happen, and you know how likely each one of them would be if you took each option, and you know how much you value each combination of a possibility and an option taken. This set of possibilities is your partition. Then if you can rank the members of the partition in order of attractiveness, you can use this ranking to compare the options.

For example, you might rank being at the beach with no rain as the top option, followed by going to 'The Godfather, part 16', followed by going to 'the categorical imperative', with being at the beach in the rain as the bottom option. If you also think that there is a 50/50 chance of rain and a 50/50 chance of a long queue, then going to the beach emerges as the risky option – it could give the best and the worse results – and going to a film as the safer option. To get further you will have to consider just how much you like or dislike these prospects. That may not be easy, but thinking in terms of a partition has given you a way of seeing the nature of the prospects for which you must do this exercise.

Different decisions involve different partitions. The choice of a suitable partition is one of the secret skills of decision-making. A good partition should reveal the important factors that can affect the outcomes of the acts being considered, in such a way that these outcomes can easily be compared. The choice of a partition also reveals a lot about the values or preferences that are being brought to the decision. Suppose, for example, the partition is: tomorrow I gain £1, tomorrow I gain £2, tomorrow I gain £3, ... Then the comparison will almost certainly be made in terms of immediate monetary gain. (A 'two dimensional' partition with elements 'I gain £n in m days' time' would tend to non–immediate monetary gain.)[2]

Under ideal conditions the choice of a partition will be a purely practical matter: choosing a different partition may make the decision easier or harder to think out, but the answer – the comparison of the options – should be the same whatever partition is used. 'Ideal conditions' means that one knows exactly how much one wants every relevant situation and how probable it is, and moreover there are no incomparabilities in one's desires. (so both desire and belief can be represented as linear orderings with no gaps.) When one's beliefs and desires are not so ideally tidy, the choice of a partition is a deeper matter.

Suppose that someone is uncertain which of two incomparable sets of values to bring to a decision. The decision might be thought out in terms of monetary gain, say, or amusement value. In each case different partitions suggests themselves. (For example, 'I gain £10, I gain £20, . . .' and I have a terrible time', 'I have a boring time', 'I have a mildly pleasant time', . . .) Now if the decision is thought through just with one of these partitions *and* in terms only of the corresponding value, the decision arrived at can obviously be very different from what it might have been if the other partition and the other value had been used. But of course this is a rather incomplete way of making the decision, since it ignores many relevant preferences (those concerning amusement, if it is just in terms of money, or vice versa). One way to meet this will be to use a more complex partition, combining elements from both. ('I gain £10 and I have a terrible time', 'I gain £10 and I have a boring time', 'I gain £20 and I have an awful time', . . .) And that is perhaps how an agent with unlimited patience and thinking-power might approach the question. But even such a being would have difficulty extracting a definite decision from such a procedure, if the two values are thoroughly incomparable. In fact, the more thoroughly one incorporates both values into the partition, the weaker the ordering that is imposed on the possible options and their outcomes.

So the way in which real people with finite capacities and a need to make decisions are actually likely to make the decision is to use a partition somewhere between those based entirely on one value and those attempting to be fully comprehensive. One might, for example, classify the outcomes in terms of 'I gain £10 and have a not unpleasant time', 'I gain £10 and have a good time', 'I gain £20 and have a not unpleasant time', etc.: that is a partition which focuses on monetary gain but includes a less-detailed consideration of pleasure; it could easily have been the other way round. A decision made with such a partition will be biased in one direction but will pay some heed to the other.

This is the way we actually make many of our decisions, I believe. We switch almost randomly from partitions with a focus on one value to partitions with a focus on another, with the result that although no value is completely neglected, in any single decision the emphasis is fairly arbitrary. And sometimes we get stuck: in some situations any way of describing the consequences of the obvious options that gives any consideration at all to competing values will lead to an incomparability in the options. (For example it can come down to gaining £10 or being thoroughly bored, and you have no clear preference between them.)

(There is a connection here with Herbert Simon's important idea of satisficing (see note 4 to chapter 1). A satisficing strategy imposes on one's deliberations an order in which options are considered and a cut-off point of value. Then one stops thinking through the consequences of options when one finds an option whose consequences are better than the cut-off point. This option may not be the best possible, but it is good enough to choose. There are obviously many possible variations on the idea, and a lot that can be said about it. The connection with the issues at hand is that before making a decision on a complex matter with a complex set of values one implicitly chooses a partition which is detailed enough for one's purposes. It will be more focused on the details relevant to some values than to others, but it will pay 'enough' attention to each. This is like satisficing pushed back to a more basic level of decision-making.)

The conclusion is important: if one's desires contain incomparabilities and if one does not require that a partition be exhaustive, then the action that is chosen, given a set of desires and beliefs, can depend on the choice of the partition. Different partition, different action.

4.3   Partition-shifting Strategies

In a dilemma to which a partition-shifting strategy applies one can see one's situation 'through the eyes of' either of two (or more) values and their associated partitions. In terms of either one can get a nice definite ranking of the options as long as one uses only a partition focused on one value to the exclusion of the other. Usually this does not matter; the rankings of options one gets are fairly stable under changes of focus in the partitions. But in some cases, those which produce the dilemmas, this is not the case: a shift in focus produces a different ranking of the options. And if one considers more detailed partitions the problem becomes too complex to think through while the definiteness of the ranking of the options is lost.

To give a partition-shifting (henceforth just 'shifting') solution to this sort of predicament one has to find a partition which works better than those focusing on either of the competing values. What 'works better' means is that it agrees with the two competing partitions when they agree, and gives a definite answer when they disagree. (That is a very strong condition. More cautious formulations are possible.)[3] If one shifts one's decision making to this new partition most of one's decisions go just as they would have, but one will get stuck in fewer dilemmas.

Different kinds of shifting – or at any rate claims that amount to claims to shifting – are at the heart of a number of common 'philosophies'. For example, hedonism suggests that instead of trying to reconcile the demands of all one's varying desires one should use a single criterion: how much will I enjoy it? (So the partition is formed from possibilities like: I get no pleasure, I get a little pleasure, I get a lot of pleasure, I am in slight pain, I am in agony, and so on.) And the appeal of hedonism is that this can seem to be roughly what one was aiming at all along: in one's past bumblings one usually steered towards pleasure, often deflected by one lesser goal or another.

Or, for a contrasting example, consider what might be called 'wisdom' or the philosophy of always taking the long view. (As in a simple reading of the 'looking back principle' of chapter 2.) It tells one to make all decisions in terms of whether, later, one would be glad, or would regret, that one had acted as one did. This tends against momentary pleasures, as they often count for little in retrospection. And it supports present sacrifice for future gain. (Or at any rate it seems to. I wonder how many people comfortably retired on more than adequate pensions wish they had saved less and enjoyed themselves more.) Again part of the appeal of the doctrine is that it provides one with a way of resolving dilemmas which generally makes sense of one's previous choices. One doesn't have to shift too far.

Shifting neither to hedonism nor to 'wisdom' will make all decisions merely a matter of calculation. For the partition one shifts to may have its own incomparabilities. This may be so although it makes some or many acts and their outcomes comparable where the previous desires left them incomparable. This is not a problem if one is thinking, as I am, of a strategy that can be used on a case-by-case basis to work through dilemmas as they arise. It is a problem, though, if one is making an all-purpose philosophy of life, which promises to identify the right action in all circumstances. For this reason versions of utilitarianism, the sophisticated and reasonable philosophical descendant of hedonism, usually claim that there is in principle a single, linearly ordered ranking of all possible outcomes. And some defences of utilitarianism, for example Mill's, can be read as arguing that we should adopt it because it presents the virtues of partition-shifting.[4] This is in a way the ultimate partition-shift, taking one to a pattern of desires which generates no incomparabilities at all.

Partition-shifting can involve a change of desire, as the new evaluations may differ from the old ones in small ways as long as the differences are small enough, or placed discreetly enough, that the new valuations endorse most of the same decisions as the old ones, where the latter endorsed any decision at all. A decision made with a shifting strategy can thus be quite delicately poised between decisions based on one's existing desires and decisions based on other – possibly better or more usable – desires. For an effective shifting strategy should feel to the person as if their existing desires are simply being summarized in a more useful form, but the long-term effect may be a subtle shift in valuation. At first it seems, for example, that deciding in terms of anticipated retrospection is just a more convenient way of carrying on with one's previous pattern of decisions. But slowly one is led into a more prudent and less impulsive pattern of choice.

That is both the appeal and the danger of shifting strategies. They give a way of overcoming the indecisiveness of one's desires without changing them drastically. But at the same time they involve subtle and sometimes insidious changes of emphasis.

4.4   Spreading Strategies

I do not have any very abstract and general definition of a spreading strategy. I shall use the term to refer to any strategy which resolves a tension between incomparable preferences by giving them different roles in a decision-making process. There are obviously many different such strategies, some suitable for some circumstances and many unsuitable for any sane purpose. They are the main topic of the next chapter ('The Price of Choice'), so here I shall just give an example of a miniature spreading strategy.

A young man from a rich but bossy family is considering which university to attend. His family have definite prejudices about which universities are desirable, based entirely on social rather than academic grounds. He also has opinions about universities, based on a number of reliable and unreliable sources of information, which are not the same as those of his parents, and opinions about what subjects he would like to study at university. His parents have few opinions on this last topic. When they were at university it seems, from their stories, that no one studied anything in particular. He does not want to go against his parents' wishes, but has no clear idea about how to rank his own preferences about universities against his desire to stay on the right side of his parents.

He solves his problem by deciding to let his parents dictate the choice of university while keeping entirely to himself the choice of a subject to study, among those available at whichever of the universities chosen by them accepts him. Is this wise?

The strategy has the advantage of allowing him to avoid balancing the force of filial obedience against that of his own preferences, while giving each some scope. It has obvious disadvantages, too. For one thing it may leave him very little scope for his choice of subjects if the only subjects available at his parents' preferred universities are ones that do not interest him. But perhaps he knows that this is unlikely to be the case. This disadvantage is a special case of something one can generally expect with spreading strategies. If different sets of preferences are at work in different parts or stages of decision making then very often one set of preferences will be working in the shadow of another, operating only with the choices that an earlier process using different preferences has left open. Another disadvantage, in the example, is that the choice of university may matter to him very much, even though he cannot weigh it against the desire not to go against his parents. This too is generally to be expected with strategies like this. And it too may not matter in a particular case. He may know that what matters most to him is the choice of subject, and that both choice of university and filial obedience come second.

Moreover, spreading strategies are more likely than others to produce pathologies such as intransitive preferences, (Where one prefers A to B and B to C, but C to A). The three spreading strategies I describe in the next chapter all tend to produce the effect that whether A is preferred to B depends on what other options they are being compared to. Still, there are quite common circumstances in which spreading strategies provide a reasonable way to proceed, as I argue in the 'Which When' section below.

4.5   The General Picture

A decision-making method should provide a way in which you can get around the obstacles to making a decision. It will generally provide ways of getting four things: a set of options, a set of values (or desires, or preferences), a set of beliefs (or probabilities), and a fairly mechanical way of choosing a best option by reference to the values and beliefs. (If the calculation is not feasible then the strategy that comes up with the material for it has not done its job.) It helps to split this process into two parts. There is the setting-up part in which options, values, and beliefs are found. The part of a decision-making method that provides these in problematic cases is a dilemma/managing strategy. And then there is the actual choice of one option to be performed. I will, very unoriginally, call that part of a method its decision-rule.

A strategy is a good one if, crudely speaking, people using it will generally get what they want. That is too crude to be much help because it leaves two questions unanswered. Is 'what they want' to be measured in terms of the values isolated by the method, or by some more general reference to the agent's motivation? And is 'generally get' to be interpreted in terms of how the world actually is, or in terms of how it would be if the person's beliefs – as isolated by the method or more generally – were true?

I think different construals of the formula are appropriate for different parts of the process. I shall follow the entirely conventional line for decision-rules: one decision-rule is better than another – when applied to the beliefs, desires, and options supplied by a setting-up process on a particular occasion – if people applying it would achieve more satisfaction of their desires, were their beliefs true, than people applying the other rule would.[5] The only justification I will give for this is that it responds to the intuition that a decision can be right although its effects were disastrous, as long as it would have given good results if the world had been the way the person thought it was and had the person's desires been reasonable. (And I take it that in many cases 'satisfying more of the desires' can be understood here as 'has the greatest expected utility', when utility and expectation are derived from the values and beliefs that emerge from the setting-up stage.)

But for the earlier setting-up stage a different, more 'objective', construal is appropriate. One way of isolating values, probabilities, options, and a decision-rule is better than another, for a particular person in a particular situation, when given the way the world actually is the person will achieve more satisfaction of their desires using that setting-up than they would have achieved using the other.[6] The justification for considering the way the world actually is rather than how it is believed to be (in practice, objective probabilities rather than subjective ones) is twofold. First it addresses questions we want answered: is this a style of decision making that will lead this person to success or disaster? And then it is manageable: we can expect sometimes to know what will in fact lead to a person's getting more of what they want. (But the question of what decision-making methods will on average give best results is in full generality hardly intelligible,[7] and the question of what will give best methods if the person's beliefs were true is best asked of the final decision-rule.)

Here is a simple example. Louise is about to see a coin tossed. She notices that it is a gold écu with the head of Louis XIII on one side. Being a fervent and slightly unbalanced royalist, she thinks it very unlikely that a coin of noble metal would fall with a king's face downwards. In fact she estimates the probability of heads at 0.8 and of tails at 0.2. She is offered a choice of two bets: (a) heads she wins ten frances, tails she loses five francs; (b) heads she wins twenty francs, tails she loses twenty francs. How should she decide what to do? Suppose that she takes her options to be simply accepting (a) and accepting (b). Then if she uses the decision-rule of maximizing expected monetary return she will accept (b). But in fact this is a worse bet than (a), given that the coin is fair. (The objective expectations of (a) and (b) are 2.5 and 0, Louise's mistaken expectations are 7 and 12.) And if she uses a more cautious decision-rule, such as the minimax rule discussed at chapter 6.2, which focuses on the worst possible outcomes of the options to be considered, she will choose (a). This would be a better choice. She would also choose (a) if she used a utility-maximizing rule but set up the decision by a procedure producing values which weigh twenty francs at considerably less than twice the value of ten francs. And she would choose (a) with a utility-maximizing rule attached to a suitable tuning of the 'pessimistic procedure' of the next chapter. (The following three chapters contain expositions of utility and money maximization, minimax, and the pessimistic procedure.)

The crude moral is that people with false beliefs about probabilities can do badly if they make their decisions by utility maximization. The subtler moral is that the setting-up process is as important as the decision-rule. A rule can give bad results if the material for it is set up in one way, and good results if it is set up in another. A yet subtler moral is that we need to make some distinctions in order to bring out the sense in which Louise, choosing (b) on the basis of maximizing her expected monetary return, is making the right or the wrong decision. Given her choice of options and the way she has formed her desires, the rule she is using is reasonable: were her beliefs true she would have done well. But if we take the setting-up into the scope of the evaluation we have to judge the combination of setting-up procedure and decision-rule to be a bad one: it makes a bad result likely.

Getting nearer to real life, consider the evaluation of shifting strategies. Shifting strategies leave many of one's previous decisions unchanged. (They just erect a new scaffolding beneath them.) They therefore respect the valuations of most options and outcomes. And thus the desires of someone using the strategy can be compared with their desires had they not used it. So we can compare the extent to which the same underlying desires would have been satisfied by two shifting strategies. For example we can compare simple hedonism to 'wisdom'. We can consider – for a particular person with a particular complex of preferences – whether resolving dilemmas by one strategy will lead to more and more strongly held desires being satisfied than they would be by the other. It may be that the person's desires really are such that satisfying most of them does give immediate pleasure, and that the amount of pleasure is proportional to the strength of the desire (as reflected in the choices made before the shift to hedonism). Then hedonism will probably turn out to be a good solution, at any rate a better solution than 'wisdom'. More likely, if the person's desires are like those of most people, there will be many strong desires whose satisfaction is not accompanied by proportionate pleasure, and some of these will be ones that the person would later regret not having satisfied. So very likely for such a person 'wisdom' is a better strategy than hedonism. (Which is not to say that it is the best possible strategy.)

Spreading strategies can be discussed in the same terms. The young man choosing a university and a subject to study could have adopted many other strategies: For example, he could have let his parents make all the decisions. And we can compare the extent to which his desires would have been satisfied in these two case. Suppose that his parents would prefer him to study Art History while he has a strong preference for studying Engineering. Then if his parents make all the decisions this strong preference will not be satisfied. And this is evidence that the parental-choice strategy is not as good in his case as the mixed-choice strategy.

Now I can deal with some unfinished business from chapter 2: saying more about indirect satisfaction. There I described a dilemma-management strategy which consisted of satisfying one desire in a straightforward way and another, competing, desire 'indirectly' by resolving to satisfy desires which underlie it. The natural way to interpret this, in the context of what I have been saying in this chapter, is to say that a strategy treats a desire as a candidate for direct satisfaction when the setting-up process produces it as one of the desires on the basis of which the decision is to be made, and produces options which could satisfy it. And a desire is treated as a candidate for indirect satisfaction when it does not find its way to the set of desires which are input to the decision-rule, but related desires do.

The most likely related desires are those which a shifting strategy will produce: they will justify many of the decisions which the neglected desire would have motivated, from a more general perspective which allows present neglect to be balanced against future satisfaction. But a mild revaluing strategy can also produce substitute desires: these will typically be desires for one aspect of a complex whole which was the object of the original desire. (You wanted to see a particular film; that desire is replaced with a desire for emotionally stirring experiences that are not linked to your everyday life.)

4.6   Which When?

If this is how to justify the use of a dilemma management strategy, then it follows that some strategies are more appropriate to some dilemmas. Spreading strategies, for example, apply to situations in which one's preferences split naturally into two or more individually usable sub-systems. For instance, the student in the example above can evaluate outcomes well enough in terms of what would please him purely selfishly, and well enough in terms of what would please his parents, but has trouble putting the two systems of preferences together. The two coincide in value on very few outcomes, though often one is indifferent between two outcomes when the other has a definite preference. (In this case the story is naturally told in terms of two easily separated criteria of evaluation. In other cases it may take some work to separate the person's preferences into disjoint systems.) Then a spreading strategy not only allows him to get ahead with the decisions he faces, it allows different ways of doing this, different spreading strategies, to be compared.

Shifting strategies would not apply in that case, since there is no body of decisions on which the competing values give essentially the same results. But they do apply when the person's preferences give a clear valuation to a large number of options and outcomes but leave some crucial things undecided. Unlike a case calling for a spreading strategy there are not two globally incomparable systems of preference but rather a single unified system with isolated incomparabilities. Then a shift to a more decisive set of valuations – or, minimally, to a partition that uses the existing valuations more decisively – will produce a coherent pattern of choice. And the choices that result can be compared to those that would result from other strategies – at any rate, other not too different shifting strategies and in some cases other non-shifting strategies – in terms of the extent to which the desires that underlie the body of undisputed past decisions are satisfied. So one has some guidance as to the choice of strategy as well as, given a strategy, the choice of an option.

(In the terminology of the last chapter, spreading strategies are appropriate when one's desires take an overall diamond-shaped form, with very few preference relations between the 'branches' of the pattern, while shifting strategies are appropriate when the pattern is that of many linked small-scale diamonds.)

Spreading strategies are more drastic than shifting strategies, in that they place a more complex barrier between one's preferences and one's choices. Or, to put it differently, the procedure they require is less like that which one would follow if one had less ambiguous preferences. Spreading strategies are for when a shifting strategy will not work.

Sometimes neither kind of strategy will work. Sometimes one has neither a body of unproblematic past decisions resulting from not-too-divergent values nor a way of spreading the decision-making work between disparate values. I think some deep incomparabilities are like this. Examples are the incomparability between the value one attaches to one's life-work and the value one attaches to one's relations with other people, or that between the value of preserving life and that of avoiding suffering, both discussed elsewhere in this book. In these cases the way forward has to be something more drastic yet.

The form this usually takes is that of a wider or deeper change of desire. One either changes a large number of one's preferences or some of the underlying values from which one's preferences stem. That is a more drastic course to take in part because it can be hard to do. (Though it is not as hard as is sometimes thought: See chapter 9, 'How to Change Your Desires'). And also, more to the point, because it can be hard to know when such a change is for the better. That is, if a person at one time is acting on one set of preferences and then later acting on another, perhaps more decisively but following a generally different pattern of choice, then it is not at all clear when we should say that more or stronger desires are satisfied.

In some cases the comparison is not so difficult. If someone is living a completely frustrated life because of their obsession with some unattainable goal then a change to desires that can actually be satisfied will be an improvement. (In terms of desire-satisfaction, at any rate. There might be other reasons for disapproving of it.) The same goes for desires which are obsessive and unsatisfying: imagine, for example, someone whose life is dominated by the need to offend authority figures of all sizes, but whose attempts at offence are so timid and oblique as to be rarely noticed. If some sublimation could turn this person into an effectively acid book reviewer or political commentator then they might for once accomplish something that mattered to them.

I am in fact more optimistic than many about the possibility of comparing the desires of different people, or of one person at different times.[8] But there certainly are difficulties. Although I will talk of desire-changing strategies as if they formed a single class, I am sure that there are in face important differences between them, depending on the kinds of comparisons between different sets of desires that they presuppose. For example the revaluing strategies I discuss at the end of chapter 3 (Incomparabilities) where my example is the conflict between commitments to one's work and to one's family, are surely very different from the changes of desire I discuss in chapter 7 (Risk: A Few Answers) where my example is the discrepancy between lexically ordered preferences and the needs of probabilistic reasoning. There must be a lot more to say here, but I am not yet in a position to say it.

4.7   Evaluating Strategies

One decision-making method is better than another – for a particular person with particular beliefs and preferences – when following it leads to a greater satisfaction of that person's desires. And for dilemma-managing strategies this means: given the actual state of the world someone using the one strategy will get more desire satisfaction (measured against their existing desires even if the decision is not made in terms of them) than someone using the other. This clearly does not provide a universal comparison of strategies, even for a particular person at a particular time with respect to a particular class of decisions. For the degrees to which a person's desires would be satisfied if one strategy were followed may well not bear a simple greater-or-less relation to the degree their desires would be satisfied if another were followed. The comparison may not be possible, or it may give a definite verdict that the two degrees are incomparable.

If we take desire-satisfaction to give a merely sufficient condition for one strategy to be better than another, we can add some other conditions. There are in fact two natural conditions to add. The first is the decisiveness of a strategy. One strategy is more decisive than another if using it will result in fewer situations in which options and their consequences cannot be compared. Decisiveness alone obviously will leave many strategies incomparable, but it also does obviously describe a definite advantage that one strategy can have over another. The other condition is conservatism. One strategy may require a major change of a person's desires while another may require very slight change. The second not only is more likely to be feasible, but also conforms to the precept of rationality: change your mind only as much as the situation requires.[9]

We should take one strategy to be better than another whenever it provides a clear advantage in terms of desire-satisfaction, I think. When the desire-satisfaction score is not clear then these or other similar conditions can provide an answer. It would be a mistake to think that because there is no single criterion of the value of a decision-making strategy there is no objective difference between good strategies and bad ones. That would be like thinking that because it is sometimes not a determinate matter which act one should perform there is no difference between the actions of a careful decision-maker and those of a maniac.

5

The Price of Choice

There are many situations in which choice is neither free nor forced. They arise when you can avoid choosing, but only at a price. The price may be expressed in terms of the alternatives you are choosing between, or it may be in quite different terms, which are hard to compare with the original alternatives.) Then you face a very difficult question: how much will you pay to avoid the choice? No account of decision making can avoid dealing with this issue in some form or other. One reason why it is important is that it is related to a pervasive moral intuition that some pairs of goods should never be balanced against one another. But the basic questions are not intrinsically moral.

Here are four ways in which the question of the price of a choice can arise: one trivial, one about risk, one awful, and one moral.

5.1   *Trivial: Vienna–Ravenna*

You are planning a holiday, and must decide where to go and whether to bring your young child. You can go to Vienna, in which case you will leave your child behind with its grandparents to save trouble and expense and because there is not a lot for children in Vienna. Or you can go to Ravenna, in which case you will take your child but will have to choose how much time to spend with it on the beach and how much time going to Byzantine sites. You think Ravenna is more interesting than Vienna, and you would enjoy both visiting the sites and going to the beach, but you dread having to steer between the competing pulls of beach and art. You decide to go to Vienna.

This choice may seem sensible, as it avoids conflicts which might ruin a holiday. Or it may seem lazily irrational, as it takes the option you want less just for fear of having to do some further deciding. The question is delicate: it depends on exactly how much you don't want to have to choose between the beach and the sites, and how you weigh the trouble of choosing against your preference for Ravenna.

5.2   Risk: Prudence and Howard

Suppose that someone – call her Prudence – has just retired and is investing her life savings, with which she must support herself and her handicapped child for the rest of their lives. She can take the advice of her bank manager or of an unorthodox but completely honest stockbroker. The best deal the bank can offer is an annuity which gives a reliable annual return of 10 per cent of her capital. The stockbroker has a more complicated story to tell. The market is going through a volatile period, so there is no completely safe investment with a rate of return matching the bank's annuity. But if she entrusts her money to him he will after a little research come up with some riskier options giving good chances of greater returns. They will be typically of two types: one (call it the little risk) gives a good chance of a high return and a definite chance of a bad return; the other (call it the big risk) gives an even better chance of an even higher return, but a very slight chance of an awful return. (If you want definite numbers, think of A as giving a 0.8 chance of a 15 per cent return and a 0.1 chance of a 5 per cent return, and B as giving a 0.9 chance of a 20 per cent return and a 0.05 chance of a 0 per cent return. In both cases there is a small chance of a return between the two extremes.) So Prudence has to decide either to take the bank's safe and adequate offer or choose between the little risk and the big risk.[1]

Prudence reasons as follows: 'If I put my money with the stockbroker I will have to choose between the little risk and the big risk. I would find this decision pretty well impossible, so I shall settle for the 10 per cent the bank can offer.'

This may seem quite reasonable. But now imagine a friend, Howard, who tries to dissuade her, as follows.

Howard: If you were forced to choose between the little risk and the annuity which would you choose?

Prudence: I'd stick with the bank. The return on the gamble isn't enough to overcome the danger of an inferior return. I couldn't have a comfortable retirement and get help for my child on that.

Howard: If you were forced to choose between the big risk and the annuity, which would you choose?

Prudence: I'd find it really hard, but I think I'd go for the risk. There is a high enough chance of a really good return to make the risk worth taking. And if the worst came to the worst I could go back to work, and probably find a charity to help my child. Not that I'd like either, but it's only a 5 per cent chance.

Howard: So you really prefer the big risk to the annuity. Isn't it crazy
            not to take it?
Prudence: No. I'd choose the second gamble if I were forced to choose.
            But I would rather not be forced to choose, so I have set
            things up so I don't have to.

Is Prudence crazy? Her claim that by choosing the annuity she has set
things up so that she does not have to choose between the risks doesn't
seem obviously true. For she seems to have chosen, and decided against
both risky options, by choosing the safe investment. Yet there are many
examples like this, in which someone would prefer one option to another if
forced to choose, but would also prefer not to act on the forced choice.
Can this be defended?

5.3   Awful: The Fugitive Child

Your child is a member of a violent revolutionary organization. You have
a general sympathy for the aims of her group but extreme disapproval of
its methods. You are on holiday when you hear on the TV news that a
government minister – responsible for bugging the telephones of citizens
and harassing those with undesirable views – has been killed by a car
bomb, together with all his family. You suspect, but are not sure, that
your child and her organization may be behind the murder. You can continue your holiday or you can return home. If you return home your
daughter may well visit you. If she has not been involved in the murder
you may then be able to help and comfort her. But if she has you will have
to decide whether to hide her from the authorities. This will be a terrible
choice: you think that terrorists should be brought to justice, but your
child is your child. You are therefore strongly tempted to remain on
holiday, rather than face such a choice.

    Let us suppose that there is a cost to not going home, a price to be paid
to avoid the awful choice. The greater part of the price could well not be
in money but in neglect of other children, impossible living conditions, or
other things. How much should you pay?

5.4   Moral: The Stricken Wife

Contrast two situations. (a) A man, Thomas, is walking with his wife in
the country when she has a heart attack. There is a farm-house nearby,

and the children playing outside it say that there is a telephone in the house, but that their mother is very suspicious of strangers. In fact, she will neither open the door to Thomas nor herself telephone for an ambulance. Thomas seizes one of the children and threatens to harm it if the call is not made. The mother gives in and telephones. (b) Thomas knows that his wife has a weak heart, but he also likes walking with her in the country. She worries about the danger of a heart attack far from medical help and among suspicious unhelpful country folk. Thomas says 'Don't worry. Street-wise is people-wise: if it comes to that I can always find the right threat.'

In (a) Thomas acts reasonably. The fright to the mother and the fear and discomfort of the child are less serious than the threat to his wife. (Or, to put it in the terms of chapter 2, Thomas can repair some of this damage later, taking the child and the mother as objects of indirect responsibility.) In (b), on the other hand, his intentions seem wrong. But why is this, since the act he is planning is the same as the act in (a) where it is, in the circumstances, justifiable?

The difference between the cases comes down to that between forced and chosen choice. (Like the risk case). In (a) Thomas has no choice but to weigh inflicting pain and fear on harmless strangers against risking his wife's life, while in (b) he freely gets himself into a situation in which he will have to weigh the one against the other. What the Thomas of (b) seems not to understand is that although he should choose as in (a) if he has to, this is a choice he should try to avoid.[2]

5.5   The price of choice

It is obviously very hard to compare the awfulness of a choice to the desirability or undesirability of the things one is choosing between. The undesirability of having to choose between loyalty to your child and opposition to terrorism seems to be incomparable both to the loyalty and to the opposition. But the world is a nasty old place, and very often we are forced to make the comparison. For example, in the trivial case above: if your preference for Ravenna over Vienna is great then you should not let your aversion to the beach/sites choice prevent you going there; if your preference is very slight then perhaps you should let it prevent you; and if it is neither great nor very slight then you should think hard. Less trivial cases are the same: you cannot avoid having to think about how bad a choice is, in terms that compare it to the possible benefits of the choice. Sometimes, even, part of the price has to be calculated in crude money terms.

In the risk case the undesirability of having to choose between two risky options has to be weighed against a possibly lesser monetary outcome, as Howard points out. In the awful case the undesirability of the choice seems to be part of what it is to be committed to another person: you would try not to get into a situation in which you had to balance great harm to them against other and perhaps more important factors. In the moral case the undesirability seems to be part of what it is to be a responsible moral agent: you should not treat the rights of others as things you can lightly balance against one another.

There are two things going on in these case, I think, which have most effect when they are combined. One of them is a decision-making heuristic. This is clearest in the risk case. Prudence's aversion to choices between risks and safe options obviously has limits, which are related to the gains and losses involved. If there were an investment like the big risk but more so, with an even greater chance of an excellent return and an even smaller chance of a bad outcome, she would take it instantly, with no protestations about not wanting to choose. So the aversion to choice involves some of the same factors as would go into the choices were they to be made.

But there is an immediate problem here. If Prudence's aversion to balancing risky options depends on the probabilities of the different possible gains and losses then to know whether she ought to prefer not to compare the options she must already have compared them. Part of the answer to the problem has to be that in deciding whether to be averse to a choice one does not go into the options in the same depth as when actually making a detailed comparison between them. This would exploit something that is an inevitable part of decision making in any case. For in any complex decision one has to decide which options to take seriously and think in detail about, and if this preliminary sorting out is indeed to be preliminary it has to work with a rougher and quicker description of the options. In a case involving risk the natural way to go about this is to apply some very rough characterizations – 'risky', 'guaranteed return', 'real possibility of disaster', and so on – in order to select those options which one will then go into in a more detailed and quantitative way.

Appeal to preliminary evaluation of options clears up one thing. To choose one thing rather than choose between others *is* to choose between all of them, and thus in a way to evaluate the hard-to-evaluate ones. But it is to do so in a preliminary way, with the kind of evaluation appropriate for deciding what is and is not a live option. So the question of avoiding choice and the question of deciding what options to take seriously are very closely connected. Moreover, if the reason for avoiding a choice is the unpleasantness or repugnance of thinking about the issues involved, then in a preliminary examination one can consider them just enough to tell whether one ought to overcome one's inhibitions. After all, however painful the topic, a preliminary evaluation just might show that the gain from one of the options could justify the unpleasantness of thinking about it.

But the heuristics cannot be the whole story. We often show an aversion to a choice even when there is enough time and energy to think through all the options, and even when the source of the aversion is not the psychological unpleasantness of a topic. (The 'risk' and 'moral' cases above could be told so as to be examples of both of these.) The other factor that comes into play is the intrinsic incomparability of the options. Affection versus citizenship, historical sites versus the beach, a comfortable retirement versus the risk of poverty. The difficulty of balancing such things makes even a preliminary evaluation of the options very hard. There are many ways of working intrinsic incomparability into a coherent procedure for the preliminary sorting out of options. I compare three of them below, which I call the pessimistic procedure, the optimistic procedure, and the sieve. They all have the effect of allowing some decisions to be avoided because of the kinds of comparisons they involve. The pessimistic procedure is definitely on the right track. The optimistic procedure cannot be right, but brings out some interesting points. And the sieve is right in conception, if not in detail.

5.6   The Pessimistic Procedure

In making any decision the range of options to be chosen between is usually narrowed down from a large and unmanageably varied list to a small number whose relative advantages can be carefully thought out. The narrowing down often happens unconsciously; perhaps some of it is always unconscious. So one nearly always makes several passes through the options, each time eliminating some, and grouping and reformulating others. The criteria one uses for rejecting options on the early passes through them must be different from those used to make the final decision, or there would be no point in dividing the process into stages. Early passes use rougher and less quantitative considerations, since human beings are not very good at handling exact probabilities. (What they are good at is imagining possible consequences.) And very often early passes use, and should use, more pessimistic criteria.

One way this might work is as follows. One has several ways of evaluating the options and several guesses about the relevant probabilities. The evaluations could be different ways of trading off one value against another; for example, one evaluation might construe each loss of life as an irreparable disaster, and the other might take losses of life to be justifiable by sufficient gains in other things. And the probabilities might well take the form of rather schematic pictures of ways in which the situation might develop: call these 'stories'. Then each option which is up for preliminary consideration gets looked at in the light of each valuation and each story. This leads to a rough picture of how bad things might be if each option were followed, for each valuation and each story. Some options will have conspicuously bad results, for some valuations and some stories. A criterion for this might be that there was a non-negligible likelihood of a something disastrous. (Rough thresholds of both have to be set.) These are the worst-case options. Throw them out and consider them no more.

On the next pass through the remaining options one narrows the range of valuations and stories, using only valuations which on reflection one trusts and stories which one thinks likely. Then exactly the same procedure is followed, except with more care and more detail. For example one thinks more carefully how bad possible consequences would be according to a particular valuation, and one uses probabilities less as rough stories and more as detailed comparisons of the likelihood of many different possibilities. But the result is the same: the worst-case options are discarded.

This procedure can be gone through until either there is only one valuation and one story left or until one arbitrarily decides to put off the fateful moment no longer and makes a definitive decision. Then one chooses one valuation and one version of the probabilities to give a detailed comparison of the surviving options. And on this basis one decides. (It would be sensible to make this final decision on the basis of something like a calculation of expected utilities, but other methods could fit in here just as well.)

This procedure does two things at once. It reduces the number of options to a manageable number, and it allows each of a variety of assessments of value and probability a role in the decision. These fit naturally together, since it makes sense to use the assessments in which one has the most confidence in a careful and detailed way and those in which one has somewhat less confidence in a quicker and more preliminary way. Nevertheless, the process can be tuned to emphasize one of these aspects or the other. For example, it could be varied in the direction of the second aspect – democracy between different assessments – by considering options in greater detail even at the preliminary stages: real detailed probabilities rather than rough stories could be considered well before the final decision. Or it could be varied in the direction of the first aspect – reduction of options – by using more drastic criteria for rejecting options in early stages: perhaps any option giving any probability at all (above zero) of the worst possible result (according to any valuation) might be rejected. That would be pretty drastic.

Of the four cases above, Prudence's reasoning in the risk case most nearly fits this pattern. In fact it fits it when it is tuned in the direction of democracy between competing valuations. She rejects both risky options without going into them in detail because she is not confident of the criteria which would make one of them better than the safe option. Rather than let rival criteria fight it out and make a decision based on one of them she rejects options which do badly on some possible criteria, those which emphasize the badness of poverty. (To take the case this way is, of course, to read things into it. When Prudence says that she would probably go for the big risk rather than the annuity if forced to choose, but the choice would be hard, I interpret this as suggesting that she has some rough valuations according to which the big risk would *not* be as good as the annuity, although if forced to choose she would probably not use these valuations.)

The trivial case (Vienna—Ravenna) fits the pattern fairly well, too. In this case the process seems to be tuned in the direction of option-reduction. 'You' anticipate that thinking through all the possible strategies for balancing beach and sites on the Ravenna option will be very burdensome, so you adopt a decision-making procedure which reduces the burden of the process. The awful case (fugitive child) is somewhere between the risk case and the trivial case in this respect. And the moral case will be discussed later in this chapter.

5.7   The Optimistic Procedure

Though the pessimistic procedure may seem sensible – one first weeds out possible disasters and then gives more careful attention to the rest – we sometimes seem to do the opposite. Doing the opposite seems the rational response to desperation. Suppose for example that you are facing bankruptcy and you are considering numbers of ways to improve your business. None of them seem to do more than stave off the inevitable for different short periods. Except for one: it might lift you out of the doldrums into real success, but it might also cost you your life. (The idea is to do some business with the underworld, say, and use the profits to advertise your product on the scale required.) You take it seriously; perhaps then you do it.

There is something right here. Desperate situations need desperate remedies. So in a tight spot one looks first at the options with an optimistic eye, and if any seem to promise really good results one goes on to give them a longer and colder look. The routine then is exactly the same as the pessimistic procedure, but upside-down; first optimistic then pessimistic. Or, slightly more precisely, during all but the final pass through the options one eliminates all of those that do not give a reasonable probability of a very good result. And then, when the options have been sufficiently reduced, the final decision is made in detail just as in the pessimistic procedure.

This is, as I said, the intuitively right response to some desperate situations. It allows desperate people to reach through the options for the straw of a course of action which will rescue their fortunes. But it is quite clearly not a strategy for general use. Neither is the pessimistic procedure an absolutely all-purpose method, if the optimistic procedure is ever appropriate. So rather than compare the two I shall try to find a more general procedure, of which they are both special cases.

5.8   The Sieve

How to reconcile the optimistic procedure and the pessimistic procedure? I am sure that there is a neutral rule, which has both the optimistic procedure and the pessimistic procedure as special cases and which captures something fundamental about our attitudes to decision making. I am much less sure that I can formulate it adequately. Here is an attempt. It is probably more complicated than it needs to be.

A decision begins with a first pass through the full list of available options, including the crazy and the ridiculous ones. The aim is, as before, to extract from the full list a smaller list whose consequences one can compare carefully. The most important thing here is to discover which options are non-starters and which ones have interesting advantages. So one notes options which might have particularly bad consequences or which might offer particular advantages. Pessimistic evaluations tend to bring out the bad possible consequences, of course, and optimistic evaluations the good ones. In both cases estimates of probability (stories) which do not minimize the likelihood of less-probable consequences will underline extreme advantages and disadvantages. Then options are discarded and others saved for the next pass. The ones which are saved are those which do not have very bad possible consequences or do have conspicuous possible advantages — for any valuation and any story. (So if an option has very bad and very good possible consequences, on the same or different evaluations, it is kept.) Later passes through the remaining options are the same, with smaller ranges of valuations and probabilities. And eventually, when one tires of this, one makes a decision. The decision is between the shortlist of options which have come through the sieve, using a valuation which one would have used if forced to make a quick decision between them with no prior sieving.[3]

The sieve turns into the pessimistic procedure if the emphasis is put on rejecting options with bad consequences, and turns into the optimistic procedure if the emphasis is put on saving options which might turn out well. In a treacherous situation, in which there are unlikely to be many surprisingly good options and many options will have hidden dangers, the pessimistic procedure will be a good approximation to the sieve. And in a promising situation, in which there are few hidden dangers but many hidden opportunities, the optimistic procedure will be a good approximation to the sieve. This suggests that one might first evaluate the situation, in terms of the likelihood of hidden benefits and dangers, and how good or bad they might be, to make the first decision of all: what procedure to use. But this is not usually a real possibility. There usually is not enough time or energy. So one has to go by tradition or intuition, roughly classifying the situation as treacherous or promising and operating accordingly. Or just using the whole sieve.

5.9 Paradoxical Advice

There is something paradoxical about this style of decision making. An option can be rejected on the basis of non-central valuations or probabilities although in a forced choice it would have been accepted. The discussion between Prudence and Howard brought this out quite clearly: if Prudence had been forced to make a single comparison between all three options she would have chosen the big risk, but because she uses a more complex sequence of comparisons the big risk is rejected in favour of the annuity. This paradoxical air remains when this style of decision is applied to other kinds of case.

Consider the awful case again. Suppose that according to pessimistic interpretations of the outcomes, both of the options you would have to choose between if you return home – sheltering your child from the law or refusing to – are worse than the option of evading the issue by staying away. Then according to the pessimistic procedure you should not try to choose between the two first options, which involve weighing your loyalty to your child against your public duty, but should take the third option and stay away. (No doubt the third option is really a family of options, and you must look at the details to decide the best way to stay away.) Suppose though that on an optimistic interpretation of the outcomes one of these two first options is not that bad. Perhaps you will discover that your child's role in the murder is pretty marginal and you can persuade her to dissociate herself from her co-conspirators and face the law, without ruining your relationship with her. Suppose in fact that on a more detailed, and more optimistic, examination this option is even preferable to any of the staying away options, for in all of them she will see you as having abandoned her. Then we have the peculiar conclusion that by applying the cautious, pessimistic, rules I have been suggesting, you will be rejecting an option that a more balanced consideration might have shown to be the best one.

This conclusion *is* thought-provoking. But it does not convince me that this style of decision making is wrong. Consider again the risk case (Prudence and Howard). There the risky options are rejected on the basis of pessimistic evaluations although more optimistic evaluations would have led to one of them being accepted. But, after all, why should optimistic evaluations be more correct than pessimistic ones? One of the things one wants to do when faced with a dilemma is to do justice to all the possible values that can be brought to bear. One way, at any rate, of doing this is to use in one's own decision making a range of valuations which express both one's own guesses or forced-choice preferences and one's acknowledgement that other valuations may also be right. What one wants ideally is a way of varying the influence a valuation or a guess about probabilities has on the decision, depending on how much confidence one has in it. All three of the methods I have described do this to some extent: the final decision is made with the valuation one would use if forced to make a choice between all the options, and along the way to this final decision one discards less trusted valuations.

There is a more abstract way of seeing the question. The paradox is that an option can be rejected from the 'long list' although it would have been chosen had it got through to the 'short list'. In fact, phenomena rather like this are fairly common in decision making; for example, many widely used voting procedures exhibit something similar. That is, very often when people are voting to establish a group preference between options or candidates they use procedures which give a preference only relative to the set of options at hand. If the set of options had been enlarged or contracted then the order of preference of the remaining options could be different. This violates a condition first formulated by Kenneth Arrow and called 'independence of irrelevant alternatives'. But it is usually thought to be harmless for many purposes.[4]

The usual illustration is of rank-order voting (where voters write down a 1 beside the name of their first choice, 2 beside that of their second choice, and so on, and the numbers given to each candidate are added up to determine that candidate's position in the resulting order). Here is a

different example, more like the three decision procedures above. A group
of people need to decide who to give a job to. It is vital that the candidate
not be disliked by any of them, and also that they be well thought of by
one particular person with whom they would have to work especially
closely. Call this person the decider. The procedure they adopt is as
follows. They consider the long list of everyone who has applied for the
job and each vetoes one candidate and endorses one. Then vetoed
candidates are removed from the list unless more than one person has
endorsed them. (Candidates who are neither vetoed nor endorsed are retained.) This process is repeated until there are only a small number
(ideally, two) remaining. Then the winner is decided by the decider. (This
is much like a common procedure when a large group forms a shortlist,
leaving a final decision to a sub-committee.)

   This voting procedure is clearly much like the sieve. And it shares its
paradoxical quality. For candidates could be eliminated at the first round
although they would have been chosen had they survived to the final
decision. For suppose that there are three voters, Albert, Barbara, and
Charles. Albert is the decider. There are four candidates, Prima, Secundus, Tertia, and Quartius. Albert prefers Quartius to Prima to Secundus
to Tertia, Barbara prefers Tertia to Quartius to Secundus to Prima, and
Charles prefers Tertia to Prima to Secundus to Quartius. So at the first
round Prima and Quartius will be eliminated, leaving Albert to choose
between Secundus and Tertia. He will then choose Secundus, although he
would have preferred Prima had she not been vetoed earlier.

   Suppose, moreover, that Quartius had not been a candidate. Then
Secundus, the actual winner, would have been vetoed in the first round by
Charles. Prima would also have been vetoed and Tertia would have been
chosen, without any need for Albert to make a decision. So eliminating a
non-winner changes the choice of winner.

   So which candidate is chosen depends on what he or she is chosen
against. Does this mean that it is a bad way of choosing candidates? Not
at all. I would try to persuade my colleagues to use it under some
circumstances. And if I was making a decision between a large number of
hard-to-compare alternatives on the basis of a number of equally plausible
guesses about the values and probabilities involved, I would consider
letting each valuation 'vote' between the alternatives, choosing a voting
system to suit the situation.

5.10   Agenda-manipulation

These are agenda-manipulating strategies. They deal with a decision-making situation by structuring the comparisons that are to be made in order

to think it through. Agenda-manipulation can take many other forms. For example, there is the strategy described in chapter 2 for choosing candidates for a job while maintaining both a preference for members of some disadvantaged group and a commitment to hiring the best person. (I don't know why job appointments seem a good source of examples here.)

And agenda-manipulation in much the form it is taking in this chapter will arise naturally in many dilemma-managing strategies. An example is the revaluing strategy described at the end of chapter 3 (section 3.8), intended to avoid the need for compromise between the claims of career and family. To follow that strategy you have to find sub-aims in each category which you can try to achieve in a direct uncompromising way. They have to be aims which will not often conflict with one another. Conflicts will still sometimes occur, but the governing idea is that you should keep the two strands of your life as unentangled as you can. So, given a choice between two courses of action, one of which will involve you in a need to balance the two and the other of which will not, you have a motive for choosing the other. And one way of thinking out how strong the motive is would be to follow something like the pessimistic procedure, seeing options first with equal scope for the point of view associated with each of the parallel strands of your life, and rejecting those which look bad from either point of view. This makes it very likely that options involving choices or balances between the two strands will be rejected, because from either point of view a concession to the other will be a disaster.

One obvious effect of all of these strategies is to prevent some options from being considered. They thus function rather like rights or side-constraints in ethics.

Naively speaking, someone has a right to something when no one else has a reason to interfere with their relation to it. And a side-constraint is a prohibition against a whole class of actions: no reason can be given for doing them. Thus we have rights to our lives and others are constrained not to take them from us. Rights can come in different strengths: perhaps rights to property are weaker than rights to life. Side-constraints are absolute: they cannot be overridden by rights or by stronger side-constraints. It is notoriously controversial whether there are any side-constraints, and whether the notion of a right is a basic concept of ethics or simply a useful heuristic.

This much is clear about such concepts: they limit the options one can consider. A right says 'think twice before taking this as one of your options', and a side-constraint says 'this cannot be one of your options'. And, to that extent, moral systems incorporating either tend to produce paradoxical situations where an act is forbidden although it would, on a more careful examination, be chosen.

One form this can take is Judith Thomson's 'trolley problem'.[5] I will put it in terms of buses rather than trolleys. You are a passenger in a bus, sitting near the driver, who has a heart attack. The bus is heading for a cyclist stopped at a red light before you. You could seize the wheel and head the bus off to the left, avoiding the cyclist. But there is a pedestrian in the way to the left, who would then be in danger. What should you do?

Many people imagining such cases have a moral inhibition against choosing an action, in this case seizing the wheel and veering to the left, which will result in death or serious injury to someone. Imagine an extreme case of such an inhibition. The person will not choose to take over control of the bus and turn it to the left even though the bicycle ahead is carrying a child in a seat as well as its adult rider and the pedestrian to the left is young and athletic and might be able to jump out of the way. The reason is that to do this is actually to choose to inflict probable harm on the pedestrian, and to allow the bus to continue on into the bicycle is not to choose anything. *But* if this person were actually at the wheel driving the bus when the cyclist/pedestrian choice arose, both options would be considered and, most likely, the result would be a left turn.

So one course of action – steering the bus into the pedestrian – cannot be put into the set of actions to be considered, even though if it were in that set it might well be chosen as the course to follow. This may seem paradoxical. But it is the result of a very appealing principle: don't even consider killing anyone.

These moral intuitions may not be best expressed in terms of rights or side-constraints. Those are just terms in theories that philosophers and others have made to accommodate the intuitions. That is not my concern now. My concern is to state an important fact, that there are deep resemblances between moral and non-moral decision making here, and to express a conjecture. The conjecture is that if we go far enough into the ways in which we do and should make decisions involving risks of disaster and decisions in which we have to take account of future decisions, we will find that the concepts we need are also ones we need in ethics.

5.11   *The Foolish Philosopher and the Starving Thieves*

These are questions on which issues about rational decision and issues about morality come together. They are difficult questions. To give a further taste of their depth and difficulty consider two contrasting examples.

First consider the situation caused by tentative revisions of our values.

For example, many philosophers have produced arguments for not attributing to all human lives the same very great value. In fact in chapter 8 I endorse somewhat similar conclusions myself. Suppose, to make it stark and simplistic, you were forced to choose between saving the life of an almost-senile, mentally ossified, person with a fairly short life expectancy whatever your actions, and saving the life of a promising young scientist, on the verge of making a basic breakthrough in cancer research. Then, according to the arguments of many recent philosophers, you should choose to save the life of the scientist.

Imagine a foolishly sanguine philosopher who understands the arguments for revising our standard views about the value of life, but not the reasons for taking these revisions as tentative and uncertain. He is faced with a choice: course A involves great costs in terms of real and possible harms to people but no deaths, and course B involves a further choice between saving the life of a senile, mentally ossified, etc., person and that of a bright young scientist. He chooses B, confident that the further choice is unproblematic and the cost of the whole course of action less than that of A.

Something is very wrong with this carefreeness, even if one accepts the revisionary views about life. And the pessimistic procedure captures the wrongness. For although one has, let us suppose, accepted a view according to which it is right to put more effort into saving some lives than others, there are other values which one knows might be right. One knows that some argument that one has not thought of, or even some painful experience, might push one back to thinking of all lives as having an equal claim. So there is a pessimistic valuation of either of the outcomes of course B, according to which each of them is worse than anything that would come up in course A. So, according to the pessimistic procedure, both should be rejected in an early stage of decision making unless the alternatives are even worse, seen pessimistically. If the alternatives are even worse then you have to choose, and in this case you know what choice, based on non-pessimistic values, you will make. But if you are sensible you would rather not get into that position.

Contrast this example with another. There are some desperately poor but gentle thieves. They make their living robbing pilgrims on the road to a temple. But no one believes in the old gods any more so pilgrims are very few and the thieves and their children are on the brink of starvation. They have two options. One is to look for work as farm workers. But the farmers know and distrust them so the risk of starvation would still be very high. The other is to rob tourists staying in a new hotel near the temple. The advantage of this is that the tourists are rich. The disadvantage is that tourists do not know the subtle conventions that have grown up between pilgrims and thieves. It is likely that there will be confrontations in which tourists will resist, think they are being murdered, or try to contact the authorities. If this happens there is a small but real chance that a tourist will be killed. The thieves do not want this to happen: thieving has always been a very civilized occupation. What should they do?

The pessimistic principle tells them not to rob the tourists. There is a chance of a death. Perhaps the lives of foreigners are more significant than those of their starving children, or perhaps it is much worse to kill to feed your children than it is to let your children die. And trouble with tourists might lead to reprisals from the authorities and the end of their way of life. These are parallel to the considerations working in the foolish philosopher case, where they do seem to give the intuitively right answer. On the other hand the optimistic principle would tell them to rob the tourists. The advantages are very great – a really decent standard of living – and the dangers may not materialize. And even if the worst happens the deaths of tourists, who are mostly middle-aged people who have already had decades of luxury, are less to be regretted than the deaths of one's own children, who have known only a few years of illness and hunger.

The reasons against robbing tourists, from the pessimistic principle, and for robbing tourists, from the optimistic principle, both seem to have some force. The sieve, which incorporates both principles, says that they should take both tourist-robbing and a change of profession seriously. And that seems right. But it doesn't say what they should do. To know that they need a final set of values, which they can use to compare the possible benefits with the possible dangers. And they may just not have that. (Or, to put the point differently, in order to decide whether to use the optimistic or the pessimistic procedure, instead of the full sieve, they would need to make just the kind of definitive comparison of very different outcome which procedures of either kind are meant to forestall.) So the thieves have a real dilemma on their hands. Both options can be justified, and both can be refuted. They are open to indecision and remorse. But I tend to think they should rob the tourists.

6

Risk: More Questions than Answers

*And if it [a child] be from five years old even unto twenty years old,
then thy estimation shall be of the male five shekels of silver, and for the
female thy estimation shall be three shekels of silver.*

Leviticus 27: 5

Decision making comes under pressure when the stakes are high and our
information is imperfect. That is risk. There are many puzzles about risk.
Most of them can be most easily presented in terms of tensions between
the recommendations of a simple theory and the complex reactions we
have to individual cases. The theory is the standard philosophers' and
economists' account of rationality in the face of risk, in terms of expected
utility, and the cases derive mostly from the intuitive sense many people
have had that there is something wrong with the theory. My aim in this
chapter and the next is to give a diagnosis of what underlies these intuitions. As you might expect, my diagnosis appeals to the fact that our
preferences are riddled with incomparabilities. The conclusion, though, is
that there is nothing wrong with the standard theory, taken as a theory of
how decisions should be made once one has a suitable set of preferences,
probabilities, and options. The real problems about risk-taking arise
before that point, in setting things up so that probabilistic reasoning can
apply.

6.1 Probability-dependence and Risk-aversion

Reasonable people risk their children's lives for monetary gain. They
really do, all the time. For example, I am offered two hundred pounds for
a book review if I write it in one day and deliver it by five o'clock to the
offices of the *London Review of Books*. I need the money and I accept, but
to have the day to work I have to hire a baby-minder I have less than total
trust in. I put the probability of his doing the child any serious harm at all

at one in ten thousand – once in twenty years the baby-minder might cause harm – and the probability of the child's dying because I left her with this inexperienced person at something even smaller, say one in a million. So I hire this baby-minder, since no others are available, and get down to work, finishing the piece on the train to London. I have accepted a gamble with a certain gain of two hundred pounds and a 0.0001 per cent chance of my child's death. (Of course I am unlikely to express it to myself in those or any other numbers, but the rough size of the risk will be essential to my decision.) Life would be impossible if one did not take such risks with one's own life and those of others all the time.

Now consider a disturbing line of reasoning. The risk I took with my child's life shows that I value a 0.0001 per cent chance of its death at less than (a certainty of) £200. If the probability of death were higher I should need a larger monetary gain before I took the risk, but I certainly would take somewhat higher risks for considerably greater sums. I would trade probability against pay-off. Does this process ever stop? Perhaps there is an enormous sum which would reconcile me to a certainty of my child's death.

The sum would have to be truly enormous, much more than £200,000,000. But to suggest any sum at all seems crazy. It seems crazy to suggest that there must be any sum of money which I would prefer to even a 50 per cent chance of my child's death.

The values we put on options seem not to be independent of the gambles under consideration. We appear to give our lives and those of others finite values when the probabilities of losing them are small, and nearly infinite value when the probabilities are large. And when a decision falls between the cases where risks to life are routinely taken and those where they are out of the question, we are usually confounded and confused. Or so it appears. The appearance may be deceptive, but let us say that the patterns of choice that suggest it exhibit *probability-dependence*.

Probability-dependence is closely linked to a phenomenon called *risk-aversion*. Here is an extreme example bringing out one aspect of risk-aversion.

Imagine a fair but unequal society. It is divided rigidly into three castes. From the top caste to the very bottom caste life becomes progressively less comfortable. At the top 'Brahmins' live lives of luxury and have satisfying careers. At the bottom 'Harijans' live lives of unvarying and unrelieved physical toil. Middle-caste people live comfortable but not luxurious lives. Children are not born into castes: they all have the same casteless upbringing until the age of twelve, when their future lives are assigned to them by a lottery.

The lottery works as follows. Any twelve-year-old may choose to join the middle caste. Children may also choose to have their castes assigned randomly. In that case a roulette wheel is spun and the child enters the caste which the pointer indicates when it comes to rest. There is an equal chance of being in any of the castes.

Would you choose the middle caste or the lottery? You would have to know more about the lives of the three castes before being sure how you would decide. But I am sure that as long as I make it clear that the lives of the Harijans are really awful, those of the Brahmins very nice, and those of the middle-caste people not awful, most people would choose not to submit their futures to the lottery. The one-third chance of an awful life outweighs the one-third chance of a wonderful one.

This is a mild form of risk-aversion. It consists in a tendency to be more impressed by the bad possibilities in a gamble than the good ones, and – closely related to this – a tendency to prefer certainties of middle values to gambles between extremes. So choosing to avoid the lottery only counts as risk-aversion as long as you think that Harijanhood is about as much worse than middle-caste life as Brahminhood is better than it. Some people are obviously more risk-averse than others, but some degree of risk-aversion is universal.

Compare the original caste society with another. The second society is like the first except that the assignment of castes is only for three years. After three years one can choose again, and choose either a certainty of the middle caste or a gamble between all three.

Most people would be more inclined to take the gamble in this situation. (One attractive strategy might be to choose the middle caste for the first few times and then to gamble. Perhaps if the gamble made you a Harijan you would next choose the middle caste to be certain of escaping Harijanhood, and after that gamble again.) This is another instance of risk-aversion, since the life one will get by gambling in either society will be *on average* the same. That is, if we give each kind of life points (−1 for each year as a Harijan, 0 for each year in the middle, and 1 for each year as a Brahmin, say), then consistent gamblers will on the average get the same score whichever of the two societies they are in. (The expectation is 0.) But of course in this second society fewer gamblers will have consistently awful or consistently luxurious lives. So if you find a gamble in this second situation less fearsome than a gamble in the first situation, it is because you think that a greater possibility of a really bad result is not compensated for by a greater possibility of a really good one. This allows a more careful definition of risk-aversion: it consists in preferring gambles with a smaller chance of bad results, even among gambles which will on average give the same value.[1]

6.2 Expected Utility

Risk is not the same as uncertainty. A decision involves uncertainty when the consequences of some of the options are not known for certain. Then the decision must be made on the basis of probabilities. There are a number of simple rules for decision making under uncertainty, of which the simplest are *minimax* and *expected utility*.[2] The essence of them can be appreciated by imagining a simple coin-tossing situation in which if the coin comes down heads you lose five dollars and if it comes down tails you gain twenty-five dollars. (You are a cosmopolitan person and will think in terms of dollars as happily as pounds. Later in the chapter you will consider roubles and drachmas.) You have to choose whether to play. Minimax says not to play, because one possible result, losing five dollars, is worse than the outcome of not playing. Expected utility says to play, because on average you will gain ten dollars: assuming that heads and tails are equally likely and that your desire for twenty-five dollars is about five times as strong as your desire not to lose five dollars. (More on this second point below.) It is important to see that expected utility recommends taking the gamble even if you will only play the game once, so that what you will get will not be the average but either a gain of twenty-five or a loss of five.

An easy way to understand both minimax and expected utility as applied to more complex cases is to represent the possible outcomes of each of the options one is choosing between as a graph in which the desirability of the outcome is graphed against the probability of its happening. Thus imagine that the choice is between options A and B. A gives you a good chance of ten thousand dollars, but also a good, though smaller, chance of nothing, as shown in Figure 1. B, also represented in the diagram, can give you anything from one thousand to nine thousand dollars, and most likely will give you five thousand. (A and B could be investment opportunities.)

The choice involves uncertainty because it is not known with certainty what will happen if one takes either option. Moreover, one of the options, A, involves a large element of risk in that the graph is a very spread-out one: there is a fair probability that the outcome may be bad. The minimax rule recommends the choice of that option whose worst possible outcome is least bad. It thus avoids risky options. In this case it recommends choosing B, since the worst that can happen to you if you choose B is that you get $1,000, while if you choose A you may get nothing.

This contrasts with the rule of expected utility, or EU as I shall call it. The EU rule tells you to choose the option with the greatest expectation, that is, the greatest mean or average value (averaged over all possible

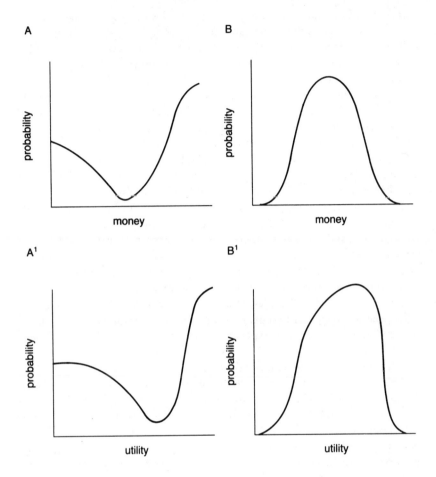

Figure 1 Risky and safe gambles. The gamble graphed in A has a higher expected monetary return than that graphed in B, but is also more risky, in that it presents a higher probability of a low return. If the gambles are graphed in terms of utility rather than money, and increases in money correspond to progressively smaller increases in utility, then the graphs are squeezed, so that A¹ represents a smaller expected utility than B¹.

outcomes). This too is most easily understood with a graph like those in figure 1: the mean is the point along the horizontal axis at which the graph will balance, with an equal area to the right and to the left of it. The significance of this mean depends on what quantity that horizontal axis represents. In the gambles above the mean was expressed in money. But if the amounts of money or other benefits are at all great the axis has to be rescaled to take into account the 'diminishing marginal utility of money', the fact that successively greater increases of money produce successively smaller increases in benefit. Utility is whatever this rescaling of possible benefits and losses results in. The central idea of EU is that for every decision there is such a rescaling, from benefits to utility, and the rational decision is the one for which the mean utility is greatest.[3]

There are three main reasons for believing in EU, and together they make a very strong case. The first is the simple and natural explanation of risk-aversion you get when you assume the diminishing marginal utility of money or other benefits. Consider a risky gamble like option A above. If a possible gain of ten thousand dollars is 'worth' much less than ten times as much utility as a thousand dollars then the mean value of gamble A will be a lot less, in terms of utility, than that of a less spread-out gamble such as B. (See the diagrams.) So people who don't like gambling are still choosing in terms of mean (or expected or average) values; they just give a smaller value to large gains – or a greater disvalue to large losses – than people who are more willing to take risks.

The second appeal of EU lies in its connections with the intuitive 'grammar' of risk taking. If one formulates rules which describe intuitively reasonable risk-taking behaviour one tends to find that one has come up with another formulation of EU. To state this in a little more detail: suppose that we have an intuitively plausible set of rules relating a person's preferences to the choices they should make between risky prospects. Several such sets of rules have been formulated. Then, almost always, there will be an abstract theorem stating a correspondence between these preferences and numerical utilities. In effect: anyone following the rules will always choose the option with the greatest expected utility. These are remarkable theorems, but they have to be taken with a little caution. They do not say that reasonable people will always maximize the satisfaction of their desires, or their expected good, or anything as thinkable as that. The 'utility' the theorems prove to exist is a purely abstract quantity, to be read off people's preferences and choices rather than introspected or prescribed.[4]

The third appeal of EU is the most intuitive, and the most controversial. The expected value of a choice is the average value that would be approached if the choice were made, under the same conditions, over and over again. (If the person's estimates of probability are correct, that is.) The rule is meant to apply to one-off choices, too, where there is no question of the situation recurring even once, let alone over and over again forever. Then the appropriate image is of alternative possible worlds branching from this one, representing things that might have happened but did not. (The coin falls heads, and you lose five dollars, but in an alternative world, which a moment ago had an equal chance of becoming actual, it falls tails and you gain twenty-five dollars.) Imagine that the number (or 'proportion') of worlds in which each thing happens is proportional to its probability. So there are as many worlds in which a coin lands tails as heads. And imagine that after each choice is made you can calculate how much you have gained or lost in each possible world. Then the expected value of a choice is the average of all these gains and losses. So if you take a course of action which is very risky but has a high expected value then although you will quite likely come out with a loss your possible selves in other possible worlds will on average have done well, because a few of them will have gained a lot. (The only question is: why should you care?)[5]

The expected utility rule, in various forms and variations, is at the heart of analyses of decision making under uncertainty given by most economists and business management experts, and by many philosophers. To use it you need estimates of the relevant probabilities and you need to be able to attach utilities to the relevant outcomes. In real-life situations neither is easy, to put it mildly.

In practice, if one's decision making is shaped by the EU rule the effect is likely to be found in one of two ways, which I call *the change of probability principle* and *backwards reasoning*. And the problems that can arise with the EU rule can usually be traced to one of these two secondary principles. Each in turn.

The change of probability principle says that one action is preferable to another to the extent that it makes a desired outcome more probable. (I say 'to the extent that' because the actions will usually have different effects on the likelihood of some other outcome.) Thus if I can buy more fire precautions for my house or make a payment on my mortgage, but not both, then I should pick the one that makes it most likely that I will continue to have my house. (Assuming for simplicity's sake that they have no other relevant effects, thus ignoring for example the danger of fire to life and limb.) If it is less likely that the house might burn down if I do not buy the precautions than that the bank might take it if I default on my mortgage, then I should spend the money on the mortgage rather than the precautions.

The change of probability principle allows one to compare different actions even when one does not know what the absolute probability of an event's occurring is. I do not know how likely it is that I will have my house in a year's time if I pay my mortgage now, but all I need to know to decide between paying my mortgage and buying fire precautions is the difference between the probability of my having it if I do the one and if I do the other. It is a pretty plausible principle, in many cases.

The other sub-principle that gives the EU rule its force is the backwards reasoning principle. It amounts to a bit of advice: think what the ultimate consequences of your actions might be, then for each such consequence think how much you want it and how likely it is, and choose your action on that basis. (This is closely related to the 'sure thing principle', one of the principles of rationality that can be proved to be collectively equivalent to EU.[6]) To do this completely by the book you have to find appropriate numbers to serve as utilities ad probabilities and then calculate the expectation of each action. But the real importance, I think, lies in the rough advice. It reverses a natural tendency of decision-makers to reason in the other direction, starting with the possible actions and asking of each 'what will follow if I do this', accumulating pros and cons and possible alternative actions until things become too complicated to follow any further. The backwards reasoning principle is a useful corrective to some of the disadvantages of this tendency and most of the effect of the EU rule on business practice is, I suspect, due to its inculcation of backwards reasoning.

6.3   Four Cases

Consider a family of related examples which bring out both the force of the EU rule and some of the problems with it.[7]

Case 1: the beleaguered general. A general has under his command two companies, A and B, which are threatened by an attack which if he does nothing will wipe out A and kill 3/6 of the men in B. But he can reduce his losses by calling for an air strike. If the strike comes to the aid of company A its losses will be reduced so only 5/6 of the men die but company B will still suffer the loss of 3/6 of its men. If the strike comes to the aid of company B then its losses will be reduced so that only 2/6 of its men die, but company A will be wiped out. Supposing that the general's only concern is to minimize loss of life, what should he do?

The general has to compare the value of reducing the probability of death (of an arbitrarily chosen person in company A) from 6/6 to 5/6, with that of reducing the probability of death in company B from 3/6 to 2/6. But it is easy to see that here the two options are equivalent: by calling for an air strike to aid either company he will have reduced his total losses from 9/12 of his men to 8/12. The two options are worth the same. The change of probability principle has an easy intuitive force applied to this case: lowering the probability of death for an average soldier by 1/6 has the same value whether that probability was initially 6/6 or 3/6.

This holds true if we replace the devastating enemy attack with two snipers, one of whom has a 6/6 probability of killing a man in A company and the other a 3/6 probability of killing a man in B company. Again the general will reduce his expected losses by the same amount by calling for a strike against the sniper threatening A, reducing the sniper's probability of success to 5/6 – he will have to take cover but will still be able to fire – or by calling for a strike against the sniper threatening B, reducing his probability of success to 2/6. That is to say, in the long run the general will reduce his losses by the same amount if he reduces either the greater or the lesser threat. But in this case the general is likely to experience some hesitation: if he calls for the strike against the sniper threatening B company then he knows that a man will die in A company. We can tell the story so that he knows who this man will be. So very likely he will call for the strike against the sniper threatening A company. But then his concern is not just to reduce loss of life: he is also trying not to have caused the death of a particular person.

Case 2: Russian roulette. A millionaire and her two children have been captured by evil philosophers. They put six-shooters to the heads of the children and propose to play Russian roulette. The pistol at Alice's head has a bullet in each of its six chambers while that at Bruce's head has bullets in only three chambers. So the probability is 6/6 that after the barrels have been spun and the triggers pulled Alice will be dead, and 3/6 that Bruce will be. There is a glimmer of hope, though. In exchange for a contribution to MAD (the Moscow Academy of Decision-theory) the philosophers will sell a bullet: they will, for a price, remove one – just one – bullet from one revolver. Two million roubles is mentioned. The millionaire cannot afford more. Which child's danger should she reduce?

Again the answer, according to the EU rule, is that the two options should have the same value for her. That is, this is so if we assume not only that the lives of the two children are equally valuable to her, but that the loss of the two children is twice as bad as that of one. If she buys the bullet in Alice's pistol then she will have increased the probability that both children survive but at the price of a greater chance that neither child will survive than the other option would have given. And the number of lives saved will be the same, on average, whichever child's danger she reduces.

(It is worth doing the calculations for oneself. Only with the figures before one does one appreciate the really painful twist of the dilemma: that the worst-case outcome, in which both children die, is more likely if she buys Alice's bullet. So in lessening Alice's risk she is not only ignoring Bruce's, but is taking the path that is more likely to lead to the ultimate disaster of losing both children. Before seeing this one might think that the intuitively more cautious option was to buy Alice's bullet.)

For all that, most people would have a clear preference for reducing the danger to Alice. For otherwise Alice will certainly die, while Bruce has a 50/50 chance of survival. The millionaire might, for example, prefer to buy a bullet from Alice's gun because if she does not her action will have led directly to Alice's death. (And later she will say to herself that she caused it, though she neither set up the situation nor pulled the trigger.) But her concern then would not just be with her children's lives but also with her role in their lives. For this reason it is hard to believe that this motivation gives the whole reason for the preference. For one thing, someone who was concerned only with the children's lives would also be likely to prefer that Alice's danger be reduced. For instance, if you were watching the scene, helpless to intervene, you would probably wish the millionaire to buy a bullet from Alice's pistol.

If the millionaire does prefer to buy a bullet from Alice's pistol, then she will be willing to pay more for it. The philosophers may thus ask more for one of Alice's bullets than for one of Bruce's. Suppose that Bruce's bullets go at a discount; she can get one for only one and a half million roubles. Should she still prefer to buy one of Alice's?

It will then matter a lot what she can do with the half a million roubles she would have left over if she abandons Alice. Suppose that she knows that the philosophers have other tricks up their sleeves, and she may need more money to get Bruce out alive after the game of Russian roulette. Then if she chooses to buy a bullet from Alice's gun rather than Bruce's she is in effect buying a small increase in Alice's life expectancy with a decrease in Bruce's. Can this be right?

These are extremely hard questions, in terms of our naive intuitions about what it is reasonable to do. The EU theory is very clear though: if the millionaire values both children's lives equally and is concerned only with the number of lives saved, so losing two children is twice as bad as losing one, then she should be indifferent between buying a bullet from either gun for the same price. And she should not pay more to reduce Alice's danger than she would pay to reduce Bruce's.

Case 3: stranded convoys. Albert works for Oxfam in Eritrea. Two convoys of trucks with food supplies destined for camps of starving refugees have been blocked. Convoy A has been held up by corrupt officials who if left to their own devices will certainly take the contents for themselves. An offer of a bribe to the chief official will help, but only so much. It will reduce the probability that the supplies will disappear from 6/6 to 5/6. Note that what is called for is the offer rather than the payment of a bribe: if the supplies are not released the bribe need not be paid. Convoy B has been captured by rebels. Though hungry themselves they are of the same nationality as the refugees and are thus more likely than the officials to let a convoy through. The probability is 3/6 that they will take the supplies for themselves; this probability can be lowered to 2/6 by offering them the same amount as the bribe that might oil the way of convoy A. Or so Albert estimates. Again what is needed is an offer rather than a payment. He has not the funds to pay off both the officials and the rebels, and his life and Oxfam's operations will be forfeit if he makes an offer and then cannot come through with the cash. Which should he pay?

Though the numbers may be the same as in the earlier cases the answer is not. If the number of lives each convoy could save is the same and Albert sees his efforts as succeeding in proportion to the number of lives saved, then he should offer the bribe to the officials rather than the rebels. For the crucial difference is that if the gamble does not pay off and the convoy is not released then the money does not have to be paid. So the chance is that if Albert makes the offer to the officials the convoy will still not be released, and the money will be saved to buy more life-saving supplies, while if he makes the offer to the rebels the convoy will probable get through so he will have to pay the money. (This verbal reasoning can be backed up with an expected utility calculation.)

(I am not looking very carefully here at the assumption that saving n lives is n times as valuable as saving one life, or at the corresponding assumption in case 2. In the next chapter – in section 7.3, 'Roulette Revisited' – I return to them.)

Case 4: Greek roulette. Our millionaire has paid to buy one bullet from Alice's gun, the triggers have been pulled, and both children have survived. Driving home, she tries to recover her equanimity by concentrating on mathematics. She explains the multiplication principle for the probability of independent events to the children, and uses as an example that the odds were twelve to one against both of them surviving their recent adventure. When they understand, Alice and Bruce are as upset as she. This does not cheer her up. Nor does the appearance of another set of gunmen who force the limousine off the road and bundle their three victims into a nearby house.

Again revolvers are produced and again Alice and Bruce are faced with a 6/6 and 3/6 probability of death. Again just one bullet is for sale. The millionaire points out that she has paid all her money to the first kidnappers. But these villains explain that they are from GRIM (the Greek Research Institute into Motivation) and that they know all about her secret reserves in Athens. Six million drachmas are suggested. So the millionaire promises that she will pay, but since she has nothing with her, all she can do is promise that she will pay for the bullet later, unless the child from whose gun the bullet was taken dies. In that case nothing they can do will extract a lepton from her. They agree, but remind her that she can only make an offer towards the purchase of one bullet. Which child's danger should she now reduce?

This time her natural inclination to reduce the overwhelming danger to Alice is backed up by the EU rule. The situation is parallel to that facing Albert in case 3: if she offers the money towards removing a bullet from the gun at Alice's head she will probably not have to pay, since the probability is still that Alice will die, while if she offers it towards one of Bruce's bullets there is a good chance that Bruce will survive and she will have to pay. And experience is rapidly teaching her that it can be a life-and-death matter to have enough money available to buy off danger.

(She buys one of Alice's bullets. Barrels are spun and triggers pulled and again both children survive. She proceeds on life's way with her children, more than ever convinced both that in this grim world you must do your sums carefully, and that madly calculating philosophers are the scourge of the earth.)

6.4 Missing Pieces

What needs explanation about these four cases is the way in which one's intuitions vary, although formally speaking the cases are so similar. I take it that most people would accept the EU analysis of case 1 (the belea-guered general) and of case 3 (the stranded convoys). (The first version of case 1 is in fact much easier to think about than any of the other cases in that the general knows exactly what his losses will be given each of his options, rather than, as in the other cases, knowing only the probabilities.) But most people would hesitate before applying the same reasoning to case 2 (Russian roulette). And in case 4 (Greek roulette) most people would accept the result of the analysis while feeling unsure that it had captured the real reasons for the decision. Something seems to be left out.

One thing that is left out is any recognition of the dilemma-like quality of the decisions. Even if the preferences sanctioned by the EU rule are right, it does not seem true that the decision is unproblematic, that the people in question can be sure that they had not gone wrong. This element is most acute in case 2, where the two options open to the millionaire are judged to be equal in value. That would seem to make the decision an easy one: she can do whatever she wants. But that is surely to miss something essential. Whatever she does she ought to do hesitantly, with a sense of the appeal of the other option.

I shall approach this issue indirectly, via some more easily managed questions. In the next chapter I give some suggestions about how we should approach decisions with risky options. To end this chapter I shall just list some of the resources which the chapter has ignored. For it has been formed around the standard analyses of risk, and it is important to see how narrow a range of ideas they bring to bear on the problems.

One way in which we unnecessarily narrow our room for manoeuvre is by trying to pick out in any situation a 'best' action or actions which a person must choose if they are not to be irrational. In truth, we think in a richer and more flexible way. We speak of what actions one *must* rationally choose (one would be a fool not to choose them), and actions that one *may* choose without being irrational (one would not be a fool to choose them), and actions one *just might* choose (one may or may not be a fool to choose them). In fact we make far more distinctions than this. So, at the very least, we should allow for a distinction between options one must take, if one is rational, options one may or may not take, and options that one may not take.

In the case of risky options such distinctions have a natural place. Suppose that someone who will take a 0.0001 per cent chance of their child's death for a sure gain of £200 is also willing to take, say, a risk of the child's life a hundred times this great for a monetary reward also a hundred times greater. This seems perfectly all right. But balking at this greater risk for this greater gain also seems alright. Both seen permissible and neither seems obligatory. Or so it is natural to think: not that I have yet backed the intuition up with any analysis. It is also natural, though more controversial, to think that the millionaire in the Russian roulette case may rationally be indifferent between buying Alice's bullet or buying Bruce's, and also rationally prefer buying Bruce's bullet. (But prefer by how much? How much more may she pay for Bruce's bullet? Then things begin to get really difficult.)

Moreover, in common sense we acknowledge a spectrum of character-types whose differences turn on the way in which they react to risk. We allow brave risk-takers and prudent hesitaters; we accept that three-year-olds and adolescents think death is a myth, while nervous parents stay at home and bite their nails. And although we allow that there are unjustifiable extremes in both directions we do not suppose that in any given situation either the adventurous or the cautious must be right. Human life may always have needed both impulse and timidity, and modern life may also call both for speculative entrepreneurs and for careful portfolio-managers. Why suppose that there is only one right attitude?

(This should not be taken as assuming that the expected utility approach must deny either the distinction between the obligatory and the permissible or that different people have different affinities to risk. Some careful things have to be said here, as I try to in the next chapter.)

The discussion in this chapter has also ignored incomparable desires. Two kinds of incomparability are particularly relevant to risk. The first comes into the picture because of the way in which probability or uncertainty can dilute the strength of a very great value or desire. The most obvious examples are irreversible disasters such as the death of oneself or of others. (There are many such disasters: bankruptcy, the loss of a war, the failure of a life's project.) Death is so much worse than the loss of something small and replaceable, like a sum of money, that one normally works by a crude rule of thumb: loss of life is worse than loss of money. But when the amount of money increases and the weight of death is diminished by the force of probability, as when one has a gamble between a certainty of a large gain in money and a small probability of loss of life, then this rule no longer applies. What emerges is a great uncertainty about the relative weighting one should give to life and money. And for many people, at any rate, the strong appearance is of a fundamental incomparability. There is a 'diamond-shaped' pattern of preferences in which avoiding a certainty of death is preferable to almost any gain in money, but many probabilities of death and many smaller sums of money cannot be directly compared. (In fact, within the diamond there is almost certainly a shifting horizon, as I discussed in chapter 3.)

(There are natural connections between issues about incomparability and the questions about 'must' versus 'may' versus 'might just' that I alluded to above. If options – as well as outcomes – are sometimes incomparable then one can expect some very complex patterns of rational obligation to occur. For example it could then be the case that one may do A or B, and may not do C, but if one does not do A one may do B or C.)

Sometimes a risky option involves a gamble between comparable outcomes. (Heads you lose all your money, tails your wealth is tripled.) These decisions are also hard. It is a natural suggestion – but a more speculative one – that here too we have a kind of incomparability. Gambles and certainties just may not fit directly on the same scales. (And another twist of incomparability enters when we are ignorant not just of what the future has in store but also of what the relevant probabilities are.) But it must be admitted that the difficulty of these gambles is most acute when the stakes are highest, and then one's attitude to them is inevitably linked to the catastrophic consequences that might follow from very great losses. So ground-level incomparability such as that between money and death may be all that we need to appeal to.

7

Risk: A Few Answers

Where would we be without worry?
It helps keep the brain occupied.
Doing *doesn't take your mind off things,*
I've tried.

Worry is God's gift to the nervous.
Best if kept bottled inside.
I once knew a man who couldn't care less.
He died.

Roger McGough

I shall present a model of risk-taking behaviour. That is, I shall describe some simpler patterns of preference than real people ever have, and then I shall describe some strategies that would make sense for people with these simple preferences when faced with choices between risky options. I then claim that these strategies can also make sense for us, with our more complicated preferences.

The chapter is built around an intuitive idea and a closely related formal one. The intuitive idea is that many risk-taking dilemmas can be traced to incomparability between two kinds of things that we value. The first kind consists of goods like money or commodities or pleasure. These can be substituted for one another: I don't mind losing a coin if I will soon gain another. The other kind consists of irreplaceable things like our lives or our self-respect, which do not allow such substitutions. And the formal idea is that there are some very natural patterns of preferences which are inherently unsuited for use in probabilistic reasoning. These preferences take some reshaping before they can be usefully combined with the information that characterizes risks. The connection between the two ideas is that these uncomfortable preferences are likely to be found when we compare the replaceable and the irreplaceable.

7.1 The Timid Snobs

Imagine a tribe of people whose dominant characteristic is fear of death, their own and others' of the tribe, followed at some distance by desire for social status, followed at another distance by desire for the basic goods of life. They see death as awful, but they also want honours, distinctions, and rank, and dread the quite common condition of having no status at all. And they know they ought to get loaves of bread and roofs to sleep under, though their hearts do not beat much faster at these prospects. I shall refer both to basic goods (like shoes and loaves of bread) and to undesirable everyday things (like leaking roofs, headaches, and hunger) as 'basics'. And I shall refer to anything that gives social status as an 'honour'.

Let us represent their desires in an extreme way, so that each of them prefers any honour to any basic, and prefers any basic to any death. Moreover, compared to basics deaths are more bad than honours are good. That is, the combination of any death, any basic, and any honour is worse than the basic alone. So not one of them would sacrifice the life of the most distant cousin in order even to become both king and rich. Their desires form what is called a 'lexical ordering'. In fact it is a double lexical ordering: the result of an increase in basics, however great, is less desirable than the least honour, and the result of any combined decrease in honour and basics will be preferable to any increase in death.[1] (See Figure 2.)

Now you might think that this preference for honours over basics is very imprudent. But the Snobs live in a world in which honour can only be had by risking lives, but in which basic goods, the bare essentials of life, can be obtained more safely. (Though basic goods may not be easy to get; time and effort may be needed.) To achieve status and renown you have to take part in wars and lead expeditions through wild country. As a result looking for honour is also looking for death, not necessarily one's own, and trying to gain basic goods becomes relatively more desirable.

Let me make some more detailed assumptions about their preferences. The way in which death is incomparably worse than honour or basics is different, I shall assume, from the way in which honour is incomparably better than basics. For in comparing one prospect with another no increase in honour or basics can compensate for an increase in death. But on the other hand 'differences' between pairs of basics and between pairs of honours are comparable. That assumption amounts to two things. First, that a change in basics is comparable to a change in honour: for example an opportunity to exchange a crust of bread for a bowl of soup may be worth the same as an opportunity to exchange a mere appearance at court

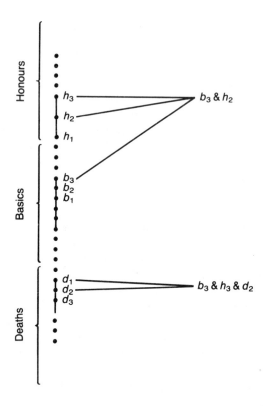

Figure 2 The Snobs' preferences. All honours are preferred to all basics, and all basics to all deaths. (And there are infinitely many of each, with for example $b1$, $b2$, $b3$, ... having the same difference of desirability between bi and $bi + 1$.) But combinations of basics and honours can substitute for increases in honour. Thus the combination of $b3$ and $h2$ is as good as $h3$. On the other hand no increase in basics or in honours can substitute for a decrease in death. Thus the combination of $b3$, $h3$ and $d2$, although better than $d2$, is not as good as $d1$.

for a mention of that appearance in the court gazette. And second, that combinations of basics and honours are comparable to honours: for example a new coat plus the right to be addressed as 'sir' may be worth the same as the right to be addressed as 'your honour'.

These comparabilities between honour and basics do not undo the fact that the least honour is worth more than any amount of basic goods. Someone without any honours would prefer any honour to any basic good, but someone who has passed the threshold of minor honour can then trade honour off against basics, as long as this leaves him at least a minor honour. (We might suppose that as the threshold of honourlessness is approached it takes increasingly great amounts of basic goods to compensate for any decrease in honour.)[2]

(These assumptions are more complex than need be, though the diagram should make them intuitively graspable. I could have made the relation between honour and basics like that between basics and deaths and honours and deaths. But I wanted to bring out the variety of preference-patterns that we can make sense of, and the variety of patterns that can cause the kinds of problems that I shall discuss.)

The final assumption is that there are infinitely many basics, so that for any basic good there is a better and for every basic evil a worse. There are also infinitely many honours and infinitely many possible deaths. But even a single death is worse than any basic evil.

Since honours can only be had at the price of deaths, the only honour-giving possibilities that the snobs can realize are combinations of an honour and a death. But these combinations are all less desirable than any basic. So as long as we are dealing only with certainties, they cannot achieve any of the honours they long for. (These all will stay in the hands of barbarians with different preferences.) This is an uncomfortable situation: not only will their lives always be blighted, deprived of what they want most, but they may be forced to accept absolutely miserable conditions, basic evils, in order to avoid causing death.

The situation might change, though, if we consider uncertain prospects. A certainty of any combination of a death, a basic, and an honour is less desirable than any basic alone; but a small probability of a death combined with a high probability of an honour might perhaps be preferable to a certainty of a basic. Might they take a minuscule chance of death in order to achieve great honour?

The Snobs' preferences have only been specified over certainties. So the question is: can they be consistently extended to gambles in such a way as to allow the snobs to take some risk of death in order to achieve honour? (Or for that matter to avoid basic evils?) There are two conflicting lines of reasoning here. The first, and simpler, says that they cannot be. Since all the attainable options which yield honours involve a chance of death, and deaths are worse than honours are good, even a chance of death outweighs any certainty of honour. So basics – even basically undesirable things like hunger – since they can be attained without danger of death should always be preferred to honours.

To put this in a sharper focus imagine a Snob faced with a choice involving an honour, a basic, and a probability of death. The honour is, of course, coupled with a danger; assume that the basic is dangerless. To be specific suppose that the choice is between an honour with a value of 100 on the scale of honours but carrying a 0.0001 probability of death, and a basic with a value of −100 on the scale of basics. The expected value of choosing the honour is honour to the value of 100 and death to the value of 0.0001 (that is, one death in a thousand tries). And the expected value of choosing the basic is −100 on the scale of basics. Let us represent these two expected values as (100,0,0.0001) and (0, −100,0) respectively. Now since any amount of death is worse than any honour is good the second of these triples is preferable to the first. So the Snob should choose the basic. In fact the Snob should choose any basic, however low it ranks on the basic scale, rather than any honour, however high it ranks on its scale and however small the associated danger of death. A lifetime of painful but non-fatal hunger is preferable to a lifetime of high office if the high office carries even the slightest whiff of danger.

That may seem a very straightforward result. There is something puzzling or disappointing about it, though. For it says that the snobs are doomed to miserable lives, even if the honours they crave are available at very little danger. It seems a shame that they cannot find a way of taking the slight dangers necessary to achieving some of their strongest desires.

The argument that they should, or at any rate may, take the dangers follows a very standard line in decision theory. Consider a highly ranked honour, ranking say 100 on the scale of honours – an appointment as general, perhaps – and the death of a single person. Then consider something between them in desirability, for example a basic ranking 5 on the scale of basics – a decent meal, perhaps. The aim is to show that this basic is either interchangeable in value with some gamble between the honour and the death, or incomparable to such gambles. And the argument to this effect, slightly streamlined, goes as follows.

Suppose that a Snob is given the choice between the basic and a 50/50 gamble between the honour and the death. Then there are four possibilities. The gamble and the basic will be interchangeable in value, or the gamble will be preferred to the basic, or the basic to the gamble, or they will be incomparable. In the first and last of these there is nothing more to do. But in the second of them – gamble preferred – consider instead a different gamble weighted more heavily to the death: say 45–55 honour–death. Similarly in the third possibility – basic preferred – consider instead a gamble weighted more heavily to the honour: say 55–45 . Again the same four possibilities arise. Continue, if need be running through all possible gambles between the honour and the death, until the process either provides a gamble – probability p of the honour and probability $(1 - P)$ of the death – which is interchangeable with the basic or shows that the basic is incomparable to all such gambles. (This gamble, if it exists, cannot amount to either the pure honour or the pure death: p cannot be 1 or 0. For basics lie between honours and deaths in desirability.)

But this fact allows there to be choices in which the honour is after all chosen over the basic. For if Snobs are indifferent between the basic and some particular gamble between a honour and a death then there will be other honour-death gambles that they prefer to the basic. If a decent meal and an 80/20 gamble between an appointment as general and the death of one person have the same value for you then you should prefer a 90/10 gamble between the appointment and the death to the meal. And if the gambles are incomparable to basics then they may be chosen over them. So, in either case, the Snobs can sometimes go for honour.

7.2 Mercator's Projection

These are paradoxical results. The Snobs seem both forbidden and encouraged to gamble with death. In fact there can be no unequivocal advice to them. For there is no way of extending their preferences to include gambles between honours, basics, and deaths, which both allows standard probabilistic reasoning and preserves the (lexical) structure of their preferences. Though the Snobs' desires are a simplification of common human desires they just do not combine with probabilities. For the structure of probability (real numbers in the interval from 0 to 1) imposes conditions on the structure of preferences which are to be used as input to probabilistic reasoning. (In the case at hand it is the 'Archimedean' property of the real numbers that is causing the problems.)

There are several ways in which the Snobs can find their way through risky situations. I shall describe two.

The first is, in effect, to refuse to reason probabilistically. Given every risky prospect they can decide what the most likely outcome is, equate it to a certainty of that outcome, and choose accordingly. This is something we often do in real life. We say 'if I do this then the result will be . . .', where the result is really just the most likely outcome. We then evaluate actions by these most likely outcomes (we use the modes rather than the means of our probabilities).

Reasoning in this way the Snobs can accept some risks of death to gain basics and honours, when the most likely outcome is that no life will be lost. Their choices will be fairly coherent, as long as they are not faced with too many borderline probabilities. They will also have problems with situations which amalgamate several gambles into one. For example, a 0.2 probability of death might well be acceptable in order to obtain a high office. So it could be that on five successive occasions such a gamble was accepted. But a single prospect of five such repeated gambles would not be acceptable, since it would present a 0.67 probability of death. And they would not have any way of trading off probabilities against benefits: for example a marginally acceptable gamble for a considerable gain, say a 0.4 chance of death for a very high office, would not become unacceptable when the gain was reduced, so that the same chance of death would be justified by the prospect of a basic good.

Only in a fairly simple and unambiguous world can you get away with identifying all actions with their most likely results. In more complex situations something closer to real probabilistic reasoning will be needed. And this is the second way in which preferences such as those of the Snobs can come to terms with risk. It consists in approximating patterns of preference which do mesh with probabilities.

A perfect approximation is not going to be possible, for there is no way of assigning real numbers to preferences such as these without ignoring some of their structure. But there will be usable assignments if we consider only restricted parts of the full range of preferences and probabilities. If we only consider options involving basics, for example, there will be no problem reasoning probabilistically – applying the EU rule – to gambles involving any probabilities at all. But for a more interesting case consider basics no more desirable than a minor banquet and no less desirable than a bad headache, and deaths of no more than one person, combined in gambles in which the probability of death is never greater than 0.1. Then the preferences span the gap between basics and deaths. Assign the banquet the desirability (utility) 10 and the headache the desirability −10, and to a single death the desirability −100. Other basics between these two are given desirabilities in accordance with their relation to them, and probabilities of death are evaluated straight-forwardly as fractions of −100. Then in the limiting case in which probabilities are near zero or one the choices which are entailed are very little different from those which would arise from the untampered-with preferences. And these choices vary smoothly and coherently as the probabilities become greater.

But we cannot extend the range of the basics further without changing the value attached to death. If, for example, we consider better and worse basics than banquets and headaches, extending the range so it runs from +50 to −50 but keeping the value of one death at −100 then some unwanted by-products will show up; for instance it will become acceptable to substitute a top basic for a bottom one at the price of a death. A different range of outcomes needs a different set of numbers.

Yet trickier cases involve more than one death or all three categories of outcomes. To tackle both at once consider gambles involving basics between a banquet and a headache, one or two deaths, and a few honours. (Up to a minor title, say.) Again give the basics desirabilities between 10 and −10, but value one death at −200, two deaths at −400, and honours from 50 to 100. Then again we have a good approximation to the original preferences when the probabilities are low, and a reasonable pattern of choices as probabilities increase. Again the values cannot be maintained if the range is extended, since it is essential that the gap between the top and bottom basic be less than that between any basic and any honour, which is in turn less than that between any basic and any death and than that between one death and two deaths.

It is important to notice the play between probability and desirability in these assignments. There is no best value for the disutility of death. The lower it is the better the approximation to the underlying preferences, and the higher it is the more manageable the set of gambles that is endorsed (and the more scope given to basics and honours in their uneven comparison with Death.) So the clue to a workable assignment of desirabilities is to find a disutility for death that is no lower than it need be. And the main factor determining this is the greatest values of other goods that are in play. For the gap between death and the least good must be greater than that between any two goods. Now suppose that one has fixed on a disutility for death, −D, but the gambles being considered all involve only fairly small probabilities of death. Then the largest positive utility that need be considered may be rather smaller than D, if there is no other source of large utilities besides gambles with death. If so, then a smaller disutility for death will do just as well. And so on, until the utilities of goods that are actually being considered put a stop to the process.

The conclusion is simpler than the argument: the lower the stakes (besides death) and the lower the probabilities of death, the lower the disutility that need be assigned to death.

These desirabilities capture local rather than global features of the preference-structure. For example they miss the fact that there can be a descending chain of evenly spaced basics, which are all less bad than a single death. (That is, a series of basic goods $b1$, $b2$, ... where the difference in value between any bi and the following $bi +1$ is the same.) Such chains are only represented approximately: even if an assignment of desirabilities includes infinitely many basics any descending chain of basic goods will find its desirabilities steadily squeezed together further along the series.

It is like mapping the earth. No single projection can reproduce on a plane the topology of a sphere, but for each limited region of the earth there is a projection which will do well enough.

7.3　Roulette Revisited

Real people and their preferences are nowhere this simple. In reality we have more, and more varied, incomparabilities, and our desires do not divide into easily separated classes like those of the Snobs. That suggests a certain degree of caution in extrapolating to real life from this simple model. But in real life it is even *more* likely that our underlying preferences are laden with incomparabilities and infinities which make them unsuitable material for probabilistic reasoning. So in thinking through risky situations we must first reform them into simpler preferences, which look more like well-behaved stretches of real numbers. But when we do this we find that we must use different such reformed preferences in different contexts. And one consequence of this, as I argued above, is that when the probability of disaster is high we will use a high estimate of its disutility. In effect, probability-dependence.

Probability-dependence is in fact found throughout human decision. And one of the most interesting and powerful ways of accounting for it, that due to Mark Machina, does in fact work by supposing that people smoothly substitute one set of valuations for another as the stakes and odds change. Machina intended his account to be purely descriptive, modelling the way people do act rather than how they should act.[3] The model I am presenting shows how such preferences can arise out of an intelligible set of underlying preferences. So one can see how such patterns of choice could be a reasonable reaction to a situation in which agents could easily find themselves.

Remember now the millionaire of the last chapter, who had to choose between changing the probability of death of one child, Alice, from 6/6 to 5/6 and changing the probability of death of another child, Bruce, from 3/6 to 2/6. The problem was that given some quite natural assumptions the two actions have the same expected utility. Moreover there are closely parallel cases, such as that of the beleaguered general, in which it is natural to take the two actions to be equal in value. But many people would think that her clear priority was to save Alice. And many who have no position on what she should do know that her decision is a deeply difficult one, and no simple calculation can show which option she must take.

Suppose that the millionaire often has to spend money to buy safety for her children. She values her children more than any amount of money. (They are, as we say, incomparably more valuable.) But in order to think through the prices she must pay to reduce different threats she needs a way of weighing money against risks to their lives. Then she is in just the situation of the Snobs. So she may well reason in the second way I suggested they might, and use different 'finitizations' of her preferences on different occasions. The result will be that she will take the value of a child's life to be higher when the probability of losing it is higher than when it is lower.

Therefore if she is confronted one day with a threat imposing a 3/6 probability of death on Bruce, which she can reduce to 2/6 by paying a sum of money, she may well impose an upper limit on the amount she will pay. She can reason 'If I pay more than that I won't have enough left to deal with future threats, for example to Alice'. Suppose then that the next day it is Alice who is faced with a 6/6 probability of death, which can be reduced to 5/6 (but no further), by a payment. The millionaire is likely to pay more then, since she will be using a different set of comparisons, relative to that degree of threat. She can reason: 'This is where my reluctance to pay yesterday pays off; if they ask for my whole fortune I will pay it, for there can be no greater threat.'

So she will pay more to reduce the probability from 6/6 to 5/6 than from 3/6 to 2/6. Alice's bullet is worth more than Bruce's. But the situation is not quite the one that I originally described. In the situation I described the two threats are simultaneous. She does not compare Bruce's threat to money one day and Alice's threat to money the next day, but rather compares Bruce's threat to Alice's. Which one has the priority?

It would be very natural for her to think of each threat in terms of the price she would pay to alleviate it in isolation from the other, and then compare the two prices. And if she does that she will conclude, as most people would, that Alice's threat has the priority. Natural, but not at all obviously right. For if she prefers reducing Alice's threat to reducing Bruce's she ought to be willing to pay more for it. The extra price might be in money. Or it might be in an increased threat to Bruce. (she might, that is, choose to reduce a threat to Alice from a 6/6 to a 5/6 probability of death, rather than reduce a threat to Bruce from 3/6 to something between 3/6 and 2/6.)

If the price is in an increased threat to Bruce, or if it is in money which is clearly going to be needed to deal with future threats, then there is a good reason to think that it is wrong to pay it. For then the millionaire's problem is essentially to get herself through the foreseen or guessed-at threats in store for her with minimal loss of life. She has to find that tradeoff between money and threats to life which will minimize the expected loss. The calculation will often be very complicated, and it will be made harder by the fact that the millionaire has desires for other things besides her children's lives. So, like the Snobs, her decision-making may make some room for satisfying these lesser but real desires. In effect, she must find temporary preferences with which to decide how much she is willing to pay now to ransom either child's situation, bearing in mind what may lie ahead of them.

If she would not be willing to pay more to save Alice then saving Alice cannot be the preferred act. And even when the price paid for preferring Alice is not an increased threat to Bruce (or an increased threat to Alice later), the situation is really one in which the millionaire must find the best way of minimizing the probability that her children will die, given all the other things she cares about. So, in the simultaneous-threat case, Alice's prospects seem bleak.

Something important has been left out, though. The calculation that equates buying Alice's bullet with buying Bruce's assumes not only that the millionaire cares equally about Alice's and Bruce's life, but that she finds the prospect of losing both children twice as bad as that of losing just one. If we vary this assumption we get different answers. If we assume that losing two children is much worse than losing one – the real disaster would be to come out of the crisis childless – then calculation shows what intuition would suggest, that the millionaire should buy Bruce's bullet. And if we assume that losing two children is less than twice as bad as losing one (while losing two is awful the threshold of disaster comes with the loss of one) then again calculation agrees with intuition: she should buy Alice's bullet.[4]

But why should she not consider the loss of two children as being exactly twice as bad as the loss of one? If children were just valuable things like any others then it would indeed be hard to justify any other assumption. (I am assuming that the millionaire is thinking entirely in terms of parental love, and is not for example thinking of her future life with a child or childless. If she is there is no problem: she should buy Bruce's bullet.) But for most people irreplaceable things like human lives are not just valuable things like any others. A simplistic way of representing this is in terms of preferences like those I gave my Snobs: lives are more valuable than any ordinary replaceable good. No doubt our actual preferences are subtler, more complicated, and less coherent than this, but in these terms we can see why the assumption is problematic. If the loss of a child is infinitely worse than any loss of money, then is the loss of two children worse by double infinity? Is double infinity more or less than infinity?

A different way of putting the point. To think through gambles of life against money the millionaire must fix an arbitrary value for the loss of a life. This is not a completely unconstrained business, but it is still fairly arbitrary, as I argued above. And fixing it at a particular value does not fix the value for loss of two lives. That is a further decision. So even if the millionaire has determined an upper limit to what she would pay to reduce a given threat to one child's life, this does not determine what she should pay to reduce threats to both children.

If this is so, what assumption *should* she make about the comparative value of one and two children's lives? There is no right answer. That is why the problem is a dilemma. And if *this* is so, how should she make her decision?

One way in which she could approach the decision is to compare the consequences of different assumptions about the relative awfulness of one or two deaths. She might, for example, consider the threshold of disaster to be crossed with one child's death, and the death of two children to be at most twice as bad. ('I love them as individuals', she might say, 'and the loss of either is as great a calamity as I can imagine.') If this is how she feels then two deaths are at most twice as bad as one for her, and may be comparatively little worse than one. And the consequences of buying Bruce's bullet are thus at best just as bad as those of buying Alice's and at worst a lot worse, since buying Bruce's bullet gives a certainty of at least one death. So, *if* this is the way she feels, caution would suggest that she buys Alice's bullet, since the consequences of this choice might be not as bad as those of the alternative.

7.4   The Risk Sieve

Worst-case reasoning is a natural tool when one is unsure what values to apply, or what the true probabilities are. It provides almost the only plausible way to rationalize the millionaire's buying Alice's rather than Bruce's bullet. (And even then it needs just the right assumptions about the possible values of the various catastrophes. But perhaps those are the assumptions she would make.) It is important to see that this worst-case reasoning is very different from the classical minimax rule. It does not say: decide on the basis of the worst possible outcome according to your favoured values. Instead it says: take account of which options are worst according to values and probabilities you take seriously. That is pretty vague, and it obviously describes just one factor one should take account of.

One way of making it precise is, in effect, what in chapter 5 I called 'the sieve'. As applied to risk-taking dilemmas it can be formulated as follows. The aim is to sift through a long list of possible options to find options whose consequences should be carefully evaluated. One begins with a long list of options and a selection of estimates of probability and assignments of utility to outcomes. (These come in pairs; the utilities have to be consistent with the probabilities.) Then one goes through the list looking for options which might have particularly bad consequences or which might offer particular advantages. Then some options are discarded and others saved. The ones which are saved are those which do not have very bad possible consequences for some pair of probabilities and utilities unless they have conspicuous possible advantages, on the same or different evaluations. Then the procedure is repeated again, with the remaining options and using a smaller set of utilities and probabilities. Eventually few enough options are left that one can choose a single set of probabilities and utilities, if need be arbitrarily, and compute their expected utilities.[5]

The line of reasoning I suggested the millionaire might use differs from this in only one respect. (But it is an important one.) It uses the sieve not just to reduce the options to a shortlist but to reduce it to a single option. That is one way of seeing it. Another is to see a shortlist of two (Alice's bullet or Bruce's), which have exactly the same value on the most natural (or compromise or forced-choice) utilities and probabilities. So the sieve is brought back to settle the tie. I do not actually think this second way of describing the process is very helpful, as presumably if the millionaire prefers buying Alice's bullet to Bruce's she would pay somewhat more for it, an option that would have to be preferred to the alternative before the final utility comparison with the most natural utilities, since it would lose in that comparison.

In fact, I think we should modify the sieve with this in mind, as follows.

> *First stage*: go through all plausible options, with all plausible probabilities and utilities, eliminating those with disastrous consequences unless they also have very desirable consequences.
>
> *Second stage* (optional): repeat, with a narrower range of probabilities and utilities. (Repeat again, if desired.)
>
> *Third stage*: Calculate expected utilities for the remaining options using any of a favoured set of utilities and probabilities. Reject those options which have the worst expectation for any such valuation, unless they also have the best expectation for some valuation.

Fourth stage: If any options remain, choose a probability – utility pair, if need be arbitrarily, and take the option with the highest resulting expected utility.

This is a more general and more flexible procedure. It can apply when there are no natural or favoured utilities and probabilities. Two things are worth nothing about it.

First, in the first stage I have not required that the options be evaluated in terms of their expected utilities. There are many ways in which one could get a preliminary hold on whether an option is likely to have disastrous or promising consequences. I think the one that we usually use in everyday life is to consider its most likely consequences. (Not only are these usually more easily and quickly thought out, they tend to be more stable under changes or errors in utility and probability, as Figure 1 in chapter 6.2 shows.) Not that I would defend this as a way of making a final decision between the live options of the shortlist.

Second, stages one and two, and to some extent stage three, are part of the way a decision is set up rather than the way it is made. Very often they will occur unconsciously over a long period of time. You may think you are drifting through life never making decisions. But in fact you are quietly setting them up so that they make themselves.

7.5   Disasters Behind Dilemmas

The reason why risky choices are so hard, and why different people can reasonably have different attitudes to them, is that we rank some things as incomparably worse than others. Typically these are irreversible disasters. Death is the central example, but there are many others: dishonour, the failure of one's life's work, bankruptcy. Once these have gone wrong nothing will make them right again, or compensate for them. The lack of compensation is what matters most, It underlies a reluctance to reason in terms of average long-term outcomes. (Why does it matter that the policy you are following is the one that will minimize long-term loss of life, if it allows this particular child to die now?) And it blocks any easy dilemma-managing strategies like the rain-check principle of chapter 2. (How could you tell someone facing the death of someone they love to expend their efforts on a lesser immediate need, because they can love someone else in the future?)

So our reluctance to reason probabilistically on some topics and our tendency to value some things incomparably more than others are two sides of the some coin. The problem this poses for decision making is also two-sided, though. On the one hand there are dilemmas about giving a weight to risks of death and other disasters, and on the other hand there is the general problem of how to give less crucial goods any weight at all in comparison. For example the basics and luxuries of the Snobs: the desire-preferences that made it possible to reason probabilistically with their value-preferences also made it possible to weigh these 'infinitely' lesser goods against risks to life.

This should not make us see probabilistic reasoning as something we can try to avoid, as something appropriate only to some very special decision-making situations. For in fact throughout our decision making we are faced with variations of a single problem. It is a resource-allocation problem: how are we to distribute the finite amount of time and energy at our disposal so as to get as much as we can of what we want? And there just isn't any way of approaching this problem intelligently, in all its forms and variations, without giving consistent finite values to the things that we want and then combining these values with our best guesses about the way the world is. Not that our desires, or even always our beliefs, cooperate with this. They are inherently shaped to make the project difficult. That is a basic sad fact about life.

Part III
Applications

8

Misery and Death

We often seem forced to balance 'heavy' goods like the preservation of life against 'lighter' ones such as pleasure or the avoidance of pain. The reason is usually a limitation of resources. Each of us has only so much time, energy, and money. And whole societies have only so much money and labour-power. This must always have been so, but in modern life the need to trade life against pain, misery, or deprivation has undoubtedly become greater. The kinds of resources that can affect one are now more than ever capable of affecting the other. The most obvious such resource is money: we can now buy life-expectancy more than ever in the past. And since such resources are in short supply we have to distribute them to best effect. So we find ourselves balancing. The problem is that the terms we have to balance seem particularly resistant to it.

We need strategies, to tell us either how to balance the preservation of life against the avoidance of pain or how to allocate our resources without having to balance them. I shall, as you might expect, describe a non-balancing strategy. My claim is that it could be a helpful part of a society's decision-making resources. But it would require social changes, a new set of attitudes and institutions. It is not something that one person could bring to their dilemmas.

8.1 *A and B Worlds*

Compare two imaginary health care systems. Each has positive and negative features.

A [Positive] In 'world' A no one dies unnecessarily. Emergency and intensive-care facilities are up to date and well staffed. A great variety of surgical and other techniques are available, both in terms of available skill and available apparatus, to reduce the probability of death whenever possible. (Organ transplants are expert and routine; artificial organs are in plentiful supply.)

[Negative] Facilities for the daily life of patients in non-crisis situations are very poor. Wards for chronic diseases are understaffed and uncomfortable. Physiotherapists, psychiatric staff, and health visitors are underpaid and hard to find, (Geriatric, psychiatric, and mentally handicapped patients live in squalor.)

(The life expectancy of new-born babies is 85 years; ten-year-olds can expect 80 more years of life.)

B [Positive] In 'world' B no one is unnecessarily miserable. A basic level of comfort is assured to all, and equipment and – especially – trained staff are available to fill gaps in people's self-sufficiency. Designated categories of people (such as the very old, the mad, and the extremely unintelligent) are cared for in special institutions where the level of comfort approximates the average in the surrounding society.

[Negative] Emergency services amount to little more than first-aid. Surgical techniques are rudimentary: there are appendectomies but no open heart surgery. The range and expense of life-prolonging machinery is very limited.

(The life expectancy of new-born babies is 50 years; ten-year-olds can expect 55 more years of life.)

Our world or society is a compromise between A and B. I think that it is closer to A than to B. That is not an assertion to be taken really seriously, without a definition of what counts as closeness here, but it does suggest a possibility which I think we ought to take very seriously: we might be better off if our world were further towards B along the A/B contrast than it is.

Moving in either the A or the B direction, or for that matter continuing at whatever point between the two extremes we now occupy, is the result of decisions between two contrasting bundles of goods. On the one hand we have goods which are given a very high value in the A world: the preservation of life from accident, disease, and natural decay. And on the other hand we have the goods which the B world values: the avoidance of pain and misery and the attainment of at least minimal standards of pleasure and comfort. Let me call these two bundles of goods *A goods* and *B goods*. (Think of these as Advanced and Basic goods, if you want, as long as you remember that the advance of the A world is in a very specific direction only and the B world is not at all primitive.) But it is important to realize that they are bundles and not simple qualities of life: it will later be important to take the bundles apart.

Choices between A and B goods are inevitable. In the world as it is we have not enough time, money, or other resources to achieve all the positive qualities of both A and B. People have always had to make these choices.

but they may be particularly acute now, since we have the capacity to prevent death (achieve A-goods) in many cases where we have never before been able to. But there is a price; although we can prevent deaths where in the past we could not, to do this we must commit scarce resources. It is just possible that in the future these choices will become less acute again, because our resources will increase to the point where we can afford what we want of both A goods and B goods. I am very sceptical; I suspect that difficult choices between A and B goods are here to stay.

But doesn't a commitment to the best attainable medical or health care ensure that both death and discomfort will be avoided as much as they can be? No. For one thing there is really no such thing as all-purpose medical knowledge. We have an enormous variety of medical technology, a steadily accumulating body of surgical techniques, and an increasingly basic understanding of the causes of disease. Some of these things may be developed in ways that yield both A and B goods, others may not, and all of them are so varied and so expensive that we cannot avoid having to decide which directions we want them to develop. And, for another thing, in our society there is a tendency for A goods to be served by high-tech developments and B goods to be served by social organization and trained staff. Dialysis machines versus social workers. So the kinds of investment required to push the balance in one direction or the other are, in part, very different.[1]

(I write as if a society makes a single decision about the kind of health care it wants. That may be not too misleading in a European context, but elsewhere in the world the decisions that lead to a particular complex of health care provisions are spread among a large number of individuals and organizations in a fairly uncoordinated way. Often they are commercial decisions. Still, they are decisions that, taken all together, determine the character of health care, and in public discussion the jigsaw ought to be put together and judged.)

8.2 Other Cases

There are many non-medical cases which present problems which are similar in one way or another. In some of them the shape of the dilemma is like that which a choice between A and B goods presents, though it does not actually turn on the contrast between saving life and avoiding pain. Here are some examples.

(1) Famine relief: One of the most basic facts about the planet is that much of it is hungry. And when we ask how much this should affect the life of an individual in a rich country the basic consideration has to be that

many lives can be saved if people lessen their well-being even a little. Weighed against this is the well-off individual's own well-being. Now the trivial – in comparison trivial – aspects of our own well-being do not, one by one, count for much against the deaths of others. But does it follow that our comfort is as *nothing* in comparison with the lives of others ? Or, to make it sound less selfish, compare one's obligation to prevent children in faraway places from starving to one's obligation to provide one's own children with minor luxuries. If I deprive my own children of Christmas presents, toys bought from shops, and non-utilitarian clothes I can use the saving to prevent other children from dying. And surely death is vastly worse than lack of luxury. But does it really follow that as long as I value the lives of children far away above the minor comforts and pleasures of my own children I must reduce my children's welfare to something near to poverty, to make a small reduction in the great mass of death and utter misery elsewhere? (Perhaps it does.)[2]

(Britain in 1988 devoted 0.28 per cent of its gross national product to overseas aid. We have a long way to go before we pose the questions in anything like these terms.)

(2) Drinking and driving: By having even one mild alcoholic drink at a party a driver raises the probability of causing deaths when driving home. If one has a good head for drink and is a competent driver then the probability is raised by only a small amount. The idea of a legal blood–alcohol limit, below which driving is permitted, reflects the idea that such a small increase in probability of death is justified by the minor social pleasures of drink. But is this right, since life is so enormously more valuable than these pleasures?

(3) Restrictions on useful commerce: The British government in the 1980s was very reluctant to introduce more stringent safety regulations on ferry boats, and tried to resist the pressure to ban furniture foams that produce poisonous gases when ignited. The governments's justification in both cases was that the death-preventing measures would impose a cost to the general public which would reduce the well-being of everyone marginally, for the sake of reducing the death toll very slightly. I predict that there will soon be a fairly sharp public debate about precautions against fire and other hazards in the Channel tunnel (under construction at the time of writing). Again the opposition will be between reductions in the probability the lives will be lost and costs that will eventually be diluted throughout the economy.

Most people's instinct is to think that economic advantages should not be too readily bought at the cost of risks to life. And to that extent we tend to be in favour of expensive safety measures. But there must be a limit somewhere, before safety becomes economically crippling, and so it is possible that official reluctance in these cases is justified, and we should have cheaper but more dangerous ferries, tunnels, and furniture, Similar questions arise throughout any country's industrial strategy. One factor that I have not made explicit is that of risk. Suppose that nuclear power stations can deliver the same amount of economic benefic as coal-burning stations at a slightly lower expected loss of life. (Being a child near a radiation-emitting station is very slightly dangerous, but being a coal miner is a lot more dangerous.) But suppose also that nuclear power stations present a real though extremely small probability of a catastrophic loss of life. How are we to weigh this rather different cost against economic benefit?

In all these cases the tension is between the preservation of life and various kinds of welfare. The famine relief case could have been described also in terms of a slightly different tension, between avoiding misery as well as death and promoting only relatively trivial forms of welfare. And in fact the actual tension is slightly different in each case.

In all of them there is what one might call an 'enlightened' or 'reformist' attitude – possibly a misuse of both words – in which the conventional balance between life and lesser goods is shifted in the direction of increased importance for life. The conventional intellectual tends to think that famine relief has more importance than society usually gives it: it is more a duty and less an optional charity. And we progressive thinkers also tend to conclude that governments risk the lives of individual citizens too easily for the sake of lesser commercial ends. But the first and central example, that of the different directions in which health care systems can tend, goes the other way. Conventional medical practice weighs life very highly relative to welfare, since after all the traditional ultimate end of medicine is to prevent the patient's death. A reformist attitude to these questions might then doubt whether we prolong life too readily when the price is to be paid in terms of misery. And in fact it is now quite often argued that medical practice over-values the prolongation of life.

We are pushed in different directions in different cases. Or so it seems: but perhaps we sense a single best comparison of A goods and B goods, from which our health-care practices deviate by over-valuing life and some of our other practices by under-valuing it. I doubt this, but the possibility shows how hard these questions are.

(4) Minor duties: My last non-central example is included to show how similar dilemmas can arise in comparatively trivial cases, trivial at any rate in that the enormous weight we attach to preserving life does not enter.

They involve conflicts between what are sometimes called perfect and imperfect obligations.

Suppose that you are a social worker with a very heavy case-load. You are one of the few people in your district with the skills and experience necessary for working with children who are victims and potential victims of sexual abuse. Your obligations are very varied and some of them are quite urgent, though none of them involve risks to children's lives. Now suppose you are also a parent, with not only basic obligations to feed, clothe, and not maltreat your children, but also 'extra' obligations to be nice to them in indefinitely many little ways, none of them individually compulsory. One of these obligations is just to spend relaxed uncluttered time with them, doing nothing in particular. So far no problem. But of course there is no room for everything: if all the duties to your clients are fulfilled, there will only be time and energy left for the basic obligations to your children. Then on each occasion on which an obligation from work conflicts with an opportunity to give one of your own children an 'extra' the obligation from work takes priority. And shouldn't it, after all, since it concerns the most basic emotional well-being, sometimes amounting to emotional survival, for the children concerned? And, moreover, your work requires you to do *this* thing *now*, while your relationship with your children asks for some action of this sort at some time or other. And yet if the stronger obligation wins every time, then the cumulative effect of all these right decisions is a kind of neglect.

There are two problems here. One is the problem of combining very specific obligations with more diffuse ones: reconciling the force of an obligation for a particular person to do a particular thing at a particular time with an obligation to do an act of a general type at some time or other. And the other is the problem of combining weaker and stronger obligations in such a way that the weak obligations have some chance of being satisfied.

These two problems can interact in many ways. (For example it is possible to have a conflict between a weak but specific obligation and a strong but unspecific one. You have promised to send someone a postcard from Paris and then at the last moment for posting it a man collapses near you. Any of a dozen people could help him. But that's not the issue now.) In particular, when the two problems coincide it is easy to mistake a solution to the first for a solution to the second. For example it would be natural in the social worker's dilemma (clients versus own children) to respond by some sort of planned inconstancy. 'You' could give different relative weights to your obligations at different times, favouring your children's less-than-vital needs more strongly at some times than at others. Your mood could determine which took priority on any given day, as long as in the long run the balance comes out about right. And indeed this would be a solution to the first problem, that of balancing the more and the less specific obligation. But it would not be a solution to the second: it would not tell you what to consider the 'right' long-term balance.

This last case introduces a new idea. The idea is that it is not always unreasonable to let one's relative valuation of two things, for example A and B goods, vary from case to case. Presumably there must be limits to the variation, and presumably different kinds of variation are appropriate to different situations. (Sometimes one might vary a little about an average, sometimes occupy all of a range of variation with equal frequency.) So the idea does not solve any really fundamental questions. But it is worth noting. It is also worth noting that the suggestion is very implausible in many public policy contexts. Suppose for example that we decided to tend towards the A rather than the B direction in the distribution of health care – setting a high value on life – but simultaneously assessed our obligations to help starving people elsewhere fairly low, on the grounds that welfare, including our own, is a good which while less valuable than that of life is still pretty considerable. Something would clearly be very wrong with this combination of views. And a first diagnosis would be that it was inconstant in too convenient a way.

8.3   Qualys

In looking for a reasonable tradeoff between A and B goods one starts with the range of comparisons shown in one's normal choices and preferences. These are no doubt somewhat inconsistent and need to be 'cleaned up' before they could claim to represent reasonable comparative values of, say, saving life and avoiding pain. I doubt, though, that any amount of minor cleaning up – removing of inconsistencies, smoothing out of obvious exceptions – will be enough to give a satisfactory set of tradeoff values. That is one of the main claims of this chapter.

But there is one sustained and serious attempt to find consistent valuations for different goods affecting the basic quality of life. That is the 'qualy' tradition in medical economics. It is the natural thing to consider first.

Medical economists, searching for ways of calculating the best distribution of health-care resources, have developed the device of a 'quality adjusted life year' or *qualy*. The idea seems at first rather contrived, but is really a very significant contribution. (And it is one of a family of techniques used elsewhere in economics, sometimes called 'bootstrapping'.) It works as follows.[3]

We want to compare the benefit brought to people by different medical treatments, for example hip replacements and heart-bypass surgery. The first thing to consider is the kind of life that one is able to live as a result of the treatment, measured in terms of things like mobility, freedom from pain, and social capacity. The next step is to look for a consensus among people about the relative preferability of these underlying aspects of the quality of life. The form in which these comparisons are to be made is: is n years with disability D (e.g. being able to walk but only with a frame) preferable to m years with disability E (e.g. being able to walk perfectly, but being incontinent)? There are a number of ways of discovering such a consensus, if it exists. Once comparisons of this sort have been established, we can draw quantitative comparisons of the quality of life afforded by different treatments, by assuming that if, for example, two years in condition C is equivalent to four years in condition D then a treatment which leaves the patient in condition C improves their well-being twice as much as one which leaves the patient in condition D. (That is a large assumption. More about it below.) Going a step further, if one treatment gives patients on average n years living in condition C, and another gives patients m years living in condition D, we can weight the added years of life which each treatment gives by the quality of each of those years, to see which actually gives the more 'quality adjusted' years of life, qualys. And then we can determine which of the two treatments is the better use of the money available.

Artificial as this may seem, it is a valuable tool. In particular, it gives a way of arguing for the effectiveness of relatively straightforward treatments which improve the quality of life without extending its length significantly, like hip replacements. And it tends to show up the extreme costliness, in terms of money spent for quality of life gained, of expensive and dramatic life-saving techniques such as heart transplants. It does have limitations, though. I list three, concerned with topic-specificity, risk, and death.

(1) *Topic-specificity*. The technique behind qualys can compare different kinds of disability. In so doing it implicitly compares different basic aspects of life, as long as those aspects of life are seen as reasonably short-term results of medical procedures. But the wider the differences in the kind of life being compared the less likely it is that we will get any answer in this way. Could we, for example, expect to find a stable set of preferences enabling us to make some of the comparisons between A and B health-care 'worlds'? Could we compare the life of someone who lives

for sixty years in institutional squalor with that of someone who lives for twenty-five years in a poor but comfortable and supportive family? The qualy technique is not meant to handle questions like these.

(2) *Risk*. Many decisions do not involve comparing certainties. Instead one is comparing one probability of one result with a different probability of another result. There are two ways of thinking these through, in line with the general qualy approach. The first is to make very simple assumptions about 'separability' over times and persons: assuming for example that three years in a given condition is three times as valuable as one year, and that inflicting a disability on three people for a year is three times as bad as inflicting the same disability on one person for a year. So, in effect, one just counts qualys, not caring how they are distributed between people and over time. Then given some firm probabilities one can calculate the expected gain in qualys of different risky options.

The other way is to search for a consensus about comparisons between the relevant risks and certainties. These could be elicited by the same kinds of direct questioning which give a qualy measure to certainties. Then, for example, a treatment which gave a 0.5 chance of permanent paraplegia and a 0.5 chance of full mobility could be compared to a treatment which gave a certainty of permanently having to walk with a frame. From a large web of such comparisons one could hope to extrapolate to a general pattern connecting different probabilities of disablement. There is great danger of inconsistency here. The results of the second method are unlikely to be consistent with those of the first method. And the second method all by itself is likely to produce inconsistent results. The main reason is that people employ no single set of separability assumptions consistently: they have no single way of comparing different distributions of quality of life over people and over times within a life. Moreover people's judgments about risky prospects will be affected by probability-dependence (see chapter 7) and in fact by our general muddledness when confronted with risks or delicate probabilities. So even when a consensus can be extracted, it will not have any straightforward relation to the values we should attach to risky prospects as a matter of public policy.[4]

(3) *Death*. The qualy technique compares years of life under various conditions. Being alive and being bedridden for a year is compared to being alive and being deaf for a year. This does not give a value to being alive itself. But many A versus B questions ask us to give a value just to being alive. Suppose one had to compare two treatments, one of which would, say, leave 50 out of 100 patients blind and the other of which would leave none of them blind but five of them dead. Then one would

have to know whether the loss of life of five people is worse than the loss of sight of 50.

One way of deriving something like a value for life itself from the qualy technique is to take the value of someone's not dying at a particular time to be the total of the number of qualys they can expect if they do not die then. This idea is implicit in many applications of the technique. Life is qualy-accumulation and the more you accumulate the more valuable your life. This has many surprising consequences, such as that the younger someone is the more point there is to saving their life. And here again there is a conflict with what would emerge from a direct appeal to consensus. For very few people would think that, for example, one should sacrifice more for the safety of a newborn baby than for that of a fifteen-year-old child.

There is a more general way of putting this point. Grant that we can make the kinds of comparisons that the qualy technique demands against a background of a fixed life expectancy. (Both normal life expectancy at various ages and life expectancy given various medical conditions.) Suppose, for example, that fifty-year-olds can on average expect twenty-five more years of life. And suppose that we are comparing two treatments for, say, angina, one of which will leave a fifty-year-old with a life expectancy of ten years, with a normal quality of life, and the other of which would leave the same person with a life expectancy of fifteen years, but with considerable pain. There might well be a standard consensus about the comparison of these options. And if the normal life expectancy of a fifty-year-old with angina is ten years, there might well be a consensus about whether extending this life expectancy by five years at the price of severe pain is or is not an improvement. (There are in fact data suggesting that people would sacrifice an average of almost five years of a fifteen-year life expectancy to reduce severe anginal pain to no pain at all. It is interesting, though, that there was a great variation in the number of years different subjects would sacrifice, suggesting that a consensus would not be easy to elicit.[5]) But it is a long way from these judgements, which presuppose standard life expectancies, to judgements about *changing* standard life expectancies. To make judgements of this latter kind we would need something that can be ignored in the less problematic cases: an explicit weight to the fact of being alive.

8.4 Direct Comparisons

Consider the special case of comparing the value of being alive with that of avoiding pain. There is a natural way of making the comparison. (But I don't think it works.) It consists in asking how much pain would be worse than death. Most people think that there is an amount of suffering which they would rather die than experience. They usually imagine themselves or someone they love suffering a fatal illness, and having a choice of dying fairly quickly or having their life sustained at the price of considerable suffering. And then they think that there is an amount of pain above which they would choose death for themselves, and wish for death for a loved one.

To use these intuitions to work out a tradeoff between preserving life and avoiding pain one would first have to make an estimate of where this crucial pain threshold lies. That would not be easy, partly because it is hard to imagine large amounts of pain and partly because it is hard to find the right terms to measure and describe differences in degrees of pain. Then one would conclude that preserving a life is better than inflicting any amount of pain up to this threshold. So, crudely speaking, one life preserved equals in value the threshold amount of pain avoided. Presumably the lives of different creatures would acquire different values on this approach, since most of us would place the threshold of pain at which preserving life becomes cruelty lower for a senile person or a newborn baby than we would for a fully functioning person. And there is a modern tradition according to which it is worse to submit many non-human animals to large degrees of pain than to kill them, even when pain of that intensity would not be worse than death for a human being.[6]

Many problems would still remain. One is that our intuitions about when pain becomes worse than death depend very much on the way in which the story is told. I told it in terms of someone facing a fatal illness – so death is not too far away whatever happens. But if one tells a story about great pain afflicting someone living a full life – engaged in work she cares about, involved in the lives of others – and whose life will continue, though with very great pain, then the threshold rises dramatically. In fact, when the story is told this way people are inclined to say that life is worth living as long as those activities which give it worth can continue. A tragic or blighted life perhaps, but one worth living.[7]

If these problems were overcome others would arise. Many decisions would require an at least roughly quantitative scale of degrees of pain. (A scale not of how intense the sensation is, but of how undesirable the sensation at a given intensity is.) This would be needed, for example, in deciding how to use resources which could be used to alleviate pain or to prevent deaths. (If moderate pain is at least one hundredth as bad as pain at the point at which it is as bad as death, then alleviating it in 1,000 people would be as valuable as preventing the deaths of ten people.) And decisions involving risks would need fairly precise measures of degrees of the badness of pain.

Perhaps – at most perhaps – such a scale could be found. It might, for example, be found by extrapolation from risk-taking behaviour: one would derive underlying (dis)utilities from data about the risks of death people will take to avoid various kinds of pain, and the risks of one degree of pain they will take to avoid another. Supposing this could be worked out, what would we get? It is hard to be sure, but I think that one consequence would be a radical undervaluation of life. Suppose that each degree of pain was given a value roughly proportional to its intensity as a sensation. (The more intense the worse, of course.) Then the alleviation of a large number of extremely minor pains would be as valuable as the prevention of a small number of deaths. (Ten thousand headaches, each one hundredth as intense as pain which would make life unbearable, would have as strong a claim on resources as preventing one hundred deaths.) Aspirin would seem very valuable.

I am sure most people would find this a repugnant conclusion. Perhaps it can be avoided. But by now there are just too many perhapses. Each of the points at which the idea urns into a major uncertainty involves a some-what arbitrary extrapolation from judgements people normally make to judgements they do not normally make – sometimes go out of their way to avoid making. And so even if one had initially allowed that our actual pat-tern of comparison of pain and death can be a guide to the comparisons we *ought* to make, one's confidence that what might result from the whole project reflects some underlying values will inevitably be quite small. The extrapolations need guidance by the very thing we are supposed to be discovering.

8.5   Revaluing Death

We do not have any way of making trustworthy tradeoffs between saving life and alleviating pain or misery. (Or between any of these and promoting happiness: in a way an even harder topic.) In fact, the more one reflects on what would be needed to get a single explicit and universally accepted for-mula to govern such a tradeoff, the crazier the whole project seems.

Is there any alternative? Can we operate without tradeoffs? In the short term No, and in the long term Perhaps. People who have to make on-the-spot decisions about the distribution of resources – that is, all of us much of the time – have no choice but to operate with the wide and uncertain range of tradeoffs embedded in current practice. Any dilemma-managing techniques we use will have to be able to take a wide spread of tradeoffs and compensate for its width and untrustworthiness. Spreading strategies, as I called them in Chapter 4, such as the pessimistic rule and the sieve of chapter 5 (see also 'the risk sieve' of chapter 7), ought to be part, at any rate, of the way in which individual agents live with the indeterminacy.

In the long term, though, this is not a satisfactory basis for a society's fundamental decisions. (It may be satisfactory, as well as inevitable, in individual decision-making.) The range of tradeoffs is too wide, and the variation in the standard range between different topics (health care and famine relief, for example) is too great. And the whole idea seems too unnatural. We may be able to go mechanically through these patterns of reasoning, given a background of acceptable comparisons which we are to extend or tidy up, but when the background itself comes into question we find we do not know what we were doing. We certainly do not find that our standard comparisons have given us a grasp of some simple quantity – goodness, or happiness, or added-up human wanting – which we may find better ways of measuring and maximizing.

Yet there is no real chance that we can find a way of thinking these problems through without doing some balancing, using some tradeoffs. And in modern life the need to trade life against misery (and misery against happiness, and happiness against life) has undoubtedly become greater. So we have to balance. The problem is that the terms we have to balance do not lend themselves to it.

Therefore: we need other terms. We need to be able to frame our death-versus-misery decisions in terms which are more amenable either to simple balancing or to non-balancing strategies. To use the terminology of chapter 3, we need to revalue, so that what we took to be preferences about life and death and pain we now take to be preferences about something else. What?

I take our aversion to pain to be a pretty simple and inevitable feature of our preferences, and thus not a good candidate for replacement with some more subtle values. (Not that no such replacement has a chance. For the intrinsic awfulness of pain might be distinguished from the way it interferes with other things we value. So perhaps part of our aversion to pain ought to be redirected to our aversion to impaired concentration, bad-temperedness, and dulled awareness.) So I shall attend instead to our desire to prevent deaths.

First of all, it is misleading to describe what we are dealing with as the value of life. For it is possible to be averse, even extremely averse, to death without thinking that there is some quantity called life, which there should be as much as possible of. All deaths may be to be avoided or regretted, and yet, perhaps, the number of people in the world should be very much less. (Or to put it differently, the Chinese government is perfectly consistent in trying simultaneously to reduce the number of deaths and the number of births.)[8] So let me ask a very naive question: what do we take to be good about preventing death? I suggest two very different kinds of thing, connected with the fullness and the irreplaceability of an individual life.[9]

The first and most obvious good about preventing death is just the *content* of a life. That is too varied a business to be given by a simple list. Take it for granted that we attach a value to getting what we want (a value to getting what one oneself wants and a value to other people getting what they want) and a value to the very process of discovering, evolving, and trying to satisfy our desires. Life is full, to varying degrees, and the longer a life the more it can be filled.

In preventing a death one is thus preserving what one might call the fullness and the fillability of life. The fullness of a life is the extent to which it contains intentions, desires, and projects which want to be developed and satisfied. And its fillability is the possibility that it can come to be full. The qualy tradition and much other work on the economic valuation of life directs us essentially towards fillability. A life can be fillable but not full, for example the life of a small child. It then lacks something.

We want our lives to be full and we value both the fullness and the fillability of others. (So that we think that it is regrettable if a child is handicapped in a way that prevents some normal means of fulfilment.) And both fullness and fillability come in degrees. Some lives have them to a greater degree than others. So there is more value in preventing some deaths than others. And that is true: there is. But that is not all that we want of our lives and value in the lives of others. It is also central to our values that there is a way in which everyone counts for the same. Handicapped newborn, senile centenarian, and Nobel prizewinner in medicine. We all very much want to be treated as if our lives were unique and irreplaceable. And so we agree to have the same attitude to others. (Perhaps that sounds cynical. Let me put it differently. Everyone *is* unique and irreplaceable, and it is part of the shared values of our society that we attach a high value to this fact about each one of us.)

One way in which this attitude can be expressed is by giving a very great value to the preservation of each and every life. That is the line that leads to balancing problems. (And it is reflected in preferences such as those of the Snobs of chapter 7, who can count one life as more valuable than another, but count the loss of life as worse than the loss of anything else.) But we can and do express the attitude in other ways. One way is by mourning. We mourn the deaths of people for whom death was a release from suffering , of suicides, and of infants who had no life to mourn. Many things go into mourning: affection's need for an object, irrational fear of death itself, one's own need for the presence of the dead person.

But besides all these there is the acknowledgement of the passing of something valued as an individual. This shows itself when we mourn – symbolically and ritually, but not dishonestly – people whom we did not know, or did not like, but whose lives we want to recognize.

Mourning is not the only practice that serves this function. We record the lives of people, including people whose lives were awful and people we disliked, in lists and photograph albums. We name buildings and park benches after people: we plant trees in memory of them. All these practices serve many functions. But one of their functions is to extend to a person the acknowledgement of their individuality.

Withholding the resources that would preserve someone's life can be also to withhold recognition of their individuality. Imagine yourself into the position of an alcoholic vagrant whose application for use of a dialysis machine is turned down because there are not enough machines to save all the people with kidney failure, and a higher priority is given to others. (Doctors, lawyers, and accountants, you would think.) Now you might be intelligent and lucid enough, at times, to appreciate that 'they' were in a way right: your life *is* less fillable than that of some others. But that would not prevent the thought that you had been classified as expendable, as an inadequate means to the end of maximizing the good life.

(I think this is one of the things behind the mysterious Kantian slogan that one should treat people always as ends rather than as means. Part of its content is that one should never treat people as *substitutable* means, differentiated only by the function they serve in one's plans. One of the reasons that murder is wrong, though death is no evil in itself and the person murdered may be better off dead, is that the motivation that leads to murder usually takes the life of a person to be just an obstruction like any other in the achievement of an end. Suicide is thus very different from murder. This point of view has trouble with the fact that hatred is directed at a particular person, just as love is.)

Withholding life-saving resources *need* not deny individuality, though. Individuality can be recognized in other ways: after someone's death by mourning and remembrance and before their death by reluctance and concern. We can hold a handicapped baby while it dies, and later bury and mourn it seriously, and list it in the family tree, although agreeing that the quality of its future life would not justify expensive life-saving resources. The committee that rules on access to the dialysis machine can deliberate in the presence of the vagrant and express their sadness at the finiteness of their resources. If time allows, some of them can attend the funeral; they can make sure that he is remembered.

The vagrant's presence would make the deliberation practically and emotionally harder. And counselling people, and for that matter attending funerals, takes time. Nothing is free. The important questions, which I go on to discuss in the next section, concern which needs are best met with which resources.

(Antigone is as distressed that her brother's body is left as carrion as she is by his death. Stalin was not the first despot to attach as much importance to erasing the memory of his victims as to killing them.)

8.6   Avoiding Compromises

I am suggesting a revaluing of our aversion to death. The suggestion is that we split it into two parts, one concerned with the goods that can fill a life, and the other with concern for human individuality. And I am claiming that if we could do this, we would find some balancing problems easier. The reason for this is that the two separated values relate to goods such as the avoidance of pain and the search for happiness in quite different ways.

The fullness and fillability of life are values of a piece with the goods against which they are balanced. It may be difficult to decide how, say, twenty years in a wheelchair, needing help to get about but capable of social life and creative activity, compares to five years in the life of a social and intellectual athlete, but in principle such decisions are like decisions we make quite routinely. And each of these is comparable in the some rough way with the effects on the lives of others of deploying the resources that would be necessary to achieve them. And techniques like those used by medical economists, and considerations about the amount of pain which makes life unliveable, can be extended to give rough but useful answers. One is not comparing totally different goods, but rather similar bundles of goods, each made up of roughly the same basic components. (Not chalk and cheese, but a plate of camembert, brie, and emmenthal and another of gouda, stilton, and cheddar.)

Moreover these tradeoffs do not become unthinkable when we question the standard opinions about the importance of one good or another, or when we consider radically different life expectancies. We can, for example, evaluate the lives people would live in a world in which the normal life expectancy is one hundred and fifty years, and in which a high value is put on athletic accomplishment during the first thirty years. That is, given a lot more detail we could evaluate lives in such a world in terms of how much people get of what they want, whether they form desires that structure their lives, how much pain they have, and so on. And to some extent we can balance these things against one another, to get a rough idea of whether we ought to envy or pity such people.

On the other hand the respect we owe the individuality of a person's life is unlike any of these other goods. But what it requires of us is also different. Resources of money, scientifically trained personnel, and technology come into it much less. It requires instead a particular and delicate concern and skill. It needs psychological acuteness, emotional flexibility, and a sense of when a conventional or ritual act is helpful and when hollow. Since the two values are quite different, and some of the resources that address them are different, we have a chance of separating the accounts, paying each debt in its own currency. We would need institutions which enabled individuality to be recognized in its own terms. And then instead of trying to find a stable tradeoff between our very different preferences for preventing death and avoiding pain we would separate each problem into two parts: maximizing the realization by people of the goods of life, and recognition of their individuality. More people would die, given the combination of these institutions and this decision-making strategy, though they would not be forgotten, unlamented, or ignored. And more resources would be directed at the alleviation of suffering and the quality of life.

(It is worth stressing that the point of institutional recognition of individuality would not be that dying people and their families should not feel demeaned by the fact that resources were not allocated to them. The point is that they should not *be* demeaned. It is a way of valuing each life independently of its contents, even if doing so has no effect on its content. Of course, in such a context the content and tone of people's lives would be subtly different: they would not expect that if others do not save them they do not respect them.)

The most basic resource of all is time. The institutions I am imagining would be highly labour-intensive, and the people whose skills they use would need a specialized training. So there would still be a background of decision about the amount of human resources to direct to them, and how much to direct at institutions that promote health and welfare in a more traditional sense. But decisions of this sort would not involve tradeoffs or balancing, for two reasons.

First, given a social decision about the level of resources to be directed at health and welfare generally, many decisions about the direction of particular resources would be made automatically. For example, many people are more suited for one kind of work than another. (Many surgeons could never have been good at counselling; many social workers would not have made good surgeons.) So while both the preservation of life and the care of the dying can absorb large amounts of time, the human forms in which such time comes are not themselves multi-purpose. There is no choice about how to use many of them.

Second, and more fundamentally, though difficult decisions would undoubtedly remain they would not be decisions that require balancing. They would instead require one to find stable combinations of death and misery and use them as targets. This would work as follows. First minimal standards could be set for the recognition of the individuality of dying people. These would be best specified in detail with respect to standard contexts (withdrawal or refusal of life-supporting equipment, neonatal death, and so on), consistent with a general ethos growing up in the culture. The resource-allocator's task would then be to maximize the quality of life of surviving people, while meeting the minimal standards for the treatment of non-survivors. This would not be a trivial task, but it would not require two incomparable quantities to be maximized. So it would not require tradeoffs.

It is important to see that there might be several ways of distributing resources which resulted in an acceptable equilibrium, in which all dying people receive decent treatment. Presumably among such equilibria the one in which the number of deaths is least is best. So in a way this reverses the usual picture. One would not first decide what level of resources to direct towards health care and then face imponderable questions about how to distribute it between the competing claims of life and health. Instead one would formulate possible target situations, in which health (and non-misery generally)was maximized relative to the constraint that all dying people must be treated properly, and then the resources directed at health care would have to be such as to make one of these targets attainable.

I fear that the recognition of individuality may seem trivial, trite, or too-easily obtained. I think the opposite. I think that to the extent that we try to balance life against suffering we make things easy for ourselves. The alternative I am suggesting would be better, but not at all easy to follow. To get a sense of this, compare two A and B worlds again, this time with more attention to their attitudes and customs.

In the A world, where no one dies unnecessarily, each approaching death is seen with dismay and warded off with all possible means. But once it happens there is nothing more to be done. Funerals are quick and the dead are forgotton. Life goes on, and staff are needed for other purposes. To mention death is in fact rather tasteless, since it is to allude to failure of one of society's central aims. (Mention of the dead is not quite so tasteless, as long as it is not emphasized that they died.) Dying people are as much a reminder of failure as the dead are. If their lives can be extended they are surrounded by technology, and if their lives can no more be extended than saved they are isolated and neglected. After all, there is nothing to be done for them. Parents rarely even see stillborn babies, or those which die in intensive care shortly after birth.

In the B world, where no one suffers unnecessarily, death is more frequent. (Since life expectancy is less than in the A world, if the populations of the two are the same there must be more births and more deaths in the B world.) Babies and old people frequently die, because saving them would require resources that would be better used alleviating suffering. But their dyings are attended by specially trained professionals, and their existence is remembered in a variety of social practices. For example the parents of very severely handicapped babies, who would require expensive and sophisticated interventions in order to survive or have non-miserable lives, are encouraged to be with their children for a few days, during which the baby is given individual attention and is recorded in archives and photographs. The they participate in their infants' euthanasia, seen as helping the baby out of a painful situation. Then the medical team and the parents take part in a funeral, in which the baby is recorded as part of the past of the human race.

I think the B world is a better place.[10] But it would not be easier to be in. It would require emotional and social resources that we have not developed. In particular, people living in the B world would think of their lives as having an inevitable finiteness which others would not try heroically to prolong, and yet would think of themselves as appreciated individually by others individually and collectively, in ways which were consistent with allowing their lives to end. (Anything short of this would be mere rhetorical cover for a simply qualy-maximizing would.) These attitudes are not ours, and they would not grow without a lot of cultivating. It is in part to avoid having to develop them, and because we have largely broken with those parts of our culture whose function it was to provide something like them – whether or not they did this very well – that we find ourselves in something much more like the A world. This is reflected in our much-discussed awkwardness about the topic of death, but it is also reflected in the way we persist in trying to balance values that are inherently unbalanceable.

9

How to Change Your Desires

For since one can, with a little hard work, change the activities of the brains of animals which have no powers of reason, it is obvious that one can do it even more with men, and that even those who have the feeblest spirits could achieve absolute domination of all their passions, if they put enough effort into breaking them in and driving them along.

René Descartes, Les Passions de l'Ame

There is profit in desires, and profit in the satisfaction of desires – because they increase when they are satisfied. For, I tell You truly, Nathanael, each desire has enriched me more than the possession, always deceptive, of the very object of my desire.

André Gide, Les Nourritures Terrestres

People are often thought to be at the mercy of their desires. If you want something you just want it, and that's that. And though I can point out to you how much happier you would be if you didn't want to be the world's first quadriplegic show-jumper, this will not make you want to be a computer programmer instead, even if this is something you can do from your wheelchair.

I think this common picture of our relation to our wants is deeply wrong. it takes the obvious fact that you cannot want anything at all just by deciding to and confuses it into the falsity that you have no influence at all over your wants. We can and do change our desires, so that we want what makes more sense of our lives. We can get rid of perverse or harmful desires. You can stop wanting to be the world's first quadriplegic show-jumper. Not that there is any infallible way of doing this, but there are definite procedures to follow. Some of the dilemma-managing strategies mentioned in the book suggest such procedures, and others, like what I call revaluing, presuppose that they can be found. But one of the things that makes changes of desire harder for us is the belief that they are impossible. To see some of the ways of changing desires begin with a comparison with the rather different case of belief.

9.1   Changing Beliefs

If you think that everyone in America is rich and I take you to a slum in New York or a village in West Virginia and show you people living in misery you will change your belief. You may not change it much, your revised belief may be just that there are a very few Americans who are misguided or stupid enough not to be rich. Or you may make a subtle distinction: all Americans are rich, but the poor people in New York or West Virginia though living in America are not Americans. And later, when the evidence is no longer vivid in your mind, you may go back to treating everyone from America as if they were rich and saying things which presuppose that everyone in America is rich. But when you are being careful or reflective you will use your best belief, which is that not absolutely everyone in America is rich. Belief responds to evidence.

None of this means that you can believe whatever you want to believe. Nor that I can make you believe anything I want you to. Nor that suitable evidence could make you believe anything. But it does mean that if you want to believe some particular thing there ways in which you can go about it. For example: your child has been arrested for narcotics smuggling. You don't want to believe that she is guilty. So you can hire detectives to find evidence that the drugs were planted on her, or search for evidence of relevant corruption among the customs officers. This may or may not succeed. If it doesn't you can try something else. If it does succeed you may or may not be able to have your child cleared of the smuggling charges, but at least you will be able to believe in her innocence.

There are completely different ways in which you can go about it, too. You can hire a hypnotist to make you ignore all the evidence against your child, or you can trust to your own powers of self-deception. You could join a religious group which would brainwash you into thinking that all government activities were actions of the devil. Any of these might well work. They would work in a radically different way from the first set of belief-changing devices: they wouldn't be based on evidence and you wouldn't be acquiring a reasonable belief. But, still, you would be believing what you want to. (There's a big old problem here, the central problem of epistemology: what is the difference between the reasonable and the unreasonable ways of changing beliefs? It doesn't concern us now, though the analogous problem for desires does.)

9.2 Changing Desires

Seeing Americans living in poverty will inevitably have some impact on your beliefs about American wealth. Seeing evidence that your child did or did not smuggle narcotics will have some impact on your beliefs about her. The impact may be shown in many ways, including a retreat into confusion or irrationality, but something will change. There is something like evidence which can have a similar impact on desires.

First two trivial, but rather different, examples, and then a far from trivial one.

You don't like asparagus. You have loathed asparagus ever since at the age of six you ate it at a hotel in France and were sick immediately after. The thought of asparagus makes you queasy and the sight of it makes you retch. Other people tell you how delicate and evocative the taste is, but you put this down to innate differences of taste. Then one day you are having lunch at the house of someone who knows you well. She serves you a home-made vegetable soup made with the Chinese lusun plant. You love it. The next day you are telling others of your friend's soup discovery and someone informs you that, 'lusun' is Chinese for asparagus. This makes you think that you might be capable of liking asparagus, and so you embark on a programme of asparagus-training. You sit at the same table as people eating asparagus, and allow yourself to smell it. You eat omelettes containing minute quantities of asparagus. Finally comes A-day. You drink a glass of excellent white wine and turn on the Mozart clarinet concerto, then your friend holds your left hand while with your right you take a whole forkful of fresh asparagus to your mouth. It is wonderful.

Another trivial example. Bruno is a slob. He dresses in torn jeans and dirty T-shirts. There is no variation in his dress from one occasion to another. He has contempt for people who find such things important and judges others in part by their ability to make social relations independent of social appearances. This works well while he is working on his PhD in mathematics. And it produces no noticeable catastrophe during his first job, as a software engineer in a small computer firm. Then he fails to get a job in a larger firm as a result of an interview at which he is made to feel extremely awkward because of his clothes. He resolves to be more practical and to dress in a way that will allow him access to positions in which he can do more to undermine (what he sees as) corrupt social conventions. So for several years he wears conservative grey suits and rises to a position of some responsibility in the small firm. He then sees himself as having to spend a lifetime in this uniform, and resolves to do something about it. He begins to vary his dress. Sometimes his tie will be of a size and shape that brings others to the brink of conscious thought about what the conventions of dress are. He finds a pair of grey jeans which when pressed match a grey jacket in a way that induces a startling double-take in his colleagues. He finds himself waking up in the morning planning a strategy which will stay just within the conventions of the day's situations while at the same time spreading scepticism about the conventions and making others aware of the real appearances of colours and textures. He finds he is very interested in clothes, and he finds he judges others in part by the strategies they adopt towards sartorial subversion.

Now the non-trivial example. You have two children. The younger one was not wanted and arrived at a difficult time in your marriage. Moreover he has a strong resemblance in appearance and manner to your mother, who abandoned you when you were ten. You find it hard to love this child; you do not easily want to spend time with him or to provide him with non-essentials, such as presents and occasions that suit his particular imagination. When the child is thirteen he runs away from home. At first you are worried by the child's disappearance, then relieved, and then horrified at your relief. When the child is found and returned by the police a month later you are as upset as the child is by your mixture of emotions, many of which you can barely acknowledge. You begin the task of rethinking your attitude to the child, at first by yourself and later with professional help. You have to face and come to terms with your feelings about your spouse, your mother, and your eldest child. Gradually you find new attitudes supplanting the old ones. (Some of the new attitudes are less convenient, though.) Eventually you find yourself willingly taking the child to films and concerts and spending afternoons looking for presents that might please him.

No real case could be quite as pat as any of these, but they all show important ways in which people's desires are made to evolve. And in all of them people set about changing their wants. Different as the cases were, they shared some important characteristics. One is particularly relevant to describing these changes of desire as not only possible but also reasonable things to undertake. It is the uncertainty of the result, its responsiveness to what is discovered during the process. The asparagus-hater, or Bruno the slob, or the unloving parent, could well have emerged from the process with very different desires from those I described. The asparagus-hater might have found that nothing at all could induce a toleration of asparagus. Bruno might have found that his dominant desire was not to worry about clothes, and thus that a three-piece uniform is just as convenient as jeans and T-shirt. The parent might have found that love for the child just could not be produced, and so have had to find ways in which other people could provide the child with affection, company, and models to imitate.

In all these ways the final result depends on discoveries about the person's capacities for wanting and on choices the person makes once these capacities are made clear. To that extent the process produces a kind of truth, a reflection of facts about the person and a responsiveness to their decisions. This is surely a positive trait, in some way analogous to the responsiveness of reasonable belief to evidence.[1]

9.3 Eliding the Distinction

It is not really that obvious what is to count as a change of desire. If someone wakes up one morning with a burning lust for prune juice, which she has hitherto despised, then pretty clearly there has been some change of desire. But most real cases are more complicated. Three factors which complicate the picture might be called 'means and ends', 'underlying desires' and 'ignorance'.

1   *Means and ends.* A man wants to meet a beautiful but unapproachable woman he sees walking her dog, a pure-bred boxer, in the park. He buys a boxer puppy and takes it to the park. The puppy gambols up to the older dog and the owners begin to talk. He admits his ignorance of dogs, but not his lack of interest in them, and she gives him the benefit of her experience. Years later their grandchildren play with the great-great-grandchildren of those two boxers. Did his desires change when for the first time in his life he wanted a dog? Only in the sense in which your desires change when you first want there to be a ten pence coin in your pocket for the parking meter and then want there to be a twenty pence coin when you find that that is what the meter takes. Many of our wants are for means to ends that we 'really' want, and these change rapidly with changes in our information about what will and will not lead to those ends. These changes certainly represent no real change of heart; one's aims remain unchanged. (They often lead to deeper changes, though. In a few years he may be more interested in dogs than she is.)

2   *Underlying desires.* Someone has an ambition to write novels. Rough sexy unpretentious best-seller novels. He trains to be a doctor, since many literary people have supported themselves with medicine. After qualifying he works as a doctor in a Palestinian refugee camp, and finds their plight so grim and the workload so high that he has no spare physical or emotional energy to write anything. This life continues for fifteen years

until his health breaks down and he retires, with no pension and not enough physical stamina for any sort of medical work. He lives very frugally in one room and begins a novel, though to his surprise it is a more reflective work than he had planned. Do his wants change when he abandons hope of writing, or later when he finds himself beginning a novel? Only in the sense in which your desires change when you learn that you can after all get a cup of coffee as well as the sandwich you had been planning to buy with the pound in your pocket. There are desires which we act on, and others which lie dormant because our circumstances do not allow us to satisfy them. The dormant desires are usually, but not always, less strong than those on which we act, but are desires for all that. When circumstances change so that desires become or cease to be dormant our actions change more than what we 'fundamentally' want does. (See chapters 2 and 3 on the distinction between desires and values.)

3   *Ignorance.* As a child Georgina was a very girly girl, in contrast to her tomboy sisters. Her teachers recognize her intelligence and her particular capacity for mathematics and urge her to study it at university. She tells them though that her only ambition is to marry and take care of a husband and children. She trains to be a secretary, and marries her boss. After a year of marriage she becomes very depressed, admitting only to herself that she loathes her husband's company and is bored sick by life at home This situation ends explosively when she falls in love with her husband's new secretary, and leaves with her to live and study in another town.

We obviously are often wrong about what we want. Do Georgina's desires change when she discovers that she can love women more easily than men? It depends on the full facts, but her desires may only have changed in the sense in which your desires change when you find out that the thirst that has been nagging you all day is not for a beer but for a glass of orange juice.

(Similarly, when a shifting strategy lures you into applying a different perspective to your decisions you may have no way of knowing whether you have found a better way of thinking out the consequences of desires you had all along or undergone a subtle change to a different set of wants. It will feel the same either way.)

9.4   *Rational/Non-rational: Self-seduction*

In the case of belief there are 'rational' ways of changing your opinions, by considering arguments and evidence, and 'non-rational' ones, such as being hypnotized or joining a religious sect. There is a similar contrast among ways of changing your desires. The non-rational ways are much the same: hypnotism, subliminal advertising, and unquestioning submission to an authority figure are not reasonable ways of developing your desires. And sober consideration of what you want most and what patterns your desires fall into obviously are reasonable ways of evolving your desires. But there is an enormous middle ground that is difficult to classify.

One way of seeing how large and uncharted the middle ground is is to consider some questions about what is fair and what is 'cheating' in moral argument. For example, consider the use of emotive photos. A photo of a young Vietnamese girl running and screaming after her clothes had been burned off by napalm pushed thousands of Americans a little further towards thinking that their involvement in the war was wrong. It made them want this involvement less. Photos of human foetuses, aborted at a stage when abortion is legal according to (say) British law but when very human features are evident, can be used to make one feel a revulsion to all but the very earliest abortions. Is this use of pictures more like presenting evidence or like hypnotism? Is it argument or propaganda?

Since desires can be non-rational there can be an analogy for desires of the phenomenon of self-deception. In self-deception one has non-rational belief that is produced by a process in some way analogous to that by which one person deceives another. One's belief is caused or maintained by a strategy, usually unconscious, of presenting and avoiding evidence which one knows may affect it. The same can happen for a desire. Call it self-seduction. A second order desire can produce first order desires by means which are more like propaganda or advertising than like rational persuasion. For example, someone may want to be interested in politics: he may want to be interested in the state of the parties and want to want some faction or tendency to be in the ascendancy. (Perhaps that is taken to be a sign of a serious person, with serious conversation, suitable for a dinner invitation.) So he overcomes his natural indifference to these things by presenting himself with a constant diet of political anecdote and, whenever traces of his underlying reluctance to form political opinions show themselves, manoeuvring himself into company which will be impressed with a show of factionalism. In this way he maintains a desire to be politically engaged. And all without knowing what he is doing.

In this case self-seduction requires some measure of self-deception. This is normal. (I imagine the converse is usually true, too.) Self-deception, though, is more than just maintaining a belief by a motivated strategy. It is maintaining a belief by a strategy which is meant to work even if the belief is false. Similarly, self-seduction must be maintaining a desire by a strategy which is meant to work even if it makes for a poorer life.

That is just as paradoxical a project to set oneself as that of believing something even if it should be false. But it is a less definite one, and so the limits of self-seduction are even vaguer than those of self-deception.[2]

9.5   Second Order versus First Order

Rather than meeting the puzzles of the last two sections, I will in fact sidestep them by concentrating on a limited range of cases. I will, for the rest of the chapter, discuss cases in which someone wants to change their desires. (As in all three of the examples in 'Changing Desires' section 9.2 above.) There is then a conflict between their second order desires – their desires about what desires they want to have – and their simple, first order, desires. How ought one to resolve a conflict between first and second order desires?

The first point to make is that it is not at all plausible that the second order desire should always win. Sometimes you should go on wanting what you want, and stop wishing you did not. An interesting and important instance of this is part of the development of our culture in the past hundred years: that is, the throwing off of Victorian inhibitions. Two generations of influential writers, from late Victorians such as Samuel Butler to twentieth-century authors such as D. H. Lawrence and Andre Gide, faced up to the conflict between what they actually wanted, particularly in sexual matters, and what their upbringing had taught them to want, and decided to be loyal to their desires rather than to their upbringing. At first, no doubt, they did sincerely want not to have forbidden wants. But real second order desires degenerated first into vague moral beliefs, then into conventional forms of words, then into nothing. And no doubt this was for the most part what should have happened.

Moreover, this process is repeated every year in the lives of many people. For many people, to some extent all people, grow up with culturally induced expectations about what they should want. And then when they find that they do not want what is normal, whether it is a conventionally successful career or a conventional correct sexual partner or something much less drastic, they at first wish that they did not have the unexpected desires. Then, later, they often slough off the conventional expectations and stick with the wants they find have become central to their lives. One interesting side to this process is that abandoning an ideal of what one's wants should be is often as hard and painful as getting out of the grip of a strong first order desire. (Giving up respectability can be worse than giving up nicotine.)

There is thus a difficult question: is there anything systematic to be said about resolving conflicts between first and second order desires? Sometimes the resolution is easy, for example when the first order desire is very strong and the second order desire very weak, or vice versa. (You want a long and healthy life more than you want to smoke, so your desire to rid yourself of the desire to smoke is very strong.) Then the 'only' problem is to eliminate the desires that must go. But in many cases it is not at all clear that one can make a sensible comparison of the strength of the competing desires. They are so different. Consider, say, the situation of an adolescent trying to decide whether to yield to or suppress unwelcome homosexual desires. Anyone who said 'well, you just have to decide what you want more, experiences of these kinds or the kind of relationship you have been brought up to want' would be completely missing the depth and difficulty of the dilemma. (And underestimating the range of options open to the youth.)

It is traditional to apply something like a shifting strategy to these cases. (That is, something generally like the 'looking back strategy' of chapter 2. See chapter 4.) One is supposed to take the long view and make the choice that gives the life one most wants to live. But this is usually to give second order desires the upper hand. For one's second order desires are usually for the kinds of motives one wants to have effect in one's life as a whole. (I say 'usually' because there are exceptions: for example a miser who wants to save money but wishes he could want to indulge in an expensive frivolity just this once.) And inasmuch as the whole of one's life is a sensible thing to care about, what is relevant is the desires about it that one would have throughout life, rather than at the moment of decision. The point is that if one stops wishing one did not want something then later one may find oneself approving of one's want for it. One may grow a whole new system of second order desires, a new ideal of one's life. And, looking at one's whole life in prospect, why should this potential ideal not be given as much weight as that which now grips one?

For all that, some kind of a shifting strategy does seem appropriate in conflicts of first and second order desires. At least, it does in what I shall call 'acute cases' where the first order desire is strong and persistent and the second order desire is important to one's conception of oneself. (An example of a *non*-acute case: someone has a silly impulse to giggle during a funeral oration, and wants to suppress the impulse.) For then some change of desire is called for, since if the second order desire is to be satisfied a first order desires must be changed and if the first order desire is to be satisfied something central to one's life will be frustrated. But the change of desire should not be too violent or drastic, if the second order desires really are central to one's conception of oneself and one's idea of the shape one's life is to take. This rules out spreading strategies, which apply when the competing desires can coexist as long as they are compartmentalized, applied to different aspects of decision making. And revaluing strategies seem a last-resort possibility here since they apply when a major change of desire is called for. Shifting strategies are the tool for subtle shifts of desire.

There are in fact shifting strategies which apply very plausibly to acute cases of conflict of first and second order desire. And they do seem to correspond to ways in which people actually work their way through these cases. One, fairly crude, such strategy is to think in terms of whole lives, but to adopt a fairly hedonistic attitude to their value. I call it 'Epicurean shifting'. Then you do not ask 'will this desire be satisfied – will I get this that I want – if I change my desires in this way?', or 'will the life I will lead be one that I now want?', but rather 'will many wants be satisfied? will I get much of whatever I will want?'

That is putting it too generally. You do not really consider a whole variety of possible lives and measure them by the number and variety of wants that are satisfied. Rather, if it is to be a true shifting strategy it must focus on future desires and future lives that give not too unfamiliar kinds of satisfaction. So, for example, if you are considering an escape from your desire for respectable wants then it must be in the direction of satisfying desires which are not too different from those that had gone along with respectability. Perhaps friendship and aesthetic appreciation should play a large part.

There are much more subtle shifting strategies which can apply to acute cases. In particular in evaluating the lives that would follow from possible changes in one's desires one can take account of the pattern as well as the amount or variety of desires that are satisfied. This is inevitable, really, since one's second order as well as one's first order desires have to come under the scope of the shift: one has to come up with new second order desires – a new conception of what kind of priorities one wants to have and what character of life one wants to live – which also make not too radical a break with the decisions that one's earlier second order desires motivated. For example one might think in terms of what in chapter 12 I call 'temporal framing', focusing on the way in which moment-to-moment experiences relate to past hopes and future ambitions. But that idea needs some setting up, so it must wait until that chapter. But even a simple strategy like Epicurean shifting has definite advantages for the specific purpose of resolving conflicts of first and second order desire. (Especially if we build into it a shift of second order desire, towards a conception of one's life as a search for some specific kinds of satisfaction.) For it begs the question neither in the direction of satisfying first nor of satisfying second order desires, and it links the judgement of what one ought to want very closely to an estimation of what one is capable of wanting. The second of these advantages is important. There are two parts to it.

First, frustrated desires hamper life more than changed desires. Suppose you wish you wanted a life of respectable conventional accomplishment, but find you don't really want all the tasks and commitments that go with it, and suppose moreover that it is impossible for you to acquire these wants (whether or not you know it.) Then to choose to let your second order desire prevail is to doom yourself to a life of frustration and failure. So in general, if one direction of resolution is psychologically very difficult, the lives it would lead to are not likely to be satisfying, and Epicurean shifting is not likely to give it the upper hand.

Second, to imagine long stretches of life is to tell stories about oneself. to think through the kinds and degrees of satisfaction that different lives would bring is to imagine them as structured wholes with imaginable characteristics, that is, as stories. Or, to put the point more carefully, the most effective way our limited minds can grasp the totality of moments that make up a life is to structure it as a narrative.[3] But to tell an attractive story is to provide a way in which both second and first order desires can change and develop. For, in acute cases at any rate, a second order desire is part of a conception of what sort of a person one wants to be. An intelligible picture of another sort of person, living another sort of life with other wants, is a sketch of another system of second order desires. Then to the extent that one takes the story to depict an attractive life one is on the way to having second order desires, desires to want the things wanted in the story. And to the extent that one can, moreover, imagine being the protagonist of the story, one can begin to work oneself into actually having the desires that it describes.

An example. As a child Martha was often physically abused by her parents, for trivial or imagined reasons. Now as a woman in her early twenties, she finds that she has a very strong desire to have children, and also has unwelcome fantasies about harming children. The fantasies are usually repressed as soon as she becomes aware of them, but when occasionally she attends to them she finds that they center on very small children committing small infractions of arbitrary rules and being severely beaten as a punishment. Naturally, this disturbs her, as she concludes that she has strong desires to re-enact her childhood, with herself as aggressor rather than as victim. She wants not to have these wants, if only because they stand in the way of her being a successful parent.

Martha had always imagined that she would find a partner and begin a family at about the age she now is. Now this seems to her just one among a range of options she should consider. One option is to have children and to watch her behaviour towards them very carefully. The more details of this she imagines the less possible it seems: She finds that whenever she imagines a parental interaction with children in any detail fantasies of abuse begin to enter. Another option is to find a man who understands her problem and can be a very comprehensive father to her children, taking over parts of roles she does not dare play herself. Martha is pretty sceptical about there being many such men. But the more she tells herself this story the more she finds that the attractions of parenthood in it are rather slight. It is an attractive option for quite different reasons: it allows her to imagine a close relationship with someone that does not centre on her being a mother of children. This loosens her hold on the original desire to have children. She decides not to act on it and to focus her emotions instead on adults. She begins to search for two essential people: for a partner who will not include parenthood as an inevitable part of their life together, and for a psychiatrist.

9.6   Routes and Destinations

This is an acute case because at its heart there is a conflict between a second order desire (not to have or act from motives of compulsive anger towards children) and first order desires (to have children). Of course there are also conflicts between second order desires and between first order desires. This is typical. One almost never finds a pure first order/ second order conflict. And in fact although pure first order/first order conflicts are common, a deep and extensive change of first order desires rarely happens without a change of second order desires.

There is a reason for this. (A reason besides the inevitable connection of second order desire with deliberation and decision.) There are two main obstacles to any change of desire. The obvious one is making the change actually occur. But before that one has to know whether the change would be for the better. And if the lives that might follow from making the change are quite unrelated to one's present life there is no way to make the comparison. But if there is a rout from here to there – if you can see how a shifting strategy can transform your beliefs from one pattern to another – then you can begin to evaluate these possible lives. 'Can' helps with 'should'. (This is pretty evident in particular cases, I think. Arguing that dilemma-managing strategies, particularly shifting strategies, generally tend to produce comparisons as well as decisions is trickier. I worry about the question in chapter 4.) But shifting strategies work by approximating to one's earlier pattern of choices, so they cannot ignore the effect of one's second order desires. Second order and first order fit together pretty intricately, and so the shift has to affect both. So a non-trivial change in one's desires and preferences is likely to be accompanied by, and to be made possible by, a change in one's conception of the kind of person one wants to be and the kind of life one wants to live.

The aim of any change of desire is to achieve a harmony between second order desires, first order desires, and the world around one. One aims to find a conception of what kind of a person one is – what one wants and what one's motives are – that fits the actual things one finds oneself wanting and the opportunities for getting these things that life affords. That is an impossible aim; no one ever fully realizes it. So there are always many ways in which one's pattern of desires can be improved. Most of these improvements are very abstract possibilities: it would be nice to be there but there is no evident path from here. These changes in desire are therefore not real options, not things one ought to consider seriously. But there are always other changes that are real options: new contracts between first order, second order, and world which not only provide a more pleasant, vivid, or satisfying life than one's present desires afford, but which can be imagined in a way that does show the way from here to there.

Imagining routes from one complex of desires to another is hard. There are cultural as well as individual resources for doing it. (Rites of passage, for example, which involve a distancing of oneself from what one had wanted, and a period of isolation in which one begins to sense the shape of one's new motivation, represent a cultural resource we have largely lost.) And there are cultural obstacles, too. One of them is an ideology, expressed both in common-sense psychology and abstract philosophical accounts of rationality, of the immutability of desire.

10

Coordination Problems

This is a chapter about changing the desires of others.

People often have to coordinate their actions in order to get what they want. That is, the consequences of an action often depend on what others choose to do, so that we can best achieve our ends if we can make our actions parts of coordinated patterns with those of others. This must have been so throughout human history. Groups of people must have always needed, for example, to stay together for protection against dangerous animals, particularly rival humans. So at the very least they will have had to coordinate their movements. And in fact one would naturally think that one of the main advantages of being an intelligent, rational, creature, would be that one could get better results by cooperation with other similar creatures than one could get solely by one's own efforts.

The need for coordination produces a practical problem and a philosophical problem. The practical problem is just how to achieve this coordination, how to make sure that one's actions mesh with those of others to best effect. And the philosophical problem is to show how individual rational agents, each trying only to achieve their own good, may find their way to a mutually advantageous coordination. The difference between the problems is that in dealing with the practical one you don't have to get hung up about rationality. You just need a way of choosing an action from the choices at hand which will not fall foul of the choices other people make. But the philosophical problem requires that one formulate a coherent account of individual rationality which allows individual rational people to make successful coordinations without compromising their rationality.

The philosophical problem is now well under control. This is one of the success stories of analytical philosophy. It is no longer a mystery how individuals bent upon their individual interests can achieve a coordinated result. (That is not to say that the subject is closed. There is a lot more work to do. But no one can now claim that the central problem is insoluble.) In this chapter I shall start with a fairly unoriginal exposition of the reasons for saying this, to the point (in 'The Taming of a Few, section 10.3 below) where it connects with the main themes of the book. That is where it becomes an essay on changing the desires of others.

10.1   The Prisoner's dilemma

Two people, Alfa and Bet, are walking through the desert. They have no affection for each other, and do not even speak the same language, but must stick together for fear of lions. They come to the crest of a dune and realize simultaneously that there is an oasis with many people half a mile away and that a lion is stalking them. Each understands right away that they have two options: run for the oasis or walk slowly towards it. Alfa knows that if she runs and Bet walks the lion will go for and kill the easier prey, Bet, and she, Alfa, will therefore arrive at the oasis unharmed. If they both walk the lion will attack them but they will probably be able to beat it off together and arrive tired, frightened, and scratched, but alive. If they both run the lion will attack both of them, and since they cannot defend themselves while running they will both be at least maimed. And if it is she who walks and Bet who runs then it will be Bet who arrives unharmed and she who is killed.

Bet knows all this too. And each knows that the other knows it and that their choices are independent: they cannot catch each other preparing to run or walk. The lion is approaching and there is no time to try to communicate. Each must immediately decide and act. What should each do? The situation can be represented with the standard pay-off matrix below.

	B walks	B runs
A walks	A hurt, B hurt	A dead, B unhurt
A runs	A unhurt, B dead	A maimed, B maimed

Alfa can reason as follows. 'Bet will either walk or run. If he walks then I am better off if I run (since being unhurt is better than being hurt). If he runs then again I am better off if I run (since being maimed is better than being dead.) So whatever he does I am better off if I run. So I should run.' So she runs.

Bet can reason in an exactly parallel way. So he will run too. The result will be that both will run. Many people find this troubling: since both will run they will both be maimed by the lion. If both had walked then both would have been hurt but unmaimed. So careful hard-to-fault reasoning has landed them in a situation which is for each of them the second worst result. If they had both walked the result would have been second best for each of them.

This situation is called the prisoner's dilemma. (It is so called because the standard example involves two prisoners who can either confess and implicate the other, or remain silent.) Real examples of prisoner's dilemmas are found throughout social and economic life. They are defined by the fact that there are two actions open to each person, one representing a cooperation with the other and the other not. Each person has to act in ignorance of the other's deliberation and action. The results of cooperation or non-cooperation depend for each person on whether the other cooperates or not, but for each of them the best result occurs when she does not cooperate but the other does. The next best occurs when both cooperate, followed by both not cooperating. The worst, for each agent, occur when she cooperates but the other does not. Each person can then reason, as Alfa did, that whatever the other does she will be better off not cooperating. So neither will cooperate. And as a result both will end up worse off than if both had cooperated.[1]

Many people find this conclusion paradoxical. Rational deliberation has led to a poor result for all concerned. (It's not just second-best: it is third out of the four outcomes for both people.) And to make it worse, both people *know* that this result will follow, as long as the other person is rational. Some use the prisoner's dilemma to cast doubt on the idea that rational self-interested agents could form a cooperative society, or that the kinds of profit-maximizing motive found in capitalist economies will always work for the common good. Others try to find a hole in the reasoning, or an alternative kind of rationality which will allow agents caught in prisoner's dilemmas both to be rational and to cooperate.[2]

It is important not to think that the prisoner's dilemma is the only, or the only important, situation in which people must coordinate their actions. There are many very different types of coordination problem. In some of them what matters most is that the people involved do the same thing, whatever it is. In some of them what matters most is that the people find a way of deciding which one is to get a small advantage, to avoid a large loss to both. Different coordination problems generalize in different ways to more than two people or more than two actions. The prisoner's dilemma has received more attention than these other situations because it has seemed to present the most intractable problems. If one can show how agents faced with prisoner's dilemmas can find their way to cooperation, then it will no longer seem implausible that people pursuing their individual good can achieve stable and mutually satisfactory social arrangements.

No attempt to construe cooperation in a single true prisoner's dilemma as rational has been really plausible. (Note the 'single', and 'true': sequences of prisoner's dilemmas are another matter altogether, and there are situations which are superficially like prisoner's dilemmas but essentially different. More on both points below.) I shall take it as a sad fact that there are situations like this, where people's best efforts to get what they want will inevitably conflict and frustrate one another. One reason that we often resist this conclusion is that we reason: the morally best option is always that of coordination with the efforts of others, and what is morally required cannot be irrational. But this reasoning must be wrong, for there are prisoner's dilemmas in which non-cooperation is the morally required action.

Consider for example a very standard prisoner's dilemma story. You are one of a group of conspirators against an oppressive regime. You and another have been arrested. You know that in another interrogation room the other conspirator has been protesting, just as you have been, that he is really a government agent sent to infiltrate the group and betray their plans. Your interrogators won't hear a word of it. They are under instructions to get confessions by any means. Several hours of torture follow, but you hold out. The torturers leave and a different officer gives you a cup of coffee and offers you a deal. If you implicate the other prisoner you will be released (and no doubt followed, in the hope of finding the group), while he will be tried and sent to a labour camp for ten years. That is supposing that the other has kept his mouth shut: if each of you has implicated the other then you will both be in for five years in the camps. And if both of you manage to hold out against the torture you will both have to be released. But not before several more rounds of torture. You can guess that at this moment one of the men who not long ago was applying electrodes to you is producing a cup of coffee and a sweet reasonable manner for the other prisoner, and offering the same deal.

There is a twist, though, to distinguish this from the archetypal prisoner's dilemma story. You know that the other prisoner *is* a government agent. (Your interrogators don't know: one tentacle of state security is keeping the information from another.) If you hold out against the torture and do not implicate him he will go off to betray the rest of your group. So if you implicate him you not only escape torture and imprisonment, you also keep him safely locked away.

This fits the pattern of the prisoner's dilemma: you should decide to implicate the other, since that is the action that gives you the best result whether or not the other implicates you. And since you know that he will reason in just the same way you know that the inevitable result will be that you will each implicate the other and both be sent to five years in the camps. If you had both held out then you would have both been released. And even given that the other is a spy you may prefer the second of these to the first. But now there is no thought of a moral obligation to hold out against implicating the other, since in implicating him you lock away a spy.

I am convinced that there is no point trying to argue that people in prisoner's dilemmas should cooperate. I think that the illusion that cooperation in a prisoner's dilemma is somehow rational can come from not realizing how artificial the situation in the dilemma is supposed to be. In real situations very much like the prisoner's dilemma it often is rational to cooperate. But the prisoner's dilemma differs from them in three important respects. First, it is unrepeatable and has no consequences for the future: one is to imagine that these two people are interacting once and either will never meet again, or that when they do their interaction will be completely unaffected by what has happened in the past. Second, each person is completely indifferent to the desires of the other, so the pay-off matrix given for the four outcomes represents all the relevant preferences of the two people. Third, each person has only two possible actions: no compromises or clever alternatives can be considered.

No real human interaction is exactly like this. I doubt that real human motivation ever fits these three features exactly. But, still, many real situations approximate more or less to prisoner's dilemmas, and to the extent that they do it is in fact difficult for reasonable people to cooperate. (Organizations as well as people: two nations with suspicions about each other's intentions but no real reason to quarrel can face a prisoner's dilemma; the cooperative solution is to disarm but one who disarms while the other does not is in danger of military threats.) Yet one cannot produce cooperation magically by adopting some alternative decision-making procedure. To convince yourself of this put yourself in Alfa's position. Dare you walk? If you do and Bet runs you will die. And you have good reasons to expect him to run, since he is surely afraid that you will run and leave him to be killed.

10.2 Sequences of Dilemmas

The problem for agents facing prisoner's dilemmas is not how to see their way to cooperation in those dilemmas but how to change the situation so that what they fact are not prisoner's dilemmas. There are many ways to change the situation. An external authority can be introduced, imposing sanctions on non-cooperation; agents can make commitments (e.g. giving hostages or making bets) which make it clear that they will cooperate. One of the most fundamental ways of changing the situation is for agents to link their actions in the situation at hand to their actions in future similar situations.

Suppose that two people are facing a series of prisoner's dilemma-like situations with each other. The pay-offs cannot include death, so the situations cannot reproduce the Alfa/Bet situation literally. But the pattern of pay-offs is the same: each person can either Cooperation or Defect – defection is the standard term for non-cooperation – and each person's ranking of the outcomes is: [Defect while other cooperates], [Both cooperate], [Both defect], [Cooperate while other defects]. So in a single isolated situation the reasonable thing to do would be to defect. But the situations are not isolated. Each will recur indefinitely, often will the same pay-offs. So each person must decide not just what she will do in the situation at hand but what strategy to adopt to the whole series of choices.

This situation has been studied extensively by Axelrod and others following him.[3] There are infinitely many strategies one could adopt: always cooperate, always defect, cooperate and defect randomly, cooperate unless the other has defected, defect until the other first cooperates, and so on. The obvious strategy to consider is 'always defect', since it is the crudes generalization of the best strategy in an isolated dilemma. Axelrod discovered the advantages of a remarkably simple alternative to 'always defect'. It is the policy of cooperating first and after that doing whatever the other did last time. He calls it 'tit for tat'.

To compare 'tit for tat', 'always defect', and other strategies we can consider long series of interactions in which they are matched against one another. (This is best done with computer simulation.) Axelrod does this in two stages: (a) take a collection of strategies and consider all possible pairings of one against another, and note the accumulated gains of each. Thus if the strategy 'always cooperate' is paired with the strategy 'always defect' the result will be a series (C,D), (C,D), (C,D), ... And if the payoffs are the standard ones – double cooperation is evaluated as (3,3), double defection as (1,1), and one-sided defection as (5,0) – then the score for agent one (the cooperator) after n trials will be 0 and the score for agent two (the defector) will be $5n$. Obviously 'always defect' beats 'always cooperate', as one would expect. Then comes stage (b) where a new population of strategies is assembled, with each is strategy being proportional to its score in stage (a). Again each is pitted against each, and then a final score for each strategy is produced, being the average of the scores of each of the players using it.

One important result emerges, and one surprising fact. The important result is that there is no best strategy, for the success of a strategy depends on the population of strategies it is set among. The surprising fact (which illustrates the important result) is that 'tit for tat' does very well, even in competition with 'always defect'. When 'tit for tat' meets 'always defect' the result if the values of the pay-offs are as in the last paragraph will be (0,5), (1,1), (1,1),..., which is not great for either, but a bit worse for 'tit for tat'. When 'tit for tat' meets 'tit for tat' the result is (3,3), (3,3),..., which is pretty good for both. And when 'always defect' meets 'always defect' the result is (1,1), (1,1),... which is equally bad for both (though not the worst possible result). So you can see that if one 'tit for tat' player meets one 'always defect' player the 'always defect' player comes off slightly better, but if there are numbers of both then the 'tit for tat' players gain more by playing against each other than the 'always defect' players can, and so will do better.

These and other results show that a person facing a series of prisoner's dilemmas could wish that all or most of the people involved were using a tit for tat strategy or some variant of it. (Another of Axelrod's analyses shows that enough tit for tat-users will under suitable conditions put 'always defect' users out of business.) Then the person could use tit for tat too, and this would have advantages of both gain and security. The advantage of gain is obvious: tit for tat players do better while playing against one another. The advantage of security is that if two players both use tit for tat their actions are in *equilibrium*: neither can do better by changing to a different strategy. (In fact they are in a coordination equilibrium: neither will do better even if both change to a different strategy.)[4]

So if you can see a prisoner's dilemma coming, one reasonable response is to try to create a situation in which most people govern their actions with tit for tat or some other strategy of conditional cooperation. (the important thing is that they use a strategy which will not defect unless defected against.) How to do this?

10.3 The Taming of a Few

Suppose you foresee a prisoner's dilemma, involving you and some other person. (Or a series of them, involving you and a fixed group of people.) You want to transform the situation so that the transformed interactions are not prisoner's dilemmas. There are two general routes to the transformation. You can change the beliefs of the people involved, or you can change their desires. Both are usually necessary.

To make the problem hard, imagine that you are faced with a number of 'wild' but intelligent others. All they are interested in is immediate gain, but they are very canny about that. (Children, for example.) Your task is to tame them, lure them into cooperative strategies. Simply being cooperative yourself will not work: you'll come out badly every time. Even adopting a cooperative long-term strategy like tit for tat will not alone do the trick. First there is the problem of convincing them that you have indeed adopted the strategy. And then there is the problem of making them care one way or the other: the motive for cooperating with a tit for tat player is to gain the benefits of mutual cooperation in the future, and future benefits do not mean much to them.

Solving the first problem is a matter of ingenuity and tact. One natural course would be to arrange a series of interactions with immediate pay-offs fitting the pattern of a prisoner's dilemma, but with the pay-offs varying in such a way as to demonstrate at small cost your willingness to cooperate if cooperated with previously. The stakes should be low at first and then rise as the others come to see the pattern of your actions. Ideally the benefits to you from mutual cooperation should be fairly low, and the gains to you from one-sided defection should be fairly high so that in renouncing them your commitment to conditional cooperation is made clear. Simple inductive reasoning should then lead them to believe in your conditional cooperation. Ideally, too, there should be forseeable interactions in which the results of double defection are fairly dire, not much better than those of one-sided cooperation, which are immediately preceded by 'low key' interactions in which the results of one-sided cooperation are not particularly bad. Then in order to gain the advantages of double cooperation at the later interaction they will be willing to risk cooperation in the earlier ones. With this as preparation cooperation in the final, high stakes, interaction, could be dared.

But this supposes that the second problem, that of making the others care about the future, has been solved. The problem is that they may discount future benefits and losses in comparison with present ones. If they do to a high degree then prospects of future benefits will not lure them into immediate cooperation. So one of your tasks in taming them is to change their desires, specifically to change the comparative weight they put on future gains and losses. The peculiar thing is that it is in their interests to act as if they put a high value one future consequences, even if we measure these interests in terms of their present, unreformed, desires!

These desires can be made to change in two ways, which I think are much like the ways we do actually mould one another into cooperative creatures. One is much like a shifting strategy, though applied to others, and the other works via pressure on second order desires. Both rely on the fact that people who do not care about the future can still learn from the past. It should be clear to them from seeing real interactions between others and imagining others that people using conditionally cooperative strategies will generally do better. So in an imminent interaction they would do better if they could believe that the person they will interact with will cooperate, and have that person believe that they will. The only way to do this is to seek out or manufacture an interaction, preferable with low stakes, before the crucial interaction arises. This can be encouraged. they will thus be acting as if they counted future consequences on something like a par with present ones, in order to be taken as conditional cooperators. (In some cases the intention may be to be taken as a cooperator and then to defect. That is still half-way there.)

Two things will follow from this 'as if' behaviour. People acting in this way will have to think ahead to calculate the actions they would take if the future mattered to them. And they will wish that everyone else valued the future on a par with the present, or at any rate acted as if they did. These are both rather cumbersome. As a short cut, at least, it would save mental effort just to calculate future consequences on a par with present ones, and wish that everyone did. With a little 'as if' tagged on the end, which will become an increasingly empty formality as time goes on, until eventually it drops. The withering of the 'as if' would be encouraged by the interaction of the two components: the nearer one got to simply wishing that everyone cared about the future the more pressure there would be on one's own calculations to conform, and the higher a weight in one's calculations one gave to future consequences the more one's norm of reasonable action for everyone would shift in that direction.

Or it could be much simpler. One could think: 'It would be better if everyone wanted to cooperate.' And so want everyone to want to cooperate, and so want to want to cooperate. And so want to cooperate. And then as an incidental result come to value future consequences more like present ones.

10.4 Signalling

I have been describing the most difficult situation, in which a single person inclined to cooperation is among others who do not see the point of it. But it was the most manageable case of that most difficult situation. Real life is usually less tidy. Two differences are particularly important. For one thing, the interactions in which people have to coordinate their actions do not consist of sequences of prisoner's dilemmas alone. Other coordination problems are mixed among them: some of them are much more complex. For example, conditional cooperation in a sequence of prisoner's dilemmas has many separate characteristics – such as being the strategy which under some circumstances will give its users the best results and being an equilibrium strategy – which can pick out different actions in more complex situations. In such situations people who want to act in a coordinated way have to decide whether it is the best mutual result or the best equilibrium they are after. (An example of this is the 'super-cooperation' game at the end of the next section.)

The other important untidiness of real life is that a crucial interaction cannot usually be preceded by a convenient series of practices, in which people's propensities to cooperation and to discount future consequences can get sorted out. For the events are usually not so manipulable, and the people involved not so constant.

The result is that in most real coordination problems the facts relevant to here-and-now gains and losses are pretty definite, and those relevant to future ones, which depend on how others react to one's present choices, are pretty indefinite. So cooperation is often a risky business: it must usually come from weighting an indefinite probability of indefinite future gains and losses against more clearly known likelihoods of present gains.

It is clear what one is trying to do, though. One is trying to accomplish two things with the same action: one wants to do as well as possible in the interaction at hand, and one wants to signal to the other person or persons one's willingness to future cooperation. If one has reason to believe that the other is conditionally cooperating then these pull in the same direction, to cooperation. But if one cannot believe this then considerations about the present push towards defection and considerations about the future push towards cooperation. And there may be no easy way of reconciling these two pushes, if you have no firm sense of the probability that your cooperativeness might spread to the other, or of the benefits this might bring. Imagine yourself again in Alfa's situation, changed so that instead of death the worst outcome is a really severe mauling. You know that the situation, or one much like it, may recur and that *if* you have persuaded Bet that you will cooperate if he does then such future situations *may* have a less unhappy outcome. But you also know that Bet's fear of a severe mauling will push him towards running, leaving you to be mauled. What is the right thing to do?

When the situation is as indeterminate as this, and the options so limited, there is no wrong action. Alfa may think in terms of the possible risks, using something like the pessimistic strategy of chapter 5. Then she will run. Or she may think in terms of opportunities, using something like the optimistic strategy. Then she will walk. (The sieve is not likely to give an answer unless it is biased in one way or another.) Either would be understandable, and neither would be wrong.

10.5 *Expanding the Options*

If the situation is this uncertain then so must be one's choice of actions. Sometimes the uncertainty is exaggerated by the way the situation is described. In particular, there are usually more options than just Cooperate or Defect. Indeed, in telling the Alfa and Bet story I allowed each of them only to run or to walk, ignoring all the pacing and jogging in between. See how the picture changes if we bring in these other options.

Suppose that two people can each act in a way that varies between two extremes, which I shall call full cooperation and full defection. There are four ultimate outcomes, with pay-offs to the two people as in a prisoner's dilemma. But with the exception of the extreme actions the actions of the two people do not achieve these pay-offs directly. Instead they produce different probabilities of them. So, for example, if each person performs an action half-way between full cooperation and full defection – half cooperation – then there will be an equal chance of any of the four outcomes. Each person chooses in ignorance of the other person's choice, but if the choices do not determine the outcome then another choice is made, which can only change the original choice by a certain amount (changing the probability at most 0.1 in either direction, say). (The outcome will be undetermined when neither has chosen full defection or full cooperation. If only one has chosen an extreme option then I am supposing that only the other has a further choice.) And so on for a fixed number of choices. After that chance determines the final outcome, in accordance with the final probabilities.[5]

In the Alfa and Bet story this could work as follows. Either person can break into a full run or a slow walk from the very beginning. Then the outcome is determined. Or they can take a few steps at an intermediate pace. Then it is not certain which of the possible results will occur. Alfa can, for example, take a first step at a fairly fast pace which while slower than running allows her to break into a run. Then if Bet has taken a first step at a full run it is very likely that they will both be maimed, just as if they had both committed themselves to full run. But it is not completely certain: for if the lion is a bit slow or Alfa slows down at the next few steps the result may be Alfa's death and Bet's escape, as if Alfa had walked and Bet run.

These intermediate actions have obvious attractions. But finding the right point between the extremes is difficult. If, for example, Alfa begins conspicuously more slowly than Bet then Bet will see the opportunity of running ahead and escaping completely unhurt, and if Alfa begins conspicuously more quickly than Bet then Bet will be afraid of being left hehind to be killed and will rush to catch up. So what is wanted is a fairly quick start which is still just slow enough to signal Alfa's willingness to walk if Bet walks. And then, if Bet recognizes this and slows down, Alfa should slow down to a pace which increases the benefit to both of them while keeping open the possibility of dashing ahead if Bet either flags or breaks into a run. In this way Alfa and Bet will be on the path to a miniature social contract.

How should each of them find the ideal balance-point between running and walking? If either has chosen irrevocably to run at the very beginning then the other must obviously get as near to running as they can, as soon as possible. (I specified only a 0.1 change in probability on each choice, so if the other has begun near a walk it will take some time to catch up.) The best initial move would seem to be the slowest speed which keeps open the option of running if that is the way the other is tending. If six choices are possible before the lion is upon them that would mean starting half-way between walking and running (that is, with a 0.5 probability of the consequences of either).

After the initial choice each of them has a further thing to consider. That is how they may signal to the other their willingness to cooperate. Suppose that on the first choice both Alfa and Bet are half-way between running and walking. On the next Alfa may want to go a bit closer to running, to keep open the possibility of running if that is the direction in which Bet's choices evolve. But to do this would signal to Bet that Alfa was heading towards running, and so make it more likely that Bet would increases his speed too. So there is a case to be made for slowing down slightly at the next choice, even if it makes it impossible for Alfa to achieve full running if need be, in order to suggest to Bet that they both might agree to walk. But then if Alfa slows down too much Bet may take it as a sign that he can achieve the ideal situation of running while Alfa walks.

In order to calculate exactly what each person should do at each stage of this process, one would have to know exactly how their choices affect the probabilities of the other person making any of their possible choices next time round. I am of course interested in what to do when this is not possible. (And that is the more realistic form of the problem, since Alfa and Bet certainly wouldn't have this information.) One strategy to follow would be an analogue of tit for tat. This would involve starting half-way between walking and running and then always moving in the direction of the other's last choice, speeding up if the other has accelerated (but never going faster than the other) and slowing down if the other has slowed down. There are also strategies that signal more actively the person's willingness to cooperate. For example Alfa might start just a bit slower than half-way between walking and running, and then respond to each of Bet's choices by aiming for a result half-way between walking and Bet's last choice.

There are obviously many other strategies. Some of them would show more fear of being trapped walking while the other runs, and other, subtler, strategies would suggest acting in accordance with the other's past several choices, reacting to their direction of change, towards or away from cooperation. They are all compromises between one relatively definite factor – the sizes of the pay-offs and the objective probabilities of achieving them, and one relatively indefinite one – the effect one person's choices will have as a signal to the other.

The natural tool to use in this compromise between the definite and the indefinite is what in chapter 5 (see section 5.8) I called the sieve. I formulated it as: keep for further consideration those options which either have particularly good consequences (seen optimistically) or do not have outstandingly had ones (seen pessimistically), and discard the rest. Optimistic and pessimistic attitudes must now be towards the cooperativeness of the other person. Pessimism takes the other to be inclined to non-cooperation, and doubts that the other will be impressed if one gestures that one oneself would be content to see two-sided cooperation as the result. And optimism takes the other to be cooperative and sensitive to signals. Then the options with particularly good consequences (seen optimistically) are those near to cooperation. And the ones without particularly bad consequences (seen pessimistically) are those not *too* near to cooperation!

It will make a difference how good or bad the possible outcomes are, relative to one another. If there is not much to choose between the best and second best outcomes for either person (that in which they defect and the other cooperates, and mutual cooperation) then the options that get on to the shortlist will include options tending to cooperation. For the goal of mutual cooperation will seem both more attractive and more attainable. It offers one something near to the best outcome, and thus provides a bait that should lure the other away from defection. But if there is a large difference between the worst and the second worst outcomes for either person (that in which they cooperate and the other defects, and mutual defection) then options near to full cooperation will be rejected, since the undesirability and the danger of one-sided cooperation will seem very salient. The ideal situation to induce serious consideration for actions near to cooperation, then, is one in which both the difference in attractiveness between one-sided defection and mutual cooperation and that between mutual defection and one-sided cooperation are small. And the situation most likely to induce defection is one in which both these differences are large.

This is what one would expect, intuitively. Suppose that Alfa thinks that getting to the oasis unscathed is not much better than being hurt, and that both are much better than being mauled or being killed, between which there is not much to choose. Then although caution will prevent her from outright walking, she will take seriously the possibility of something near to walking, in the hope that Bet will take the hint and they can both proceed slowly together. Suppose on the other hand that she thinks that getting back unscathed is a lot better than suffering any injury whatsoever, that any injury is just about as bad as any other, including being mauled, and that being killed would be a great deal worse yet. Then she will surely feel desperately afraid that Bet will run and leave her behind, and will not be attracted by a possible cooperation which would lead to something well below the best outcome. So she will set off at a run.

10.6 Socialization

So here is another resource, another route to cooperation. Single interactions between people can be seen not only as members of sequences of similar interactions, but as parts of larger complex interactions with their own pay-offs to the people involved. And this corresponds to a very basic aspect of social life: our individual actions not only have immediate effects but also contribute to larger results. (Societies themselves are among those results.) Put this way, the 'expanding the options' route seems very similar to the 'sequences of interactions' route. After all, in cooperating for the sake of the benefits of later cooperation one is taking a step towards the creation of a result, mutual trust, which is of general benefit. But there are important differences. The choices that are little contributions to larger results need not themselves have pay-offs, or pay-offs of the same kind as those of the individual choices, And the route to cooperation need not depend on people's rewarding or punishing individual others for their degree of cooperativeness.

There are obviously many variations on the pattern, as many as the variety of ways people can contribute to a collective result. There may or may not be pay-offs along the way to the final result, which may or may not be comparable with those of the final result; there may or may not be random elements.[6] There may be sequences of such step-by-step interactions. (So, in this last case, a strategy could make the first step in a new interaction be a function of the history of the earlier one.) But whenever any such pattern can be found people are to some small degree acting as members of a society.

Social life changes people; socialized people want things that they would not have wanted had each not gone through particular formation in a particular society. Solving coordination problems is only part of social life, of course, but if what I have been saying does describe some of what goes into solving them then we can see some part of the ways in which trying (or being forced) to coordinate one's actions with others puts a pressure on what one wants.

There are two fundamental factors, which I shall call the conceptual factor and the variability factor. It is their interaction that exerts the pressure.

The conceptual factor is this. If someone is thinking through a co-ordination problem, for example a prisoner's dilemma, just in terms of immediate gains and losses then, most often, no coordinated solution will emerge. The situation changes magically with the addition of a single concept, that of long-term strategic gain. The interaction might, for example, be part of a sequence of actions. Then the magic idea is that there are long-term strategies like conditional cooperation, and strategic gain consists in being labelled a cooperator who will be cooperated with in future. Or the interaction might be one that leads with others to some potentially useful result. Then strategic gain consists in being well-placed to receive the benefits of the eventual result (for example, in the Alfa Bet case above being either able to run and leave the other behind, or by threat of running persuade the other into walking, so that neither is left behind.)

Merely having the concept of strategic gain, and knowing that others have it, transforms one's actions. Social life without it is like playing chess just to capture pieces one move at a time, understanding neither that checkmate depends as much on position as on numbers nor that a sacrifice of a piece now can mean one is placed better to make gains later. So while it is important that people who have to coordinate their actions find ways of signalling the particular long-term strategies they are using, a more fundamental task is accomplished simply by making sure that the idea of strategic gain is abroad.

While that conceptual factor promises magical transformation, the variability factor threatens to bog things down in details. The point is that there is both an enormous variety of types of coordination problem, and an equally great variety of strategies which can be used on them. Consider for example situations like that discussed in the last section, where two agents can start with any of infinitely many actions and then change their relative positions in infinitely many ways. Given the uncertainty of how each will respond to the other's choices, there is no automatically best way of thinking out the situation. Instead, there are a number of reasonable strategies. Moreover, full cooperation cannot be forced upon the players by a threat of non-cooperation in later interactions, since the loser if one person cooperates and the other defects may be dead, eaten by a lion. And yet it is a situation in which the idea of strategic gain, that each one's choices can influence those of the other to avoid the double defection trap, applies and can transform the situation. You would expect two people in the second Alfa/Bet situation to reach a compromise nearer to walking than to running (more precisely with a greater probability of leading to the results of their both walking), even though they have no language in common and no love for one another.

(You would expect this as long as the two were human beings, already socialized enough to have the idea of strategic gain, even if through the norms of different societies. If one was a rational robot, or an intelligent but completely asocial creature, anything could happen.)

And this is while we are still playing variations one the prisoner's dilemma. The variety becomes more confusing when we consider very different coordination problems, especially when they are mixed up together. Imagine that you have participated in a series of interactions with immediate pay-offs making prisoner's dilemmas, with fairly low stakes, with someone who is using a tit for tat strategy. You catch on, and begin to use it yourself. (From that point it isn't really a prisoner's dilemma any more.) Then another interaction comes along, with the same person, but for higher stakes. But this one is rather different from a prisoner's dilemma. In this new interaction there are three actions you can choose: call them defection, cooperation, and supercooperation. The pay-offs for combinations of defection and cooperation by the two people are as in a prisoner's dilemma, but the pay-off for mutual supercooperation is better for both people than for mutual cooperation. Yet the pay-offs to each person from combinations of supercooperation and any other option are the same as the same combinations of defection and those options. In effect, supercooperation is just like defection, except that two-sided supercooperation is very good for both parties.[7]

Should you choose cooperation or supercooperation? What you need to know is whether the other person will count supercooperation as cooperation or as defection. Perhaps the other person will count cooperation as defection, to be punished with future non-cooperation. Perhaps the other person does not even realize that supercooperation is an option. You know that you should take account of strategic advantage, but you don't know what will give it.

So the variability factor tends to cancel out the conceptual factor. A hyperintelligent Martian dropped among us in human form would know that he should play for strategic advantage, but he would not be able to do it. But socialized human beings do know how to do it. At least, they know how to coordinate their actions in the types of situation for which their socialization has prepared them. They do not do it by knowing what others in their society want and aiming for situations of greatest mutual gain. For as we have seen that is not always something that will be reinforced by people's long-term strategies. Instead, we have fairly arbitrary coordination conventions, which define in topic-specific terms how coordination is to be achieved. (And, closely related, equally arbitrary conflict-resolution conventions.) These conventions must have some equilibrium properties. For example, to modify Robert Sugden's formulation slightly: it must be the case that most people who conform to a convention find it in their interest that others conform to it, and that if most others conform to the convention it is usually in any person's interest to conform too. And it must be the case that having some such convention is more in most people's interest than having no convention. But these conditions fall far short of determining the conventions. They are arbitrary social inventions.[8]

Examples of such conventions are those governing possession and transfer of property (including conventions of what can and can not be owned, and what rights ownership entails. Conventions' of leadership and authority, conventions of the division of labour, and conventions of entitlement to benefits are also usually part of the patchwork. And as long as people know what these conventions are, they know how to coordinate their actions in many situations.

Socialization consists in part in coming to understand these conventions. Once one understands them and sees that they are generally obeyed by those around one, one must realize that it is in one's interest to conform to them. The interest is partly strategic: if one does not conform then one will not get the benefits of cooperation from others in a vaguely defined variety of ways in the future. (Of course people do not usually put things to themselves this explicitly: the conventions are largely internalized before one can put anything very explicitly.) Then the effect on one's desires works just as it does when one finds oneself pressured towards counting the future on a par with the past: what may at first be a rule of thumb or a short cut, acting as if one wanted various things for their own sake, becomes more and more ingrained until it is absorbed into the pattern of one's desires.

This is pretty abstract. Let me illustrate it with an almost ludicrously down to earth example. Suppose you are one of a team of people building a house. There is one tool which is shared between you: a spirit level, say. Each of you will from time to time need to use it, but much of the time it is not being used. The question is where it should stay between uses, so that it can easily be found. When you join the team a convention has already been established. The level is to be put back in a standard place to the right of the main entrance. By now most of the work is being done on an upper floor, and there is a lot of going up and down stairs to get the level from its place and return it. Moreover you very often know who will be needing it next, and where, so you could just take it to where it will be needed instead of going all the way downstairs. So there are alternative conventions which might well be more in everyone's interest. Still, when you join the team you don't want to seem presumptuous, so you go along with the convention, and always take the level back to its home just to the right of the main entrance.

Sometimes someone else forgets to return it. Very often there is then a time-wasting search. But sometimes it can be clearly seen near where it will be next needed. The standard practice then is to return it to its proper place, even if this means a later trip down to get it. The rationale for this is that if it begins to get left around soon no one will know where to find it.

When you first join the team you think 'now I must put the level back, or the others will be annoyed at me'. Then, when looking for it because someone else has failed to put it back you wish that they had, and wish that it were beside the door. Then, when you have finished using it your-self you want to take it back, and when you are not sure what you did with it you hope that you took it back. Sometimes when you think someone may have left it upstairs near where you are working you still hope that they have not: it is not worth saving a few steps at the price of encourag-ing workmates who don't put things back where they belong. Eventually, the others leave and you are left to work alone. Where before you would have been torn between leaving the level in a memorable place and having it near at hand, now you find your desires are simple: you want it to be in its proper place by the door.

There are morals here about the arbitrariness of many of our desires. And about the pressures which form them. Some of the arbitrariness and some of the pressures result from the same thing: there is no mechanical way of thinking through the full range of perfectly natural and non–exotic coordination problems.

11

The Disunity of the Moral

*I shoved the whole thing out of my head; and said I would take up
wickedness again, which was in my line, being brung up to it, and the
other waren't. And for a starter, I would go to work and steal Jim out
of slavery again; and if I could think of anything worse, I would do
that, too; because as long as I was in, and in for good, I might as well go
the whole hog.*

Mark Twain, Huckleberry Finn

I spoke to my accountant yesterday and I told her that my work was going
well and that I seemed for once to be living within my means. 'What
about your pension', she said. 'Are you satisfied with the university's
scheme?' 'Not really,' I replied, 'but I don't find myself losing much sleep
over it.' 'You should take pensions more seriously', she said. I agreed that
it was easy to ignore what one really ought to do when it wouldn't make
any difference for years. We went on to discuss a sum of money I had sitting on deposit earning less interest than the rate of inflation. I suggested
an investment trust I had seen advertised. 'Don't touch it,' she warned
me, 'not with a barge-pole. Their main investment is in companies
specializing in quick and barely-legal toxic waste disposal. You shouldn't
have anything to do with them.' My accountant has a wide conception of
her responsibilities.

At first, on the subject of pensions, my accountant was reminding me
of the demands of rationality. Or prudence, or forethought. Later,
dissuading me from making a quick buck out of toxic waste, she was
talking of morality. Or was she? Perhaps she was just telling me that it was
a foolish investment. But then perhaps when telling me to consider my
pension more carefully she had been concerned less I irresponsibly
become a burden on others in my old age. When people say 'ought',
'should', 'must', 'good' (as in 'good investment') and the like, in everyday
life, it is very hard to put what they mean into a small number of separate
boxes, labelled 'rationality', 'morality', 'conventional behaviour' and so on.
(I asked my accountant which of her recommendations were specifi-

cations of moral requirements and which ones derived from her conception of rationality. She just gave me one of those funny looks.)

11.1 Moral Dilemmas

In spite of the difficulty of classifying the kinds of advice we routinely give one another, there is in the popular rhetoric of our culture a general contrast between morality and self-interest. We contrast moral motivation, as a problematic thing, with the apparently straightforward motives of self-interest, and we contrast moral dilemmas, in which you have to find an acceptable action in the midst of conflicting responsibilities and obligations, with practical or prudential dilemmas, in which the problem is getting as much as you can of what you want.

Conflicts between responsibilities can be particularly acute. There is no shortage of examples. You have promised to take a child to the zoo and then just as you are setting off a friend comes around in a crisis, needing immediate advice and comfort. The child won't understand and forgive you for breaking the promise, the friend knows that her need is more important: whatever you do is in some way wrong. This quality of inevitable regret is sometimes thought to be characteristic of moral dilemmas. Moral obligations have some sort of a hold over you even if they are overruled by stronger considerations, so that in retrospect you will feel this hold as regret, or even guilt.

I doubt this. Or at any rate to the extent that I understand the contrast between moral and non-moral dilemmas I doubt it. Non-moral dilemmas can just as easily produce inevitable regret; consider for example the dilemma faced by the millionaire in chapters 6 and 7, who had the options of reducing a great danger to one child or reducing a lesser danger to another. The more one thinks about her situation the less clear it becomes which option she should take (particularly because one sees that if she reduces the greater danger she increases the chance that both children will suffer). And the more she thinks about her situation the more she realizes that she will regret whatever she does. And this need not be because she is driven by duties, moral responsibilities, or a concern to maximize the general good. As long as she loves her children equally she will be liable to inevitable regret.

The same can be said of one of the original and central examples of inevitable regret, Bernard Williams' Agamemnon example.[1] In that example Agamemnon, the leader of the Greek expedition against Troy, decides to sacrifice his daughter to secure a good wind for the fleet. Regret is inevitable because if he does not make the sacrifice he will be failing in his public responsibilities as general-in-chief, and if he does make it he will lose his daughter. Now if we see the situation anachronistically, imagining Agamemnon to be morally sensitive to his obligations both to the army and to his child, then we do indeed get both a moral dilemma as well as a situation offering inevitable regret. But the example works just as well if we see it in a historically more likely way, in which Agamemnon is a typical Homeric thug, out for glory, a good scrap, and trophies in the form of treasures and women. He still loves his daughter, wants neither to see her die nor to be seen as not defending his family, and cares above all for his honour as king and general. And still he will find himself regretting whatever he does.

The contrast between moral and non-moral is generally vague – nothing necessarily wrong with that – and in some ways very misleading. If we want to understand what is agonizing about decision-making dilemmas, and what are the helpful ways of dealing with them, it just does not help to classify them as moral and non-moral. My aim in this chapter is first to undermine the contrast between morality and self-interest. (Not that self-interest is the only thing morality can be contrasted with.) To do this I have to undermine both sides of the contrast: I argue that neither morality nor self-interest is a single clear thing. There are other, more helpful, contrasts to make between dilemmas.

11.2   The Ageing Addict

First consider a case of confusing altruism. In the example someone can satisfy someone else's desire rather than their own. But it is not only not clear that it is morally better for the person to do so, it is not even clear how the language of morality can be applied. It is a case that cries out for a more helpful way of speaking.

An ageing heroin addict – actually he is only thirty-five but he looks and feels ninety – is walking with a teenage addict through the park. They both realize that a bag left on a park bench belongs to a neighbourhood pusher and contains enough heroin for the fix that they both desperately need. The older man is a bit nearer but thinks of his minimal life expectancy, thinks how much less his companion is used to the withdrawal symptoms that will affect the one who does not get the fix, shrugs his shoulders, and lets the other get there first.

Is this altruism, of the morally admirable kind? The older man is acting against his own inclination, and from affection for the younger one. He is resolving a conflict of desires by giving precedence to that of another. But the moral significance of this is unclear. He is perpetuating the other's addiction and helping him stay in a hopeless way of life. Suppose that instead he had rushed ahead and taken the heroin, knowing that this might be the fix that was finally fatal for him but that it gave the other a chance of escape from addiction. This action might be seen as morally heroic, although it satisfies his own achingly dominant need to the exclusion of someone else's.

11.3   Silas Marner meets Père Goriot

Here is a different kind of example, pointing to different kind of conclusion. The example combines the plots of two famous novels, each clearly making a quasi-moral point. George Eliot's *Silas Marner* is about an unhappy miser. He is unhappy because his desire to accumulate cash narrows and burdens his life. Contact with a young girl lures him out of his selfconcern and allows him a more satisfying life. (Trite, you may say, but there's obviously a truth here, about the burden of slavery to one's own 'interest'.) Balzac's novel *Le Père Goriot* concerns a different kind of miser. His central concern is not his own wealth but the welfare of his two daughters. He accumulates great capital, deprives himself, and ruins others in pursuit of his obsessive need to provide his daughters with as much wealth as they think they need. Now although père Goriot is clearly not living a good life, Balzac's main point is not that, but rather the harm he does others, the restriction of his moral universe. It is a striking point: blind concern with another's welfare can be as 'immoral' as blind concern with one's own.

Now let us combine the two cases. Imagine a Goriot obsessed with the welfare of his daughters, suffering the weight of his obsession in the way that Silas Marner does. (But this is a modern novel and so it is on insider dealing, pork-belly futures, and selling junk food to famine-striken regions that his wealth is based, and it is cocaine rather than carriages that his daughters 'need'.) And imagine that some person's capacity to inspire real non-obsessive affection in him frees him from this burden. (But to keep it modern this person should be a touchingly unorthodox object of ambiguously sexual interest, perhaps a woman thirty years older than him, or someone whose face he sees in television footage of a famine relief camp.) He is then freed not only to have concern for other people besides his daughters but to have concern for himself. For the first time he can buy himself decent clothes and eat pleasant meals. He becomes a better person as he becomes more self-centred.

Assume that our modern Goriot is a better person after his conversion. And assume that his conversion represents some sort of moral progress.

(Neither of these assumptions follows directly from the story as I have told it, but it would not be hard to fill in details so that they both became pretty hard to deny.) This makes it hard to say that his self-indulgent actions after his conversion are performed out of self-interest in a way that is opposed to morality. Better just to say two related but independent things: first that he used to harm a number of people, including himself, and now does not, and second that he is now a better person leading a better life.

11.4 Two Kinds of Egotist

Alf looks out for number one. Very intelligently and very efficiently: he plans and plots and manoeuvres to get himself what he wants. What he wants is money and power: he hasn't considered wanting anything else. Alf lives in a society of gentle rational cooperative people. Individually they are easy prey and Alf's power grows. Eventually, though, they have had enough and they take action to isolate and contain his activities. The result for Alf is no disaster but stagnation. He still has a lot of money and a fair amount of power, but can accumulate very little more. And that is a dull life, especially when one has no real friends and no other interests.

Brenda also takes care of herself, just as intelligently and efficiently. Brenda's projects, moreover, involve the ruination and sometimes the death of her rivals and opponents. Brenda, however, lives in a society of similar people. Any of them would conspire to ruin or kill a vulnerable fellow-citizen. But there is very little conspiring against Brenda; no one dares. After forty years of struggle and watchfulness Brenda achieves a degree of security and success and can rest somewhat. It is even now hardly a quiet life, but it never becomes dull.

Alf and Brenda are very different. Although their basic character may be very similar, and the character of their acts – scheming, heartless, calculatingly self-centred – may also be similar, the lives they live and the ways we should judge their lives are very different. They are different because of the difference in the societies that surround them. Alf's life is a second-best one: with a wider class of desires and a more cooperative attitude he could have had a better life. 'Better life' can mean many things, of course. Alf will not allow himself even to understand some of them. But many other qualities of a good life would be easily acknowledged by Alf, and absent from his life: cooperative enterprise, satisfied ambition, respect, peace of mind (to name a few). Moreover if there are more than a few Alfs around the society will be held back from developments of benefit to everyone. Brenda's life, on the other hand, is not second best: in her society you can't do better. To put the contrast differently: if you were advising a baby about to be born into Alf's society you would think twice before advising it to imitate Alf, but for a baby about to be born into Brenda's society Brenda should be a model to follow. It would be the best life available.

11.5   Better Distinctions

In each of these cases contrasting morality to prudence or rationality or self-interest is positively unhelpful. It obscures other more illuminating things one can say. For the contrast is really a large number of contrasts rolled into one. Below I run through four different things one can mean by morality-as-opposed-to-self-interest. The most important thing about them is that they are all different. (Another important thing to note about them is that they are not all the things that can be meant by 'morality': how could they be? Rather, they are different senses of morality which are generated by, or correlative with, different ambiguities in 'self-interest'. For the concepts of a person's own interest and that of morality live in reciprocal obscurity, taking in each other's unclarity.)

1   First there is the distinction between satisfying the wants one happens to have and satisfying wants one would be better off having. There are many things that could be included under 'wants one would be better off having', or wants that would be part of a better life. One fairly straightforward class of desires to included are those which would give one more satisfaction that one's present desires. For example the desires some-one now has may involve them in inevitable frustration, and other desires which they could easily have might make a better life. The other desires might be more easily satisfied or satisfied at the expense of fewer compet-ing desires. More satisfaction, more harmony. That is not all that is desir-able in desires, of course. (Or else the perfect life would be to be addicted to some safe and easily obtainable substance, and to want nothing else. Learning or wisdom, as described by some writers, sounds like such a substance. That would indeed be a not bad life, but hardly the perfect one.) But to the extent that someone's desires are unsatisfactory, compared to available alternatives, there is a vague but perfectly intelli-gible sense in which they are wanting the wrong things. They ought to want and do differently: it is in their interest to do so. And according to one school of moral philosophers, stemming from the work of G. R. Grice, the root of morality lies in the distinction between what would satisfy your wants and what is in your interest.[2]

2   There is the distinction between acts which support a coordination

of different people's actions to mutual advantange, and those which do not. People in coordination problems, such as prisoner's dilemmas, can see in terms of their own interests that it would be better to act cooperatively. But very often in the situation before them they have little choice but to act non-cooperatively. (Typically the gains from cooperative and non-cooperative behaviour are often very hard to compare, as I argued in the last chapter, so that it is not at all obvious what they should do.) These dilemmas can be resolved in many ways. One way is by changing the conditions that determine the pay-offs to the interacting people, so that there is no longer an obstacle to rational cooperation. Another is to act in such a way as to set a precedent for future cooperation, even at a cost to oneself. Acts like these are certainly central cases of one common understanding of morality. And again there is a school of recent philosophers, most notably David Gauthier, who see them – acts promoting social cooperation for the good of all – as central examples of the moral.[3]

3 Morality is standardly conceived of as directed at concern with the good of others. This is as ambiguous as the concept of another's good, of course, so it might be subdivided into promoting the satisfaction of others' desires and promoting the quality of their lives. (Your child is a heroin addict. Do you help her to get what she wants or help her to have different wants?) But taken either way there are obviously many circumstances in which what is good for some is not good for others, where there is no common good to be aimed at, but just zero-sum competition. Sometimes, for example, people compete for resources which each need to survive and which cannot support both. (Two drowning swimmers come upon the same small log; two tribes escaping drought come upon the same small patch of grazing land.) The most acute dilemmas presented by these situations arise when there is a range of possible actions, giving different combinations of benefit to a person and to others. (If you can grab the log or drown you don't pause to let someone else take it. But suppose there is a lifeboat and you can keep it all to yourself and be both alive and comfortable, or let others on it and be alive but uncomfortable. Then you have more to think about.) These are moral problems if any are.

4 Motivation is also essential to morality. A very crude construal here is to think of acts as morally acceptable when the motivation behind them is not malicious. By malice I mean something that can be very undramatic, for example very insignificant actions motivated by spite and jealousy, as well as evil actions motivated by hatred or sadism. They are malicious just in that they take harm to someone as an end to be desired in itself. It is important not to underestimate the role this plays in our motivation. for we often deceive ourselves when we think that a harm to someone else is a sad but unavoidable consequence of an action which is, all

things considered, the right thing to do. Often part of the reason why this action is desirable is that it appeals to spite, jealousy, or petty revenge. And the basic human desire for social standing does not have to change very much to develop into a desire for the humiliation of others. At the same time, it is clearly true that malice is not the main force behind most actions of most people. We generally see the welfare of others as something which we want, but whose priority with our own welfare is not a determinate matter.[4]

11.6   The Distinctions Clash

We have here four contrasts between morality and self-interest. The problem is that they are all different. They cut in different directions.

For any two of the contrasts there are situations which link the 'moral' side according to one contrast with the 'non-moral' or merely self-interested side according to the other. Thus in the case of the ageing addict self-interest as getting what you want and self-interest as getting a better life conflict. (As do altruism as getting someone else what they want and altruism as getting someone else a better life.) And the case of Brenda (in 'two kinds of egotist') shows that absence of social coordination is compatible with living a pretty good and satisfying life, or at any rate the most satisfying life available under the circumstances. (Alf combines several anti-moral features: he disregards everything except a small list of benefits to himself, he makes any coordinated social action involving him very difficult, and there's a whiff of evil about him, as it is hard not to suspect that he persists in his life in part because it harms others. Brenda has none of these, but is definitely no altruist.)

An important conflict is that between benevolence and coordination. There are situations in which the most easily available coordination available to a group of people is not the one that is of most potential benefit to them. Suppose, for example, that some people are engaged in a social interaction which offers them two equilibria E1 and E2. (E1 might, let's say, be based on simple and stable property rights while E2 was based on some form of common ownership.) Each of these is a pattern of actions which everyone would be better off conforming to provided that everyone else also conforms. One of them, E1, is the one they actually follow. In the situation in question they usually choose in accordance with E1 and expect others to do likewise. *But* if everyone were to choose E2 rather than E1 consistently then everyone would be better off.

Robert Sugden has argued persuasively that many conventions of social life are like this. His chief example is conventional construals of property rights. Everyone is better off with the status quo than they would be if occasional or even large numbers of people deviated from the norm, but there may well be better equilibria: patterns of action which would also benefit everyone as long as everyone stuck to them, and in which everyone would be more benefited than in the status quo.[5]

What are we to say, in a situation like this, about a lone deviator from the norm, bravely swimming off to another equilibrium, from which he plans to call others to join him? On the one hand he is promoting a situation which is in everyone's interest, perhaps at a cost to himself. But on the other hand he is undercutting a coordination that works, and works for the benefit of all. Such people typically see themselves as prophets of a better morality, and are typically seen by the conventional as immoralists.[6]

Here is a last illustration of the tensions between the moralities. A complete absence of malice may interfere with the maintenance of a convention of coordinated behaviour. For one way, at any rate, in which conventions can be maintained is if individuals adopt 'tit for tat' strategies, according to which someone who deviates from the convention is 'punished' by others with non-cooperation on future occasions. This non-cooperation may sometimes not be in the interest of the others. So in order to motivate it they must either think of themselves as investing in the general social good or, much easier psychologically, be just a bit vindictive, bloody-minded. Knowledge that there are malicious people out there, waiting for an excuse to punish some poor sinner, can go quite a long way towards persuading backsliders to act cooperatively.

11.7 Morality as Conflict Resolution

There is a natural reply to what I have been saying. In all the cases I have been describing people are pulled in different directions by conflicting motives. The conflict of motives is difficult enough in simple cases of self-interest versus other-interest, but in the cases I have described it is made even harder by the fact that self-interest and concern for others have themselves fragmented into different competing motives. Still – according to the objection – that is just the business of morality, to resolve the claims of competing and often incomparable motives. So there *is* a single thing called moral reasoning: it is what we do when we think through a mass of competing and essentially different considerations to decide on a course of action. And all of the moralities described in the last section are particular cases of it.

The objection makes one valid point. It is that there is yet another thing which can be gathered under the umbrella of the moral. And that is the balancing of incompatible, incomparable, and generally imponderable demands on one. The important thing to note about this 'morality', though, is that is has no intrinsic connection with the conflict between one person's interest and that of another. They come into it only inasmuch as that is one among many conflicts that need to be thought out or muddled through. We might as well just call it reason.[7]

Moreover, the general business of resolving and managing dilemmas has some of the formal characteristics which are sometimes ascribed to moral reasoning, taken as a more limited business. This, at any rate, was one of the conclusions of chapter 5 ('The Price of Choice') where I argued that agenda-manipulation strategies capture much of the force of moral prohibitions and moral rights. (So that what is characteristic of the de-ontological is not peculiar to morality in any narrow sense.)

There are three large families of concepts of morality, it seems to me. None of them forms a very tight unity, and there are connections between them, but the contrasts between them are fairly definite. First there is what Rawls calls the good (as opposed to the right), that is, conceptions of what makes a better or a worse life for a particular person. Second there are conceptions of the relation between the actions of an individual and the good of others. This includes conceptions of morality based on the resolution of coordination problems as well as conceptions based on the maximizing of the common good. And third there is the general topic of resolving conflicting desires, obligations, commitments, and the like. We have seen how many different sub-conceptions can be found in each of the first two. And the third is the topic of this book.

11.8   Parochiality and Wickedness

Our culture is marked by its having, and being puzzled by, the concept of morality. If am right some, at any rate, of the puzzles are unreal, for there is not single thing to be puzzled about. There would be, if some actually distinct attributes of action coincided. If, for example, actions that tend to social coordination also tended to good lives for the people involved then two sub-concepts could be combined. And two different sub-concepts, those of morality-as-cooperation and morality as maximizing the common good, would combine if actions which tended to the most salient general good also tended to the maximum public good. (If local and global maxima of public good coincided.) Both of these may be true under some or even many circumstances. But they are certainly not always true.

In a culture which assimilates these different things, two contradictory ideas can easily be prevalent. One is that there must be wonderful satisfying lives waiting for the wicked. For if morality involves restraining one's own desires in the presence of the needs of others then once freed from these restraints one ought to be able to go in for some untrammelled satisfaction. But this ignores two things. First, that a lot of standard wickedness amounts to going against conventions which are in the interest of everyone, including the would-be sinner. And second, that a large proportion of anyone's desires concern the good of others, so that before going in for unrestrained selfishness one would have to change one's wants out of all recognition. (Or, to put the point differently, in order to become a monster of selfishness one would first have to be able to solve the 'ownership of sakes problem': one would have to be able to distinguish things one wanted for one's own sake from those one wanted for the sake of others, so that one could renounce all the latter desires. But for typical human beings the ownership of sakes problem is unsolvable.)

The other prevalent idea is the opposite of the first. It is that the 'good life', the life that reason and reflectiveness would lead one to, must be a life of concern for others. For morality cannot make one lead a bad life and morality is concern with others. But in fact it is extremely unobvious how much concern with others is essential for a fully satisfying life, one guided by reflection and in which on wants what one desires and gets what one wants. Deep and close relations with other people *are* no doubt essential for a fully satisfying life. But it should be clear in the half-starved world that surrounds us that one can have deep and close relations with some people while completely ignoring the needs of far more others. (I don't mean that it is clear that the good life is a life of callousness to the world-in-general. It is not clear at all how the good life and the altruistic life relate.[8])

These contradictory ideas embody incompatible conceptions of the bad, stemming from the conflation of incompatible conceptions of the good. I think that our culture exists in a sort of a superposition of these and other contradictory moral ideas. The deeper roots of this are not at all obvious. Why do we run just these things together and not others? Which are the root conflations and which their effects? I really don't know.[9]

People are neither purely self-interested nor free from evil, and trying to act in coordination with others is the same neither as trying to live a good satisfying life nor as trying to achieve the greatest general good. As a result we cannot classify our decision-making dilemmas into moral and nonmoral. Other classifications may be more helpful but in the end, I think, we should use no simple classification at all. We should recognize only that any person at any time is trying to accomplish many essentially different things, and that there is no automatic way of reconciling or even weighing the demands they make. In short, that we are always surrounded by dilemmas.

12

Moments in Good Lives

If every event which occurred could be given a name, there would be no need for stories.

John Berger

There are many ways in which the thing I am trying in vain to say may be tried in vain to be said.

Samuel Beckett

Imagine a reasonable, well thought out, and unsatisfying life. Someone early in life formulates a general conception of the kind of career and accomplishments he will have. Suppose that it is a plan that requires years of preparation and self-denial. (Perhaps he wants to rise to eminence in an academic field where years of accumulated scholarship count for more than any amount of brilliance.) Years of obedience to his plan follow. 'Details' of life – family, recreations, social relationships – are chosen and managed so as to serve the ultimate end. Finally the end is achieved. (A full professorship at Harvard.) But – as is traditional in such stories – success is disastrous. He does not enjoy his position, feels suddenly that the years of struggle were wasted, and has no idea how to summon an appetite for the rest of his life.

The story does not have to end this way. The struggle may be interesting and the final achievement deeply satisfying. (But that makes the story duller. Perhaps it arouses too much envy.) So I shall not argue that the planned life must be boring, unsatisfying, or shallow. What I shall do is much more modest. I shall try to describe just one of the many attributes that a worthwhile life can have, one which connects both with the experience of the satisfyingness of life and with the dilemma-managing strategies that are the focus of this book. I claim that an extremely unstructured, fragmented, life can have this attribute. And without it a life which successfully fulfils a perfectly reasonable plan can be seriously deficient.

12.1   Plans of Life

Assume that people have both 'simple' and 'patterning' desires. Simple desires are for particular things – cups of coffee, jobs, saving their souls, world peace, getting rich. Patterning desires are for the overall kind of life one lives: one wants not to be such a spineless coffee-addict, one wants to be kind to one's children, one wants not to be the kind of person who gets pushed around by others at work.

One main focus of patterning desires is the content and pattern of one's life, seen as a story or a history extended in time. People often want such things as progression through the stages of a career, or marriages that progress from romance to childrearing to mutual support in old age. And they want their lives to have contained intense experiences, deep relationships with others, and worthwhile accomplishments, at some point in the story. (These wants may seem naive or over-optimistic. But that is the nature of such ideas, always lying just beneath the surface.)

It is standard in recent philosophy to assume that people have both simple and patterning desires. (It is usually thought that many patterning desires centre on second order desires, desires about what one's wants should be. Clearly most of one's desires about what kind of life one wants will have consequences about the kinds of wants one will have. but there will be a lot in them that is not second order, too.) Moreover it is a pretty widely accepted view that there would be something deeply deficient about someone who did not have a complex set of patterning desires, which affected most of the important decisions they made. (Some would use a condition much like this as a criterion for what sort of a creature could be a 'person', something whose interests one must respect and which can be praised or blamed, admired or loathed.)[1]

A life governed by patterning desires is a greater or lesser extent planned. In an extreme case a life might follow a single master plan. (Like an ideal socialist economy.) The most definite and authoritative description of the planned life is by John Rawls:

We are to suppose that each individual has a rational plan of life drawn up subject to the conditions that confront him. This plan is designed to permit the harmonious satisfaction of his interests. It schedules activities so that various desires can be fulfilled without interference. it is arrived at by rejecting other plans that are either less likely to succeed or do not provide for such an inclusive attainment of aims. Given the alternatives available, a rational plan is one that cannot be improved upon; there is no other plan which, taking everything into account, would be preferable.[2]

Rawls adds some qualifications to avoid the impression of a life compulsively planned in advance:

> A plan, then, is made up of subplans suitably arranged in a hierarchy, the broad features of the plans allowing for the more permanent aims and interests that complement one another. Since only the outlines of these aims and interests can be foreseen, the operative parts of the subplans that provide for them are finally decided upon independently as we go along.

Still, it is conformity to a plan that makes a good life. Rawls goes on to say:

> Revisions and changes at the lower levels do not usually reverberate through the entire structure. If this conception of plans is sound, we should expect that the good things in life are, roughly speaking, those activities and relationships which have a major place in rational plans.

The planned life is for Rawls not only the norm for a human life; it is, as the last quotation suggests, the source of value in life:

> Indeed, with certain qualifications we can think of a person as being happy when he is in the way of a successful execution (more or less) of a rational plan of life drawn up under (more or less) favorable conditions, and he is reasonably confident that his plan can be carried through.

It does not really matter that our lives are in fact much less organized than this. It is, after all, meant as ideal. Nor does it matter too much that the general ideal could be satisfied in ways rather different from those Rawls is considering. (For example a life might be organized by a 'third order' intention to have a plan of a certain kind, which a person could struggle towards formulating during their life even if they never managed to arrive at a particular plan, let alone carrying it out.) What does matter much more is that Rawls is insisting that in a worthwhile life there should be some sort of harmony between individual decisions and overall patterning desires. And the important questions to ask are: How central a value is this? Could there be a worthwhile life without it?[3]

Several of the dilemma-managing strategies I have discussed earlier in this book link choices to the overall pattern of the decision-maker's life. For example the rain-check strategy of chapter 2 required one to take that option which could least easily be satisfied indirectly during the rest of one's life. It is an instance of what in chapter 4 I called a shifting strategy, for it shifts decision-making attention from the immediate available options to longer-term patterns of which they could form parts. Other shifting strategies will often have the same effect of liking an immediate decision to a choice of possible longer stretches of life. And the revaluing strategy of chapter 3 required one to find those values which make most sense of the choices one had made in the past and which minimize the need for delicate compromises in the future.

All of these strategies resolve dilemmas by relating the incomparable desires that produce them to more nearly comparable preferences for kinds of lives. (The direction of fit can go either way. One can either choose an action so as to conform to some aspect of what one has decided is to be one's life, or choose some aspect of one's life to fit the decision one is now making.) These strategies could be crudely summarized as: take the option which will give you the better life. Or rather, they could be summarized this way *if* one accepts that lives are good when they conform to plans.

So you might expect me to be defending Rawls' position. And in a way I am: I am convinced that moment-to-moment decision making can only be made sense of by relating the question to be decided at the moment to larger patterns in time. And a whole human life is one such larger pattern. But that is not to say either that human lives are the only things that can give this patterning, or that the good life has to be the planned and unified life.

12.2 Temporal Framing

Accept that a person's wants and choices have to be made with reference to the past and the future, if they are to part of anything more than a moment-to-moment animal existence. But to change the focus slightly, let me ask now why it is that connections with the past, the future, and the long term are often among the things we care most deeply about. Some examples.

Imagine the father in chapter 1 whose handicapped daughter finds in music her road to progress. Imagine him watching her at a concert, as she plays a solo. Perhaps the music is good and he enjoys it, and perhaps her sense of accomplishment communicates itself to him. But neither of these compares with his joy at seeing months of labour bear fruit and his hope that his daughter's future may now fall into place. That joy relates to his past, but also to her future.

Imagine you are a research scientist who makes a conjecture in your first published work which is unanimously derided by the scientific establishment. You recover your reputation with twenty years' orthodox and acclaimed work. Then a PhD dissertation, written under the supervision of the professor, about to retire, who most roundly condemned your earlier work, uses new techniques to confirm that you were right all along. But you were wrong in one respect: the fact that has now been established is of very little scientific importance. You would experience both the satisfaction of seeing your past self vindicated and the frustration of knowing that your past efforts will not be linked to anyone's future work.

Lastly, imagine a young idealist growing up in a repressive society. He is enough of a realist to realize that the revolutionary ambitions of many of his contemporaries are not going to succeed. And so he dissociates himself from their activities, though he shares their abhorrence of the regime. In fact after an unsuccessful uprising he denounces some of his friends, who were to have been shot anyway, in order to make clear his suitability for a government position. His aim then and during his subsequent rise in the official hierarchy is to burrow his way to a position of authority, and then begin the program me of reform that he has been secretly committed to. His chance comes during his late forties, when his is appointed interior minister. Then, when he is about to put in motion a stealthy plan which will eventually disband the secret police and release political prisoners, he learns that he has lung cancer. On his death bed he wishes that he had died with the friends that he betrayed twenty-five years before.

All of these stories are centred on a family of emotions , in a way a family of pleasures and pains, in which we accept or reject our lives in the light of how our present situations realize past ambitions and lead to future possibilities. There are many such emotions.[4] Our vocabulary for describing them seems particularly rich in negative attitudes to the past: we speak of regret, remorse, shame, guilt, and embarrassment. And it is rich in positive attitudes to the future: hope, desire, yearning, expectation. As for attitudes to the present, we have a wealth of both positive and negative: we can speak for example both of satisfaction and delight and of frustration and disappointment. Stories which focus on these emotions show us that satisfactory ways of resolving dilemmas are not merely intellectually acceptable procedures for maximizing one or another quantity: they should actually lead to situations in which we can appreciate the present, as a resting point between ambitions and possibilities.

One can appreciate the present from different perspectives: one can not regret the past that leads to it, or find it satisfying as a present experience, or be buoyed by hope for a future. My interest is in the present perspective on the present: satisfaction. Inasmuch as satisfaction is a attitude to one's life and not just a kind of pleasant experience its source is a particular class of relations between a momentary experience and a long-term history. I think the way we should think of these relations is as follows. A person has desires about the evolution of some thing or process: the obvious example is the person's own life. Let me call these patterning desires, although the person's own life is not the only object they can have. And a person also has moment-to-moment pleasant experiences. The type of satisfaction that is important here occurs when the patterning desires are what make the momentary experiences pleasant. (Or more subtly, when the richness or character of the pleasure comes from the presence of the patterning desires.) Let me call this *temporal framing*, because the significance of a moment is gained by framing it in a larger-scale temporal pattern. (As a scene can become beautiful when we see it as a pattern within a real or imagined frame, or as a chord becomes interesting because we hear it as a way from one key to another.) The framing has two sides. The present is satisfying because it represents the satisfaction of past desires and because it embodies hope for the satisfaction of other, related, desires in the future.

That is the ideal case, at any rate. I think that temporal framing is deeply connected to what gives the sense that one's life is all right and to what one loses when that sense becomes unattainable. And I would argue for this if I knew how.[5] Certainly temporally framed satisfaction does not come just because one has got what one has always wanted. The man in the story which began the chapter for example: he gets what he has wanted and no doubt still values it – he wouldn't throw it away – but he doesn't like (in a way doesn't want) the present experience of getting it. And, the other way round, enjoying a present moment is certainly not enough: it can have the hollowness of mere enjoyment if there is no fitting with past and future. So you might well suspect that temporal framing is at least an important part of any life that a real person would actually appreciate living. But I shall not argue for anything so grand.

Instead I shall argue for something much more modest, that desires about the pattern of one's own life are not the only ones which can go into temporally framing a satisfying present. That is not a completely toothless conclusion, however. For it allows me to claim that some kinds of quite extreme disunity can be found in satisfying lives. A life that is very unplanned can have some basic kinds of value.

12.3 Objects of Identification

Your own life is one of the things you can use to frame your choices and experiences. But it is far from being the only one. You can have the same deep and experience-shaping involvement in the long-term career of many more things. I am not sure there is any purely logical restriction on the range of possible frames.[6] But here is one natural class of them. These are based on a pattern of acts and intentions by one or more people – people-at-particular-times I should say, anticipating what follows – which are concerned with the development of some object. The object can be anything that can have a long-term career. For example: the lives of a particular group of people (perhaps the people whose acts and intentions are at issue), the future of a country, the flourishing of a species, the progress of an artistic or scientific tradition, the health of a social institution, life on earth. All of these are objects of concern to individuals and groups. And for all of these, individuals can put their own actions and intentions among those of others, to produce a complex history which can frame their moment-to-moment experiences.

Consider a life lived for a cause. Someone early in life becomes committed to racial equality. At various times in the subsequent thirty years he finds that he is working for the anti-apartheid movement, for a campaign to reform the immigration laws of his country, and for a consultancy advising companies and government departments on ways of reducing bias in their recruitment and promotions procedures. Most of the ambitions he has are for the success of these projects. Very few of the ambitions are achieved. But there are occasional successes. And these successes give him the satisfaction that allows him to continue.

Consider now a moment of satisfaction, in which a minor victory against racism is savoured because it has been struggled for for so long and because it points the way to other tiny steps forward. The satisfaction is just as great, we may suppose, if the struggle behind that particular action consists largely of the actions of others, or if the further steps that are now possible will be taken by others So the sense that the person has that this is a moment to be savoured, which gives a sense of worth to the life it is part of, does not require that the past and future actions be those of that person's life.

But the victory of the moment is still a satisfaction of that person's desire. And to that extent is might seem that though one's satisfactions can be framed by the action of others they have to consist in the satisfaction of one's own desires. Rather than retell the story so as to show how this need not be so, let me tell a different story.

Someone is a member of a closely knit extended family. She and her family are Vietnamese boat people who, as the story begins, are living in appalling camps in Hong Kong. There are family ambitions, first of all to escape from poverty and to make a life together somewhere. She manages to get a visa to go to Canada, and then she and some distant cousins are able to help the rest of the family to reunite in Toronto. Montreal is too cold for the older generation and so her limited command of French is not much use, and her English never becomes very good. An uncle helps her find work in a restaurant and she then contributes to the education of the younger member of the family. One of her younger cousins combines a degree in electronic engineering with a shrewd financial sense in founding a company which sells the skill of linking networks of microcomputers to gain the power of mainframes. He becomes very rich, so they are all quite well off. They are able to ransom three grandparents who had been abandoned in Hanoi. (Little does she know that the family has implanted itself in a strongly individualistic culture, so that their grandchildren will think of all this clannishness as an embarrassing foreign trait.)

This is a good life. But its satisfactions are based on actions of other people and very often framed by ambitions of other people. The only thing that is unequivocally hers is the satisfaction; everything else is part of an inseparable mixture of the actions and intentions of a dozen people. In particular, she will find satisfying accomplishments whose nature she does not understand well enough to have coherent wants for them: for example, she will rejoice at her cousin's winning relief from an arcane piece of Canadian corporation tax law. What she rejoices at is that someone who is part of the project that structures her life has got something that they wanted as part of the project. The want need be no more specific than that.

The point I want to make about this last life can be put in a very general way. The satisfaction that the person gets from her family's accomplishments comes from a patterning desire: that her family flourish. (This isn't quite the same as a desire that people in her family get what they want. It is a desire that they get what they want when getting it would be part of the flourishing of the family. And no doubt her tradition gives her a picture of what that consists in.) She will try to see that the ambitions of others are accomplished, and they will try to see that hers are. Moreover, many of the plans that the family shares will not be for particular people to do particular things, but for particular things to be done. Inasmuch as they all think of themselves as part of a larger family unit, they do not care particularly who it is who does what, as long as the family interests are advanced. And when these interests are advanced, each person's satisfaction – the satisfaction at that moment in that person – will be framed between the ambitions of the family and the future that opens for them.

Many things besides individual people have long-term histories, about which we can care. And whenever we can care about something that has a development in time our actions and experiences can be framed temporally by our plans for it. Moreover the framing need not be in terms of things that one wants to do oneself or to have happen in one's own life: it can be just in terms of things that one wanted to be done or have happen, as long as one's past history and one's present experience form part of some larger pattern. (Presumably there are as many ways in which this can happen as there are larger patterns.) So a life without an intrinsic structure can form part of something that does have a structure. Indeed it can be an essential part of such a structure. And this can serve the function that a plan of life would serve in a individually organized life. Perhaps it can serve it better.

(But are these not artificial and parasitic ways of giving meaning to the moments of a life, which we would not see the point of unless we had the idea of an individual life whose satisfaction derives from its individual coherence? I suspect that historically things are the other way around: in most cultures most momentary satisfactions have been framed by the histories and ambitions of groups, and the idea of a single person's life as an object of planning is a development of recent times.)

12.4   Fragmented Lives

I have been arguing that the sense of the satisfyingness of one's life need not come from any plan or pattern to it. Still, in all my examples the life in question has had a single direction. It has been organized by its connection with a single object of concern. I think we can get even further from the idea of a life governed by a plan, and still have individual moments framed by attitudes to larger histories. A good and satisfying life can have even less unity; in particular it need not be structured by a focus on any single object of concern. Again it is easiest to begin with an example.

Imagine someone, Polly, moved by intense and well thought out enthusiasms. (A bit like Rupert of the first chapter, perhaps, but less impulsive.) Possessing no dominant motive in life she earns her living as an accountant with a large accounting firm. But finding this unsatisfying, as it seems not to lead anywhere except up an unappealing career ladder, she quits after five years, and works for Friends of the Earth. At first she organizes publicity against industrial polluters, but then finds that her skills as an accountant can be used by the ecological movement. She specializes in digging uncomfortable facts out of the public and sometimes not-so-public records of large companies. During this time she marries another ecological campaigner. Each says that they could not live with anyone not totally committed to the cause. Her husband develops muscular dystrophy. Polly finds, to her surprise, that she is quite happy to reduce her work for FOE in order to give him more practical help. After a few years she finds that taking care of her now severely handicapped husband is occupying nearly all of her time. So she becomes the most efficient support person possible. And since their life now is centred on their home they have two children. Shortly after the birth of the second child her husband dies, and Polly finds herself a single parent. For the next dozen years her life centres on taking care of her children. (She finds a firm of accountants that will employ her part-time, allowing her to meet her children every day after school) When the children are in their teens she decides to get back to work that interests her. A stray conversation with a friend leads her into work for international disarmament, and she becomes the office manager of an organization of scientists working to pressure politicians into reasonable views of their national interests. This occupies the next ten years of her life. And so on.

There are many admirable people like Polly: Capable and energetic people who bear the world on their shoulders. (There would be something impudent about a philosophy that dismissed their lives for want of structure.) Very often their lives, like Polly's, are not focused on a single dominant object of concern, and are not held together by any plan uniting their different successive and parallel concerns. In fact, the patchwork of their lives is often even more fragmented than Polly's. For we can combine a Polly story and a boat person story to describe a life which at each stage is focused on a joint enterprise with others, but in which not only are the individual's ambitions and activities inseparable from those of others, but there is no single group of others throughout the individual's life. (But a description of such a life would have to be like a real and detailed biography rather than a one-paragraph story.)

In fact even more fragmentation is perfectly intelligible. The groups and their concerns may overlap, so that not even in a brief period of the individual's life is there just one set of other people whose shared concerns frame the person's experience. No individual plan, no single shared plan, no shared plan that lasts for long. And while this may be an extreme of fragmentation, it is truer to the lives of most people – most people who enjoy their lives – than the ideal of a single individually tailored unifying plan of life.

12.5 Parfit

The fragmentation of a life into its many episodes is a theme of one of the most influential of recent works in philosophy, Derek Parfit's *Reasons and Persons*. Rawls' conclusions and Parfit's are generally incompatible, but on the question of valuing individual lives I think we can have both Rawls' insight, in my distillation of it, and Parfit's.

The central image of Parfit's work is that of a very loose relation of connectedness between the different stages of person's life. The looseness of the connection, its fragility, is essential. What is connected are persons-at-a-time. We can call them person-stages, a term Parfit seems to avoid, as long as we are clear that a person-stage is not a person, and that a person-stage lasts for more than an instant:[7] for example you on your thirteenth birthday, or you during your twenties. The minimum person-stage would be a person during the smallest span of time over which it makes sense to attribute states of mind. (It is pretty clear that one cannot identify someone's emotions and beliefs during a millisecond. What is he smallest span during which it makes sense to attribute these things? Twenty seconds? An hour?) For Parfit whole persons are not morally significant: benefits to a person are benefits to some or all of the person-stages, and moral principles should be formulated in terms of benefits and harms to person-stages and relations of continuity between them. (Including the continuity relations which add up to full personal identity.)

As Parfit says:

> It becomes more plausible, when thinking morally, to focus less upon the person, the subject of experiences, and instead to focus more upon the experiences themselves. It becomes more plausible to claim that, just as we are right to ignore whether people come from the same or different nations, we are right to ignore whether experiences come within the same or different lives.
>
> Consider the relief of suffering. Suppose that we can help only one of two people. We shall achieve more if we help the first; but it is the second who, in the past, suffered more. Those who believe in equality may decide to help the second person. This will be less effective; so the mount of suffering in the two people's lives will, in sum, be greater; but the amounts in each life will be made more equal. If we accept [Parfit's] View, we may decide otherwise. We may decide to do the most we can to relieve suffering.[8]

If this view is extended to the value of individual lives it runs into problems. It seems to suggest that we should not think of whole lives being better or worse. We should instead evaluate particular experiences. But of course the value of many experiences consists just in their connections with earlier and later states of the person. So if we apply this point of view to evaluating the quality of people's lives, there is some danger that it will collapse into a clumsy hedonism.

Perhaps because of this, when in an appendix to the book Parfit discusses 'What Makes Someone's Life Go Best', he takes rather a different line. There he treats the values of whole lives rather than of isolated experiences within them. He does not endorse any conception of the good in a life, but two views emerge from the discussion as particularly attractive. The first is the 'Global Success' view. According to it a life goes well when the person's desires about the pattern of their life over a period of time are satisfied. The other is the 'Objective List Hedonism' view. According to it, a life goes well when, or to the extent that, the person is achieving a fixed list of the good things in life (love, knowledge, family life,) and is enjoying achieving them.[9]

There might seem to be a contradiction between these views of a life's going well and Parfit's scepticism about the moral importance of whole lives. For to say that there is a scale of better and worse whole lives might seem to make whole lives into moral units. And he denies that whole lives are morally important units. But the contradiction is only apparent. For the characteristics of a good life, on either of Parfit's favoured views, are stable under reduction to limited stretches of a person's life. That is, they can be applied just as well to saying why someone's thirteenth year went well or their fifth decade was a disaster as to saying why their whole life was good or disatrous. Either a year or a decade can have, or lack, the satisfaction of desires about the pattern it takes, and a year or a decade can have or lack enjoyable attainments from any list of the central goods of life.

There is a very important point here. A small part of a life can go well or badly because of desires which are formed, satisfied, or frustrated in it and which concern the pattern of a much larger section of life. Your fifth decade may be a bad time because during it you realize that your life-long expectation that eventually you would be loved for your character and respected for your accomplishments will never be fulfilled. Then what makes these ten years bad is the failure, during them, of plans which you have had for decades before and which concern the content of subsequent decades. Beliefs and desires which are held and satisfied during a short span of time may concern much larger spans.

The point can be strengthened. If a short part of a life can go well because of desires about larger parts of that life, then too it can go well because of desires about larger parts of other lives, or larger parts of other long-term things, or because of its connections with other people's desires about other long-term things. Remember the examples of the boat person and of Polly: their lives were surely not uniformly good, but those parts of them which went well did so because they represented the satisfaction of ambitions not for their own lives but for other projects, other histories.

Put this way, Parfit's fragmentation of life into sub-lives can be combined with Rawls' conception of the good life as governed by a plan. This means a pretty large redrafting of Rawls' idea though: instead of a plan of one's own life one has a collection of plans of a collection of histories, each of which contain parts of one's own life and parts of others'. And then a part of one's life goes well if it satisfies its plan as formulated in the past and opens up ways for the plan to be fulfilled in the future. But different parts of a life go well or ill according to different plans. Perhaps in a really fragmented life different moments go well or ill according to completely unrelated plans.

It is interesting that when we break the evaluative link between a part of someone's life and the whole of that life we make other links possible, between a part of someone's life and parts of other people's lives. Deeply united communities of fragmented people are more easily imagined that deeply united communities of individuals each focused on their own career. This makes it seem as if a dose of Parfitian disintegration radically changes a Rawlsian picture of the good. But it is also important to see how this liberalization brings out the important point on which both Rawls and Parfit agree: that the good in life is a matter of the satisfaction at particular moments of plans conceived at particular moments but concerning patterns of accomplishment over longer stretches of time. Or, as I put it, temporal framing.

12.6   Platonic Existentialism

I must retreat slightly. I am claiming to describe just one aspect of life's going well: the savour of a moment as framed by a history. And yet Rawls' and Parfit's larger ambitions are luring me into discussing the Good Life in general. And I have a book to finish, so the temptation to overstatement is strong.

If a life has many moments of satisfaction – in which the person gets, and moreover appreciates getting, something important as part of a project such as their own life or some other larger history – then it goes well in that respect. It can go badly in other respects. And there is no easy weighting of the different ways in which it can go well or badly. For there are inevitably incomparabilities here, too.

Three kinds of incomparable factors are worth mentioning. First there is desire-satisfaction, the extent to which you get what you want. (Like Parfit and others I assume that pleasure, inasmuch as it is relevant to judging a life, is a kind of desire-satisfaction.) Then there is plan-satisfaction, the extent to which your life fits into a larger history. (The right kind of larger history. But I have said enough about that.) Then, third, there is temporal framing, the extent to which plan-satisfaction is an experienced feature of life. None of these need coincide. A stretch of life in which plans are made which are not satisfied until much later, perhaps after the person's death, exhibits plan-satisfaction and desire-satisfaction without temporal framing. An unplanned but hedonistically successful life exhibits desire-satisfaction but not plan-satisfaction. And so on. Moreover, it can be hard to compare lives in terms of even just one of these factors, especially when (for example) one of the lives to be compared has few ups and downs and the other exhibits extremes of success and failure.

So very often one life cannot be said to be better or worse than another. But, equally often, one life is objectively better than another. To give the standard examples, the typical life of a brutalized slave is much worse than that of rich European male intellectual in the years just before the First World War. And, more to the point, of the lives open to a person at any moment in their life, some are clearly better than others. They win on all scores. And some are better than others in that a reasonable strategy for overcoming the incomparabilities between them (for example 'the sieve' of chapter 5) will cause them to be chosen.[10]

(Shifting strategies and revaluing strategies, as I have described them in earlier chapters, have tended for focus decisions on the desirability of the whole lives that they might be part of. Chapter 10, on Coordination Problems, is a partial exception. It should be clear from this chapter, though, that the decision-maker's whole life is just one among many larger structures which can do the job.)

This may seem to give a lot of objectivity to a matter of value. It does. But many other things can remain far short of objectivity. Most importantly, there can be very little in the way of single objective answer to the question what a particular person should do in a particular situation.

So the generally existentialist temper of our times is in part right. There are usually many things you can reasonably do, and the choice is usually largely up to you. But you can't choose just anything. Some things are stupid. Why? Because there is no good life, nor any other desirable larger structure, that they can be part of. In particular, we can compare lives in terms of the satisfaction they afford – the desires whose satisfaction can be framed by plans the person can reasonably form. And this is a much more determinate matter. Many lives are more satisfying than many others. And this is an objective fact. Though its instances are infinitely varied, there is a form of the good life.[11]

Which are the best forms of life? What dilemma-managing strategies, what conceptualizations of strategic advantage, what assimilations of stages in individuals' lives to larger social projects will lead to the most satisfying lives? We don't know. (Though we can certainly eliminate some candidates.) Different strategies, conceptualizations, and assimilations mark different societies. I believe they provide a very profound characterization of a culture, of what it is like to be a member of it. And inasmuch as I think that there are better and worse lives, I must think that there are actual and possible cultures which point the way to better lives more clearly than others. Which are they? That knowledge can be gained, I fear, only by painful experience.

UNIVERSITY OF BRISTOL

Department of Philosophy

9 Woodland Road
Bristol
BS8 1TB

Notes

INTRODUCTION

1   This is a good point to acknowledge some books that are closely related to this one. The closest connection of ideas is with Isaac Levi (see Levi 1986). It was not until I was working on the final draft that I came back to Levi, having put it aside earlier to read when I had more time, and realized that his project is very close to mine. Jon Elster's earlier work (see Elster 1979 and 1983) expresses a scepticism about simple utility maximization as a solution to real-life problems. And sometimes he diagnoses the difficulty as I would, in terms of how to find the right place for maximization in the complex decision-making process. (I think that is a fair description of the atmosphere of chapter 2 of Elster 1979.) But on the other hand large parts of both books are about the explanation of action rather than about how we should make decisions, and seem to be searching for a replacement for maximization as a descriptive-explanatory tool. (I think he could use the distinction I make in the 'General Picture' section of chapter 4, between setting-up procedures and decision-rules.)

I should also mention some works that I am convinced have important connections with my project, but where the connections have eluded me. Two such works are Arrow and Raynaud 1986, and Keeney and Raiffa 1976. These are dealing with solutions to very similar problems to those I apply my account to, and run into some of the same problems. I am sure that if I understood them well enough I could find in them refutations or improvements of my attempts. The papers on 'muddling through' in Lindblom 1988 seem generally on my wavelength, but don't go into much detail.

The last work to mention is one that complements this one, giving the subtlest and most powerful account of rationality and value yet produced from within a generally maximizing perspective. That is John Broome's forthcoming *Weighing Goods*.

CHAPTER 1   PATTERNS OF DESIRE

1   Talk of trumps in this context comes from Ronald Dworkin. (see Dworkin
    1977). For Dworkin moral and political rights are trumps. It has been
    objected to me that qualified trumps aren't really trumps if they do not over-
    come all competition. But then rights don't always trump either. And the ace
    of trumps beats the king. I pick up the idea that decision making is subject to
    shifts of perspective from Edward McClennen's rather different use of the
    idea (see McClennen 1985). McClennen does not make the connection
    with remorse, or more generally with temporal perspective shifts in moral
    dilemmas, but I think it is fair to say that it is implicit in his work.
2   For more on decision making with preferences that do not fall into a linear
    ordering see the introduction and chapter 6 of Sen 1982.
3   Philosophers take second order desires very seriously largely because of
    the work of Harry Frankfurt. See Frankfurt 1971, and also Jeffrey 1974
    (reprinted as an appendix to Jeffrey 1985.) Note that in my examples the
    immediate conflict may be between first order desires and consequences of
    second order desires. So a more subtle diagnosis of the conflict is that it is
    one that the person would not have had if they did not have the second order
    desires that they do.
4   Thus nearly all real decisions involve some degree of what Herbert Simon
    calls 'satisficing' (see also sections 3.5 and 4.3) (See Simon 1982, or the very
    readable Simon 1983; see also chapter 8 of Hollis 1987.) One of the few
    attempts I know to connect Simon's ideas with moral philosophy has been
    made by Michael Slote (see Slote 1985).

CHAPTER 2   DILEMMA-MANAGEMENT: EASY CASES

1   Paula Boddington suggests an eighth course of action: go to the film and
    sleep through it.
2   This sort of argument stems from the work of Kenneth Arrow: see Arrow
    1963 and, for a nice exposition, Blair and Pollak 1983. In this case a con-
    dition from social choice theory, that of the 'independence of irrelevant
    alternatives', applies interestingly to one person's choices. I had thought of
    making 'one person social choice theory' the theme of a more technical book
    to follow up this one. But Susan Hurley seems to have got there first (see
    Hurley 1989).

CHAPTER 3   INCOMPARABILITIES

1   James Griffin almost denies that the values by which we evaluate individual
    lives are incomparable (see Griffin 1986). But what he really means is (a) per-
    fectly sensible decisions are possible in situations where apparent
    incomparables conflict, and (b) incomparability is rarely of the extreme kind

where there is no relation at all between the values. Thus I suspect Griffin would be happy with my diamond-shaped and zig-zag-shaped patterns of incomparability. Incomparability is made trivially impossible by analyses of preference in terms of 'revealed preferences' according to which to choose A over B is always to prefer A to B, and to be unable to choose between A and B is always to be indifferent between them. Such theories must allow that people change their preferences with great rapidity, since a person for whom A is incomparable to both B and C, which the person is not indifferent between, will often give the appearance of ranking A with B on one occasion and A with C a moment later.

2   See chapter 13 of Raz 1986 for a discussion of incomparable political values.

3   Preferences thus fall into a partial ordering. Expositions of the theory of partial orderings are found in decision theory texts but the clearest treatments are in undergraduate algebra books, for example Birkhoff and MacLane 1979. For a thorough discussion of some of the consequences of using partial orderings see Herzberger 1973.

4   These preferences are not representable by partial orderings. That is, the person's preferences correspond to a *set* of partial orderings. These are unified by their conformity to a single 'hypercomparative' preference relation' a is preferred to b by more than c is preferred to d'.

5   Shifting horizons on diamond-shaped preferences are sets of diamond-shaped preferences, differing in the extent of the incomparability exhibited. A simple example over six outcomes is the set of two orderings, the partial orderings generated by extending by transitivity the two lists below:

(a,b), (b,d), (d,f), (a,c), (c,e), (e,f)

and

(a,b), (b,d), (d,f), (a,c), (c,e), (e,f), (b,e), (c,d)

6   See Jeffrey 1987, Raiffa 1968.

7   For more on these issues see chapter 5 of John Broome's *Weighing Goods*, forthcoming, and chapter 5 of Hurley 1989.

8   Superia might seem just to need enormous speed and memory. But in fact it is doubtful that she could be simulated by a Turing machine. See Osherson et al. 1988, and Maung and Paris (unpublished). See also Paris and Vencovska 1990.

9   A similar view has been defended by Philip Pettit (see Pettit, forthcoming). Pettit's view is not quite the same as mine because he seems to be describing two kinds of preference relation, each of which could be a sufficient basis for decision. See also David Milligan's discussion of 'feature wants' in chapter 3 of Milligan 1980.

10   Do standard decision theorists assume the ultimate descriptions model? Richard Jeffrey certainly seems to suppose that desirability is defined over all propositions expressible in a person's language, and that is almost enough,

since that will nearly always include propositions one cannot grasp. But he is not explicit on the point. (See chapter 4 of Jeffrey 1985.) In other writers a more complex ontology of actions and states of nature makes it even harder to see what they think. But inasmuch as agents are supposed to have utility functions that remain unaltered during deliberation, and inasmuch as changes of belief are usually taken to produce changes of desire in the way the model suggests, something near to the model seems always tacitly assumed. (See also note 3 to chapter 6.) One also approaches the model to the extent to which one handles risk-aversion in the way Jeffrey and Broome do: see Jeffrey 1987 and chapter 5 of Broome (forthcoming).

11 For a rather diffuse discussion of the elasticity of desire see chapter 5 of Morton 1980. (The term there is 'plasticity of desire', referring to a rather more general phenomenon.) There I make connections with Freud's account of motivation.

12 Revaluing means abandoning some values and thus living what might be called an incomplete life. Stuart Hampshire, in chapter 4 of Hampshire 1989, argues eloquently for the reasonableness of choosing an incomplete life. His argument is in effect an attack on the authority of compromise in these matters.

CHAPTER 4   GOOD STRATEGIES, GOOD DECISIONS

1 See Jeffrey 1985, chapter 1 (where a partition is referred to as a set of conditions). Gibbard and Harper (1978) bring out clearly how carefully one must state one's definition of a partition. I have evaded the issues they raise, wanting to stay clear of the issues about causal decision theory.

2 See Raiffa 1968, chapter 2 (where a partition is a set of ultimate nodes of a decision-tree).

3 For example a more cautious condition might be: given most sets of options the shifting partition provides an ordering of options that differs from the orderings provided by initial segments of the two original partitions roughly in proportion to the extent that they differ from each other. Note the signs of vagueness – 'most', 'initial segment', 'roughly'. Note also that this definition is more general as well as more cautious than the definition in the text.

4 Compare John Stuart Mill: 'The principle of utility does not mean that any given pleasure, as music for instance, or any given exemption from pain as for example health, are to be looked upon as a means to a collective something termed happiness ... They are desired and desirable in and for themselves; besides being means, they are a part of the end. Virtue, according to the utilitarian doctrine, is not naturally and originally part of the end, but it is capable of becoming so, and in those who love it disinterestedly it has become so, and is desired and cherished, not as a means to happiness, but as a part of their happiness.' (Mill 1885, chapter 4.)

5 Note that this definition is problematic if applied to people whose beliefs are too drastically false, so that thoughts about what would have been the case

had they been true become too tangled. Decision theorists usually think of people as having beliefs amounting to a probability distribution over events involving real properties of real things. If people believe in unicorns and the magical power of innocence then the whole apparatus fails to apply.

6   It is tempting to take this as an expectation, so that one strategy is better than another if its expected utility is greater, taking utility from the person's desires and probability from the world. But there won't always be enough objective probabilities to make this well defined. If we do adopt this reading, and run together setting-up and decision-rule, we get essentially Hugh Mellor's suggestion in Mellor 1983.

7   The question is hardly intelligible because it requires a probability distribution over objective probabilities. Something like this would be needed if one were to give an argument for what many people assert unreflectively, that utility maximization will give on average better results than other decision-making procedures. I am not sure that the idea is in general even intelligible. But for a defence of some special cases see chapter 4 of Skyrms 1984.

8   See Gibbard 1986 for a sophisticated yet commonsensical defence of interpersonal utility comparisons.

9   The foremost defender of conservatism as a principle of belief change is Gilbert Harman. See chapters 4 and 5 of Harman 1986.

CHAPTER 5   THE PRICE OF CHOICE

1   I intend this example to be read more as an 'Ellsberg case' than as an 'Allais case'. That is, Prudence's hesitation is to be ascribed mainly to a sense that the probabilities reflect imperfect information rather than objective chances.

2   This example is adapted from Thomas Nagel: see section 4 of chapter 9 of Nagel 1986.

3   The sieve tends in the direction of minimax reasoning, to the extent that the criteria for rejecting options on early passes depends on their worst possible outcomes. It has a closer relation to gamma-minimax (see Gärdenfors and Sahlin 1982, and 7.7 of Levi 1986). This is a rule for choosing an option on the basis of a collection of probability assignments. It says to associate with each option the lowest expected utility that any probability assignment in the collection gives it, and then to accept the option for which the expected utility as thus defined is highest. This sieve gives the same results as this in the special case in which there is more than one estimate of probability and the evaluation of options at early passes is done by expected utility calculation. The sieve also resembles procedures such as satisficing in which the full consequences of the options are not explored (see Simon 1982, 1983) in that the criteria used to evaluate options on earlier passes may not require a full estimate of their desirability. For example, options might be admitted to the shortlist as long as there is an element of some partition, with probability above some threshold, whose utility given the adoption of the option is above

some threshold. (And similarly for rejection.) In fact gamma-minimax style reasoning and and satisficing style reasoning fit together very naturally in a procedure like the sieve, because the preliminary rejection of options can work by worst-case criteria (and retention by best-case) although the options on the shortlist are evaluated by something nearer to a full exact calculation. It is interesting to see considerations of risk and considerations of human boundedness fitting together like this.

4   Paradoxes like this stem ultimately from Arrow 1963. See also 4.2 and 5.2 of Levi 1986, sections 2, 3 and 4 of chapter 12 of Hurley 1989, and Scriven 1981.

5   See Thomson 1977.

CHAPTER 6   RISK: MORE QUESTIONS THAN ANSWERS

1   Risk-aversion is a pervasive feature of human psychology: see Kahneman and Tversky 1979. The 'caste-by-lottery' example was suggested by the role risk-aversion plays in John Rawls' justification of his principles of justice (see Rawls 1975).

2   For an exposition of minimax reasoning see chapter 4 of Luce and Raiffa 1957. And for expected utility reasoning see chapter 1 of Jeffrey 1985.

3   This is a very weak formulation. It claims that for every agent and every decision problem there is a suitable utility function. Most exponents of the theory would turn the quantifiers around, to say something much stronger: for every agent there is a utility function which is suitable for every decision problem. (But see 11.6 of Elster 1979.) For the history of the theory see Page 1968. For the theory of diminishing marginal utility see Friedman and Savage 1948, also reprinted in Page, and 14.3 of Deaton and Muellbauer 1980.

4   For the 'reasonableness entails maximization' theorems 'see chapter 2 of Luce and Raiffa 1957 and 14.2 of Deaton and Muellbauer 1980. The warnings about the interpretation of the theorems come from conversations with John Broome. Chapter 6 of his forthcoming book should be very helpful on the point.

5   For justifications of utility maximization in terms of averages over possible futures see chapter 4 of Skyrms 1984. See also Peirce 'On the doctrine of chances', in Peirce 1955. I owe both these references to an unpublished paper by Susan Hurley.

6   See 2.6 of Luce and Raiffa 1957; Broome (forthcoming); Jeffrey 1987; chapter 4 section 9 of Raiffa 1968.

7   These examples are a mixture of the 'Sophie's choice' examples found in the literature on moral dilemmas and Zeckhauser's paradox, as related by Jeffrey 1987. Zeckhauser's paradox is itself a refinement of Allais' paradox, which is in effect the topic of the works cited in the last footnote. Jeffrey's discussion is a bit confusing because it in effect runs together my cases 2 and 4. I have put all the examples in terms of someone's attitude to prospects involving the loss of another person's life, to avoid complications arising from connections

between one's life expectancy and the value to one of money and other goods.

CHAPTER 7   RISK: A FEW ANSWERS

1   There are many different kinds of lexical (very often called 'lexicographical') ordering. In particular, given a lexical ordering relating two kinds of good, so that any amount of A is less than the smallest amount of B, there are infinitely many ways of extending it to an ordering relating bundles of amounts of A plus amounts of B. It is also worth nothing that preferences represented by a lexical ordering are not the same as preferences represented by utilities within a finite interval but such that all utilities assigned to amounts of A are less than utilities assigned to some fixed amount of B. The crucial difference is that in the latter case there cannot be a sequence of amounts of A to all of which that fixed amount of B is preferred but which are 'evenly spaced' in that the difference in desirability between successive members of the sequence is the same. This is not a contrast that can be made on a purely ordinal construal of preference. (Though it can be made using hyper-comparative preferences, as alluded to in note 4 of chapter 3.) As John Broome points out to me, the implausibility of inferring a finite monetary value to life from the fact that one will take risks of life for finite amounts of money can be accounted for without a lexical ordering of life and money if one supposes that the value of money has a finite upper bound in terms of utility. For discussions of lexical orderings see 111.3 of Elster 1979, chapter 9 of Sen 1970, 5.7 of Levi 1986, and 3.2 of Fishburn 1988.

2   These can be represented algebraically as follows. (d,b,h) represents a combination of a number of deaths, a quantity of basic goods, and a degree of honour. In each coordinate there is a bottom level, indicated by 0. The first coordinate ranges through the positive integers and the other two through the real numbers. The underlying lexical ordering of pure quantities of death, basics, and honours amounts to

$$(0,0,h) > (0,b,0) \text{ when h and b are not } 0$$
$$(0,b,0) > (d,0,0) \text{ when b and d are not } 0$$
$$(0,h,0) > (d,0,0) \text{ when h and d are not } 0$$

Then the two different extensions of this to combinations of death, basics, and honours amounts to

$$(d,b,h) > (d',b,h) \text{ whenever } d > d'$$

and

$$(d,b,h) > (d,b',0) \text{ whenever h is not } 0.$$

3   See Machina 1983. Chapter 3 of Fishburn 1988 puts Machina's ideas into a very general setting.
4   Anyone waiting to understand these issues better must read the discussion of 'separability' in John Broome's forthcoming book.
5   See Levi 1986 chapter 7, and note 3 to chapter 5 of this volume.

CHAPTER 8   MISERY AND DEATH

1   Jonathan Glover is one of the few writers on this subject to have faced up to the finiteness of our resources, without thereby being forced to a view of the comparability of death, suffering, and the goods of life (see Glover 1978b). Culyer 1976 gives a good view of the economics of health care in a British-style system. (See also Boyd 1979.)
2   See O'Neill 1986 for a thought-provoking and definitely non–consequentialist account of the ethics of famine relief that, perhaps because of its non-consequentialism, does not seem to meet the question of how much of their own family's welfare it is reasonable for a concerned person in a rich country to sacrifice. Singer 1977 and Fletcher 1977 give roughly utilitarian analyses of this, arriving at rather different conclusions. Fishkin 1982 meets the question head on, and concludes that one cannot be obliged to impose heroic sacrifices on those near to one.
3   See Alan Williams 1985, 1989, and Office of Health Economics 1985 for a defence of the 'qualy' tradition. And Broome 1989 for scepticism about it. For bootstrapping see Fischhoff et al. 1981.
4   See Broome 1989.
5   See Pliskin et al. 1980.
6   See Tooley 1983 and Morton 1988a.
7   See Parfit 1984, pp. 493–4.
8   One principle which would support this conclusion is that to create someone is not to do them good. See Dasgupta 1989, Seabright 1989, Broome 1984.
9   Thomas Nagel argues, against a tradition going back at least to Lucretius, that every person's death is a great evil in comparison with the goods of life. (See his 'Death', in Nagel 1979.) Nagel does not say how appreciating this evil makes any difference to any decisions, but presumably his argument tends against the reasonableness of most forms of euthanasia. What I am doing here might be seen as providing a reason for regretting the death of each person, which does not enter into direct comparison with the goods (and evils) of being alive. Thus on my account one could regret the death of a person, though it was right for that person to seek death. I am here influenced by Becker 1974. (See also Rosenberg 1983 and Beauchamp and Perling 1978.)
10 This sentiment would probably be shared by Kuhse and Singer 1985. Helpful remarks about the kind of resources the B world would need are found in Hollis 1989. Glover 1978a seems to come down on particular issues roughly where he would if he had at the same time a general conviction that we

overvalue life and a sense that people cannot be taken merely as qualy consumers.

CHAPTER 9   HOW TO CHANGE YOUR DESIRES

1   Analogies to evidence for emotions and desires are explored in chapter 6 of de Sousa 1987. Some plausible patterns of change of desire enter in the argument of Harrison 1981/2.
2   See the essays in McLaughlin and Rorty 1988.
3   Compare de Sousa's idea of a 'paradigm scenario' in chapter 7 of de Sousa 1987.

CHAPTER 10   COORDINATION PROBLEMS

1   For an exposition of the ins and outs of the prisoner's dilemma see the introduction to Campbell and Sowden (1985). I have tried to state the dilemma so as not to beg the question of what the line of reasoning that leads to defection is. For it is worth seeing that you get defection by dominance reasoning and by expected utility and by minimax. Interesting things happen when the dilemma is generalized to n persons. See Pettit 1986a.
2   For a refutation of one class of such attempts see Pettit 1986b.
3   See Axelrod 1984, 1985, and Taylor 1987.
4   Axelrod's approach differs from Taylor's here. Axelrod looks for conditions under which 'tit for tat' players will do better than ' always defect' players. Taylor on the other hand looks for conditions under which playing 'tit for tat' will be a equilibrium, that is, conditions under which if players are using 'tit for tat' they have no motive for shifting to another strategy. These two approaches can give different results for other games. See pp. 69–75 of Taylor 1987.
5   The set-up could be varied in many ways. The pay-offs could be values varying continuously between two extremes and correlated with actions between full cooperation and full defection in such a way that the pay-offs for combinations of similarly intermediate actions form a prisoner's dilemma. For example, if 1 is cooperation and 0 is defection and the pay-offs for combinations of these are (3,3), (0,5), (5,0) and (1,1) in the usual way then the pay-offs for combinations of 0.8 and 0.2 – eight-tenths cooperation and two-tenths cooperation – might be (2.8, 2.8), (1,4), (4,1.6) and (1.6,1.6).
6   Randomization provides a mechanical way of creating actions between cooperation and defection. Then instead of just cooperation and defection one has a range: cooperate with probability x. (Cooperation with probability 0 = defection.) One could for example toss a die with the intention of cooperating if it lands with a 1 or a 2 upwards. Then one's act would be one-third of the way between defection and cooperation. This would then allow strategies like those of the last section, for example the strategy of being always on the

cooperation side of the other's last action. If the other cooperates with probability p one might, for example, respond by cooperating with probability $p + 1/2(1 - p)$.

The structure of large actions composed of smaller actions having a delicate relation to the large action is considered in Harrison 1978. (See also Morton 1985b.) Actions which are performed by the joint actions of a number of people are discussed in Graham 1986/7 and 1988.

7 The pay-off matrix might be:

	S	C	D
S	(6,6)	(5,0)	(1,1)
C	(0,5)	(3,3)	(0,5)
D	(1,1)	(5,0)	(1,1)

8 See Sugden 1986, chapter 9. I am not taking these as sufficient conditions for a working coordination convention. For example, one might want to add that people know that it is in their interest to follow the convention.

CHAPTER 11   THE DISUNITY OF THE MORAL

1 There is an enormous literature on moral dilemmas. It was all started by Bernard Williams, in 'Ethical Consistency' and 'Consistency and Realism' in Williams 1973. Greenspan 1983 and McConnell 1986 are good articles, and an excellent view of the state of the debate is given by Sinnot-Armstrong 1988.
2 See Grice 1967, Bond 1983, Hollis 1983.
3 See Gauthier 1985a, summarized in Gauthier 1985b.
4 Mary Midgeley argues eloquently for the usefulness of the concept of evil (See Midgeley 1984). I think she runs together hard core evil, wanting something *because* someone else is harmed by it, and various other kinds of undesirable motives and actions.
5 See chapters 4, 5, 6 and 8 of Sugden 1986.
6 The really interesting cases are those in which the optimum situation for everyone is not an equilibrium; for example the situation given by the matrix below.

	U	C	D
U	(3,3)	(0,0)	(0,4)
C	(0,0)	(2,2)	(0,1)
D	(4,0)	(0,0)	(1,1)

Here the pair (C,C) is an equilibrium, but (U,U) is better for both people. But agents choosing U are taking risks for themselves and others. If there is a settled convention of choosing C then someone choosing U is at the same time pointing to a better convention and rocking the boat.

7 See Thomas Nagel's 'The Fragmentation of Value' in Nagel 1979.
8 See chapter 10 of Nagel 1986, and Fishkin 1982.
9 Marxists usually both reject the moral tradition as ideology and appeal to a distinctly moral rhetoric. One thing they may be doing is appealing to some of the things we bundle together as morality while rejecting others. There should be a discussion of this in Graham (forthcoming).

CHAPTER 12 MOMENTS IN GOOD LIVES

1 The standard work on the concept of a person is Harry Frankfurt 1971. See also D. C. Dennett's 'Conditions for Personhood' in Dennett 1978. I express some scepticism, scepticism tempered by admiration, about Frankfurt's line in Morton 1989.
2 Rawls 1975, P. 408. The following quotations are from pp. 411 and 409.
3 For some sharp remarks on Rawls on the planned life see Wolff 1977.
4 See Gabrielle Taylor 1985 for a discussion of these emotions. The connection between attitudes with different temporal aspects are interestingly discussed in Annette Baier's 'Mixing Memory and Desire' in Baier 1985. I sense a connection between this discussion and the temporal aspects of emotion discussed in chapter 8 of de Sousa 1987.
5 Richard Wollheim 1984 and Mary Warnock 1987 argue for the centrality of retrospection in the good life. They both make a connection with Proust's evocation of the value-giving power of memory in *A la recherche du temps perdu*. (I have some hesitations about both Wollheim's and Warnock's analyses, as well as a general sympathy. See Morton 1985a and 1988b) David Carr 1986 brings out well how the temporal structure in which we live our lives often takes the form of a story. Non-narrative temporal framing fits some of the qualities isolated by psychological studies of what makes people enjoy being alive: see Csikzentmihalyi and Csikzentmihalyi 1988.
6 A valuable source of ideas about what it is reasonable to value is the exchange between Harry Frankfurt and Annette Baier in *Synthese* in 1982: see Frankfurt 1982 and Baier's 'Caring about Caring' in Baier 1985. The exchange is valuable not for its definite conclusions as much as for the number of interesting loose ends it leaves. I am sorry to have discovered it only when this book was essentially finished.
7 Parfit's doubts about person-stages are most explicit in his discussion with Dennett and others in Parfit 1982. They come down, really, to the insistence that person-stages aren't persons.
8 Parfit 1984, p. 341.
9 I am simplifying Parfit's classification slightly. For a good discussion of objective list hedonism see Chapter IV of Griffin 1986.
10 This view is like Griffin's. See especially chapter VI of Griffin 1986.

11   This is a bit like Thomas Nagel's views in chapter 5 of Nagel 1986. But how-
     ever objective the betterness relation between lives is, there will still be a
     large and serious problem about the relation between the ideal of a good life
     and various ideas of the moral life. See Nagel 1986 chapter 10.

References

I SELECTED BIBLIOGRAPHY

John Elster, *Ulysses and the Sirens*. Cambridge: Cambridge University Press, 1979. A very readable source of information about the troubles of standard decision-making models, which conveys the impresssion that the issues are deep and important.

R. C. Jeffrey, *The Logic of Decision* (2nd edition). Chicago: Chicago University Press, 1985. The early chapters present the most painless way to absorb the standard theory while later chapters present a novel version of the theory which simplifies and brings together many loose ends.

Thomas Nagel, *Mortal Questions*. Cambridge: Cambridge University Press, 1979. A collection of sharp and profound papers on life, death, right, and mind.

Derek Parfit, *Reasons and Persons*. Oxford: Oxford University Press, 1984. A large and difficult book, but very clearly written, that has already had an enormous influence.

Robert Sugden, *The Economics of Rights, Co-operation and Welfare*. Oxford: Basil Blackwell, 1986. Both a very clear exposition of the moral relevance of game theory and an argument for a controversial position about the relation between rights and welfare.

Helge Kuhse and Peter Singer, *Should The Baby Live?* Oxford: Oxford University Press, 1985. A brave and strongly argued approach to one of the most troubling moral issues of the time.

II REFERENCES CITED IN THE TEXT

Arrow, K. J. (1963) *Social Choice and Individual Values*, 2nd edn. New York: Wiley.

Arrow, K and Raynaud, H. (1986) *Social Choice and Multicriterial Decision-Making*. Cambridge, MA: MIT Press.

Axelrod, R. (1984) *The Evolution of Cooperation*. New York: Basic Books.

Axelrod, R. (1985) 'The Emergence of Cooperation among Egotists'. In R.

Baier, A. (1985) *Postures of the Mind*. London: Methuen.

Campbell and L. Sowden (eds) *Paradoxes of Rationality and Cooperation*. Vancouver: University of British Columbia Press.

Beauchamp, T. and Perling, S. (1978) *Ethical Issues in Death and Dying*. Englewood Cliffs, NJ: Prentice-Hall.

Becker, E. (1974) *The Denial of Death* (ed. R. Wallace). glencoe, IL: Free press.

Bell, J. M. and Mendus, S. (eds) (1989) *Philosophy and Medical Welfare*. Cambridge: University Press.

Birkhoff, G. and MacLane, S. (1979) *Algebra*. New York: Macmillan.

Blair, D. H. and Pollak, R. A. (1983) 'Rational Collective Choice'. *Scientific American*, 255, 76–83.

Bond, E. J. (1983) *Reason and Value*. Cambridge: Cambridge University Press.

Boyd, K. M. (1979) *The Ethics of Resource Allocation in Health Care*. Edinburgh: Edinburgh University Press.

Broome, J. (1984) 'The Economic Value of Life'. *Economics* 52, 281–94.

Broome, J. (1989) 'Good, Fairness, and QUALY's'. In J. M. Bell and S. Mendus (eds) *Philosophy and Medical Welfare* Cambridge: Cambridge University Press.

Broome, J. (forthcoming) *Weighing Goods*. Oxford: Basil Blackwell.

Campbell, R. and Sowden, L. (eds) (1985) *Paradoxes of Rationality and Cooperation* Vancouver: University of British Columbia Press.

Carr, D. (1986) *Time, Narrative, and History*. Bloomington: Indiana University Press

Csikzentmihalyi, M. and Csikzentmihalyi, I. S. (1988) *Optimal Experience*. Cambridge: Cambridge University Press.

Culyer, A. J. (1976) *Need and the National Health Service*. London: Martin Robertson (York Studies in Economics).

Dasgupta, P. (1989) 'Population Size and the Quality of Life. *Proceedings of the Aristotelian Society*, supplementary vol. 63.

Deaton, A. and Muellbauer, J. (1980) *Economics and Consumer Behavior*. Cambridge: Cambridge University Press.

Dennett, D. C. (1978) *Brainstorms*. Medford, MA: Bradford Books.

de Sousa, R. (1987) *The Rationality of Emotion*. Cambridge, MA: M.I.T. Press.

Dworkin, R. (1977) *Taking Rights Seriously*. London: Duckworth.

Elster, J. (1979) *Ulysses and the Sirens: Studies in rationality and irrationality*. Cambridge: Cambridge University Press.

Elster, J. (1983) *Sour Grapes: Studies in the subversion of rationality*. Cambridge: Cambridge University Press.

Fischhoff, B., Lichtenstein, S., Slovic, P., Derby, L. and Keeney, R. (1981) *Acceptable Risk*. Cambridge: Cambridge University Press.

Fishburn, P. (1988) *Nonlinear Preference and Utility Theory*. Brighton: Harvester.

Fishkin, J. (1982) *The Limits of Obligation*. New Haven: Yale University Press.

Fletcher J. (1977) 'Even if It Helps but Not if It Hurts'. In W. Aiken and H. LaFollette (eds) *World Hunger and Moral Obligation*. Englewood Cliffs, NJ: Prentice-Hall.

Frankfurt, H. (1971) 'Freedom of the Will and the Concept of a Person'. *Journal of Philosophy* 68, 5–20.

Frankfurt, H. (1982) 'The Importance of What We Care About'. *Synthese* 53, 257–72.

Friedman, M. and Savage, L. (1948) 'The Utility Analysis of Choices Involving Risk'. *Journal of Political Economy* 56, 279–304.

Gärdenfors, P. and Sahlin, N.-E. (1982) 'Unreliable Probabilities: Risk Taking and Decision Making'. *Synthese* 53, 361–86.

Gauthier, D. (1985a) *Morals by Agreement*. Oxford: Oxford University Press.

Gauthier, D. (1985b) 'Maximization Constrained: The Rationality of Cooperation'. In R. Campbell and L. Sowden (eds) *Paradoxes of Rationality and Cooperation*. Vancouver: University of British Columbia Press.

Gibbard, A. (1986) 'Interpersonal Comparisons: Preference, good, and the intrinsic value of a life'. In J. Elster and A. Hylland (eds) *Foundations of Social Choice Theory*. Cambridge: Cambidge University Press.

Gibbard, A. and Harper, W. (1978) 'Counterfactuals and Two kinds of Expected Utility'. In C. A. Hooker, J. J. Leach and E. F. McLennen (eds) *Foundations and Applications of Decision Theory*, vol. I. Dordrecht: Reidel. (Reprinted in shortened form in Campbell and Sowden (1985).)

Glover, J. (1978a) *Causing Death and Saving Lives*. Harmondsworth: Penguin.

Glover, J. (1978b) 'Assessing the Value of Saving Lives'. In G. Vesey (ed.) *Human Values*. Oxford: Basil Blackwell.

Graham, K. (1986/7) 'Morality and Abstract Individualism'. *Proceedings of the Aristotelian Society*, 87.

Graham, K. (1988) 'Morality, Individuals and Collectives'. In J. D. G. Evans (ed.) *Moral Philosophy and Contemporary Problems*. Cambridge: Cambridge University Press.

Graham, K. (forthcoming) *Karl Marx*. Brighton: Harvester.

Greenspan, P. (1983) 'Moral Dilemmas and Guilt'. *Philosophical Studies* 43, 117–25.

Greenspan, P. (1989) *Emotions and Reasons*. London: Routledge.

Grice, G. R. (1967) *The Grounds of Moral Judgement*. Cambridge: Cambridge University Press.

Griffin, J. (1986) *Well-Being*. Oxford: Oxford University Press.

Hampshire, S. (1989) *Innocence and Experience*. London: Allen Lane.

Harman, G. (1986) *Change in View*. Cambridge, MA: M.I.T. Press.

Harrison, A. (1978) *Making and Thinking*. Brighton: Harvester.

Harrison, R. (1981/2) 'Discounting the Future' Proceedings of the Aristotelian Society, 81.

Herzberger, H. (1973) 'Ordinal Preference and Rational Choice'. *Econometrica* 41, 187–237.

Hollis, M. (1983) 'Rational Preferences'. *The Philosophical Forum* 14, 246–62.

Hollis, M. (1987) *The Cunning of Reason*. Cambridge: Cambridge University Press.

Hollis, M. (1989) 'A Death of One's Own'. In J. M. Bell and S. Mendus (eds) *Philosophy and Medical Welfare*. Cambridge: Cambridge University Press.

Hurley, S. L. (1989) *Natural Reasons*. Oxford: Oxford University Press.

Jeffrey, R. C. (1974) 'Preferences among Preferences'. *Journal of Philosophy* 71, 377–91.

Jeffrey, R. C. (1985) *The Logic of Decision*, 2nd edn. Chicago: Chicago University Press.

Jeffrey, R. C. (1987) 'Risk and Human Rationality'. *The Monist* 70, 223–36.

Jones-Lee, M. W. (1982) *The Value of Life and Safety*. Amsterdam: North-Holland.

Kahneman, D. and Tversky, A. (1979) 'Prospect Theory: An Analysis of Decision under Risk'. *Econometrica* 47, 263–91.

Keeney, R. and Raiffa, H. (1976) *Decisions with Multiple Objectives*. New York: Wiley.

Kuhse, H. (1987) *The Sanctity of Life Doctrine in Medicine*. Oxford: Oxford University Press.

Kuhse, H. and Singer, P. (1985) *Should The Baby Live?* Oxford: Oxford University Press.

Kyburg, Henry E. Jr (1981) 'Principle Investigation'. *The Journal of Philosophy* 78, 12, 772–8.

Levi, I. (1986) *Hard Choices*. Cambridge: Cambridge University Press.

Lindblom, C. (1988) *Democracy and Market System*. Oslo: Universitetsfolaget.

Luce, R. D. and Raiffa, H. (1957) *Games and Decisions*. New York: Wiley.

Machina, M. (1983) 'Generalized Expected Utility Analysis and the Nature of Observed Violations of the Independence Axiom'. In B. Stigum and F. Wenstop (eds) *Foundations of Utility and Risk Theory with Applications*. Dordrecht: Reidel.

Maung, I. and Paris, J. (unpublished) *A Note on the Infeasibility of some Inference Processes*. University of Manchester, Dept of Mathematics.

McClennen, E. (1985) 'Prisoner's Dilemma and Resolute Choice'. In R. Campbell and L. Sowden (eds) *Paradoxes of Rationality and Cooperation*. Vancouver: University of British Columbia Press.

McConnell, T. (1986) 'More on Moral Dilemmas'. *The Journal of Philosophy* 83, 345–50.

McLaughlin, B. and Rorty, A. (1988) *Perspectives on Self-deception*. Berkeley: University of California Press.

Mellor, H. (1983) 'Objective Decision-making'. *Social Theory and Practice* 9, 289–309.

Midgeley, M. (1984) *Wickedness: A Philosophical Essay*. London: Routledge.

Mill, J. S. (1985) *Utilitarianism*, 9th edn. London: Longman's Green.

Milligan, D. (1980) *Reasoning and the Explanation of Action*. Brighton: Harvester.

Morton, A (1980) *Frames of Mind*. Oxford: Oxford University Press.

Morton, A. (1982) 'Freudian Commonsense'. In J. Hopkins and R. Wollheim (eds) *Philosophical Essays on Freud*. Cambridge: Cambridge University Press.

Morton, A. (1985a) review of Wollheim's *The Thread of Life*, in the *Times Literary Supplement*, 21 June 1985, p. 688.

Morton, A. (1985b) 'The Variety of Rationality'. *Proceedings of the Aristotelian Society*, Supplement to vol. 59, 139–62.

Morton, A. (1989) 'Why There is No Concept of A Person'. In C. Gill (ed.) *The Person and the Human Mind: Issues in Ancient and Modern Philosophy*. Oxford: Oxford University Press.

Morton, A. (1988a) 'A Note on Comparing Pain and Death'. *Bioethics* 2, 2, 127–35.

Morton, A. (1988b) review of Warnock's *Memory*, in the *Times Literary Supplement*, May 1988.

Nagel, T. (1970) *The Possibility of Altruism*. Oxford: Oxford University Press.

Nagel, T. (1979) *Mortal Questions*. Cambridge: Cambridge University Press.

Nagel, T. (1986) *The View from Nowhere*. Oxford: Oxford University Press.

Office of Health Economics (1985) *Measurement of Health*. London: OHE Publications.

O'Neill, O. (1975) *Acting on Principle*. New York: Columbia University Press (published under the name Onora Nell).

O'Neill, O. (1986) *Faces of Hunger*. London: Allen and Unwin.

Osherson, D., Stob, M. and Weinstein, S. (1988) 'Mechanical Learners Pay a Price for Bayesianism'. *The Journal of Symbolic Logic* 53, 1245–51.

Page, A. (ed.) (1968) *Utility Theory: A book of readings*. New York: Wiley.

Parfit, D. (1982) 'Discussion'. *Synthese* 53, 251–6.

Parfit, D. (1984) *Reasons and Persons*. Oxford: Oxford University Press.

Paris, J. and Vencovska, A. (1990) 'Modelling Belief'. In J. Tiles (ed.) *Evolving Knowledge*. London: Pitman.

Peirce, C. S. (1955) *Philosophical Writings of Peirce*. New York: Dover.

Pettit, P. (1986a) 'Free Riding and Foul Dealing'. *The Journal of Philosophy* 83, 361–80.

Pettit, P. (1986b) 'Preserving the Prisioner's Dilemma'. *Synthese* 86, 181–4.

Pettit, P. (forthcoming) 'Decision Theory and Folk Psychology'. In M. Bacharach and S. Hurley (eds) *Essays in the Foundations of Decision Theory*. Oxford: Oxford University Press.

Pliskin, J., Shepard, D. and Weinstein, M. (1980) 'Utility Functions for Life Years and Health Status'. *Operations Research* 28, 206–24.

Raiffa, H. (1968) *Decision Analysis*. Reading, MA: Addison-Wesley.

Rawls, J. (1975) *A Theory of Justice*. Oxford: Oxford University Press.

Raz, J. (1986) *The Morality of Freedom*. Oxford: Oxford University Press.

Rosenberg, J. (1983) *Thinking Clearly About Death*. Englewood cliffs, NJ: Prentice-Hall.

Seabright, P. (1989) 'Population Size and the Quality of Life'. *Proceedings of the Aristotelian Society*, supplementary vol. 63.

Scriven, T. (1981) 'Preference, Rational Choice, and Arrow's Theorem'. *The Journal of Philosophy* 78, 778–85.

Sen, A. (1970) *Collective Choice and Social Welfare*. San Francisco: Holden Day.

Sen, A. (1982) *Choice, Welfare, and Measurement*. Oxford: Basil Blackwell.

Simon, H. (1982) *Models of Bounded Rationality*. Cambridge, MA: M. I. T. Press.

Simon, H. (1983) *Reason in Human Affairs*. Oxford: Blackwell.

Singer, P. (1977) 'Famine, Hunger, and Moral Obligation'. In W. Aiken and H.

Lafollette (eds) *World Hunger and Moral Obligation*. Englewood Cliffs, NJ: Prentice-Hall.

Singer, P. (1980) *Practical Ethics*. Cambridge: Cambridge University Press.

Sinnot-Armstrong, W. (1988) *Moral Dilemmas*. Oxford: Basil Blackwell.

Skyrms, B. (1984) *Pragmatics and Empiricism*. New Haven: Yale University Press.

Slote, M. (1985) *Common-sense Morality and Consequentialism*. London: Routledge.

Sugden, R. (1986) *The Economics of Rights, Co-operation and Welfare*. Oxford: Basil Blackwell.

Taylor, G. (1985) *Pride, Shame, and Guilt*. Oxford: Oxford University Press.

Taylor, M. (1987) *The Possibility of Cooperation*. Cambridge: Cambridge University Press.

Thomson, J. (1977) *Acts and Other Events*. Ithaca, NY: Cornell University Press.

Tooley, M. (1983) *Abortion and Infanticide*. Oxford: Oxford University Press.

Warnock, M. (1987) *Memory*. London: Faber and Faber.

Williams, A. (1985) 'The Value of Qualys.' *Health and Social Service Journal*, 18 July, 3–5.

Williams, A. (1989) 'Ethics and Efficiency in the Provision of Health Care'. In J. Bell and S. Mendus (eds) *Philosophy and Medical Welfare*. Cambridge: Cambridge University Press.

Williams, B. (1973) *Problems of the Self*. Cambridge: Cambridge University Press.

Williams, B. (1985) *Ethics and the Limits of Philosophy*. Cambridge, MA: Harvard University Press.

Wolff, R. P. (1977) *Understanding Rawls*. Princeton: Princeton University Press.

Wollheim, R. (1984) *The Thread of Life*. Cambridge: Cambridge University Press.

Index